Framing Decisions

Instructor materials for *Framing Decisions* include teaching points for each chapter, homework assignment questions, exam questions, and video links for each chapter. The *Instructor's Guide* is available free online. If you would like to download and print out a copy of the guide, please visit www.wiley.com/college/Frame

Framing Decisions
Decision Making That Accounts for Irrationality, People, and Constraints

J. DAVIDSON FRAME

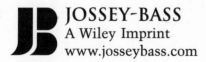

JOSSEY-BASS
A Wiley Imprint
www.josseybass.com

Published by Jossey-Bass
A Wiley Imprint
One Montgomery Street, Suite 1200, San Francisco, CA 94104-4594
www.josseybass.com

Cover art by Michele Constantini/Getty

Jossey-Bass books and products are available through most bookstores. To contact Jossey-Bass directly call our Customer Care Department within the U.S. at 800-956-7739, outside the U.S. at 317-572-3986, or fax 317-572-4002.

Wiley publishes in a variety of print and electronic formats and by print-on-demand. Some material included with standard print versions of this book may not be included in e-books or in print-on-demand. If this book refers to media such as a CD or DVD that is not included in the version you purchased, you may download this material at http://booksupport.wiley.com. For more information about Wiley products, visit www.wiley.com.

Library of Congress Cataloging-in-Publication Data
Frame, J. Davidson.
   Framing decisions : decision making that accounts for irrationality, people, and constraints / J. Davidson Frame.
       p. cm. – (The Jossey-Bass business & management series)
   Includes bibliographical references and index.
   ISBN 978-1-118-01489-9 (cloth); ISBN 978-1-118-22186-0 (ebk); ISBN 978-1-118-23564-5 (ebk); ISBN 978-1-118-26078-4 (ebk)
   1. Decision making.   I. Title.
   BF448.F73 2013
   153.8'3–dc23

                                        2012027908

Printed in the United States of America
FIRST EDITION

HB Printing   10 9 8 7 6 5 4 3 2 1

The Jossey-Bass
Business & Management Series

To my extended family of siblings: Sally, Deborah, Matthew, Pia, Marinella, Giancarlo, Mark, and Derek

Contents

List of Figures

Preface

I'm a "self-pincher," meaning that I pinch myself from time to time. The pinching is not a product of masochism or a symptom of an exotic neurological disorder (I hope). Rather, it is driven by a desire to determine whether I am awake or dreaming when I come across things that many people accept as true but don't make sense to me.

My self-pinching proclivity is not new. Following are examples of events that triggered self-pinching actions over the years:

- As a child, when my parents told me about the activities of the tooth fairy, Easter Bunny, and Santa Claus

- As a young adult living in Washington, D.C., in the 1970s, when for two years I witnessed a large portion of the American public embrace Nixon's story that he had nothing to do with the Watergate break-in

- In the autumn of 2008, shortly before the implosion of the global economy, when I heard Federal Reserve chairman Ben Bernanke assure the public that the U.S. financial system was on solid footing

- During the spring of 2010 as I watched the Congress and news media foment hysteria by accusing Toyota of producing defective cars that accelerate out of control—this without solid evidence to support their claims

The conventional word for self-pincher is, of course, *skeptic*. I am a skeptic. I may have a genetic predisposition toward skepticism, since my earliest memories have a skeptical flavor to them. My mother jokes that the first time I used the word *mom* when addressing her, I placed a question mark after it, as in, "Mom?" I enjoy standing conventional wisdom on its head, which sometimes makes me *curmudgeonesque*. I don't do this to be ornery. It comes naturally to me. If something doesn't make sense, this bothers me, and I strive to figure out what's going on.

Recently I turned my skeptic's eye toward decision-making theory and practice. I have taught this subject for more than thirty years, and as a practicing manager and consultant, I have personally contributed to significant decision-making efforts in academia, business, and government. I approached the subject uncritically for many years, but I now believe that the great majority of decision-making courses and books view decision making too narrowly. Works that fall under the umbrella of decision science often concentrate on decision-making tools that typically focus on optimizing an objective function, prioritizing alternatives in a logical and consistent fashion, or building models to carry out what-if analyses.

Works that approach decision making more broadly go beyond mere tool use and may suggest useful heuristics and good-sense nostrums to follow, but they still adhere to the underlying precepts of traditional decision science: decisions should be based on logical and rational thinking, should seek to maximize benefits and minimize costs, should focus on core issues and push nonpertinent distractions to the side, and so on. On the surface, these precepts sound 100 percent compelling, but a bit of skeptical reflection raises questions on this matter.

In my view, works directed at "how to be a better decision-maker" are especially off-target, because they promote the view that if readers assume the right perspective and do the right things, they will be better decision-makers, making smart, high-impact decisions. What is bothersome here is that these works implicitly assume the reader is in a position to make decisions in isolation from the rest of the world. The fact is that nontrivial decision making occurs in a social environment that requires decision-makers to recognize that the viability of their individual decisions is often shaped by forces that lie outside their direct control. How useful is a book titled *How to Be a Better Decision-Maker* to a committee of senior managers of a company trying to determine whether to acquire a new company, or to a field commander pondering whether to launch an attack against enemies entrenched in civilian homes? Can anyone seriously believe that the president of the United States will improve his decision-making skills by reading the hypothetical *How to Be a Better Decision-Maker*?

What is missing in these traditional perspectives is conscious consideration of a host of factors that have a significant impact on how decisions are actually made but are not usually covered in decision-making courses and books. I am referring here to things like politics, legacy, competence, honesty, selfishness, altruism, personality, cognition, and acts of God. No one would deny that these factors can strongly affect decision making, yet they are seldom discussed in formal treatments of decision-making theory and practice. People routinely discover the importance of these factors in the school of hard knocks, but they are unlikely to encounter them in a university classroom. These factors should not be viewed as interesting sidelines in the business of decision making but as part of the core process.

Consider, for example, the reality of dissimulation. How often do decision-making courses and books address lying and liars? Informed decisions require acquiring facts. When the facts are consciously twisted, decisions based on these facts will be poor ones. At the risk of sounding overly cynical, I would argue that there are plenty of times that the facts going into a decision-making equation have been consciously distorted, with distortions ranging from small white lies to the Big Lie. It seems obvious that smart decision making should accommodate the possibility that the facts decision-makers work with are not truthful. Ordinary car buyers bargaining with a salesperson on the showroom floor know this and factor it into their purchasing decision. TV viewers watching late-night advertisements describing miracle wrinkle-removing creams know this as well, and they too factor it into their purchasing decision. Yet you do not come across much treatment of lying and liars in traditional decision-making books and courses. Is this an important topic that decision-makers should highlight? Certainly! Consider how the lies of Bernard Madoff, Enron's Kenneth Lay, and WorldCom's Bernard Ebbers distorted the decision processes of countless investors, causing them collectively to lose billions of dollars.

Another example of the narrow outlook of conventional decision science thinking can be found by examining its approach to decision making under conditions of uncertainty. While this topic is routinely covered in decision-making courses and books, the treatment of the nature of uncertainty is largely mechanical and shallow. Generally in decision science, it refers to making decisions with incomplete data. For example, when conducting a market research study for a new product, market researchers can only guess at potential market size and the price at which the new product will sell. The lack of information on market size and product price defines uncertainty from the viewpoint of traditional decision science. Decision scientists attack the problem of uncertainty by computing probabilities of events and employing clever statistical techniques to fill in the blanks. They tend to deal with it mechanically. Researchers affiliated with the sixteen-university Decision-Making Under Uncertainty Multi-University Research Initiative have developed a detailed list of worthwhile research topics, such as "basic methods based on probability, decision and utility theories," "real-time inference algorithms," and "fusing uncertain information of different kinds." (For a full list of suggested topics, go to http://www.cs.berkeley.edu/~jordan/muri/.)

Personally I love this stuff. When I get stuck at a central Nebraska airport during a snowstorm or after missing a connection to Yunnan province in southwestern China, I work on problems like these to pass the time and maintain my sanity. I also use them to guide decisions in well-defined, highly structured circumstances. But although these are interesting and valuable topics worthy of study, none touches on a more profound aspect of uncertainty that scientists and philosophers regularly address: uncertainty rooted in the limits of what humans can know.

The most famous treatment of this subject is Heisenberg's uncertainty principle, which holds that you can know a particle's location or its momentum, but you cannot know both at the same time. To the nonphysicist, this revelation is too abstruse to have meaning, so let's ignore its physical interpretation and focus on its deeper, nontechnical implication: it tells us that no matter how smart you are and no matter how powerful and precise your instruments are, there are things you simply are incapable of knowing. There are absolute limits to your knowledge. The emergence of quantum physics in the early twentieth century was a humbling experience for science. After Newton's revelations of his amazing laws of motion, scientists saw no limits to their mastery of knowledge. It seemed that through the gradual accretion of knowledge, they could ultimately have a full understanding of all natural phenomena. Quantum physics dashed this vision.

While we have no clear mathematical demonstration of the limits of knowledge in the arena of human behavior that is comparable to the uncertainty principle, it is evident that there are many things that we are unsure of—often profoundly so—despite our efforts to study them diligently. To see this, consider the lives of nine of the most significant decision-makers in the United States: the justices of the U.S. Supreme Court. Their principal mission is to adjudicate. The point of adjudication is to decide the disposition of a legal case after careful review of the facts. Anyone who has been unfortunate enough to be involved in a legal dispute has learned that in legal proceedings, facts are examined with far more care than in typical business proceedings or when making personal decisions.

If truth were unambiguous and clearly discernable, all Supreme Court rulings would be unanimous. This is an important point. But in reality, most rulings entail split decisions. As a skeptic, I enjoy reading the justifications of the affirmative and dissenting views of the Supreme Court justices on specific cases. They are all over the map. Here you have nine men and women who stand at the apex of the legal profession, have studied at the top schools, have undergone a rigorous screening process in getting hired, and whose decisions guide the law of the land—and yet they often hold opposing views on how decisions should be rendered.

What the legal system teaches us is that in the real world, the facts decision-makers rely on do not speak for themselves. They must be interpreted contextually. Assumptions must be made about their veracity. A decision scientist who suggests that due diligence clearly paves the way to correct decisions has not experienced the workings of the legal system in general or the Supreme Court in particular.

In this book, I am not rejecting the traditional perspective on decision making. Rather, my goal is to expand its purview because I believe the traditional outlook is too narrow. I am not a lone pioneer in this effort. I am one individual in a growing crowd of men and women currently looking at decision making from a non–decision science perspective. The scope of decision-making theory and practice is being broadened because of interest in the topic arising in other disciplines. Practitioners of traditional decision science have not displayed much curiosity about the social dimensions of decision making; however, we find that social psychologists, political scientists, and economists are pursuing investigations on topics such as the impacts of group dynamics on decision outcomes, the achievement of decisions through coalitions, and the psychological dimensions of market behavior. Similarly, practitioners of traditional decision science have not devoted much effort to examining the biology of decision making, but this subject is being studied actively now. Since the 1990s, there has been a burst of activity among neuroscientists, ophthalmologists, and psychologists examining the biological roots of decision making. Researchers in these fields are employing new technologies and psychosocial experiments to examine brain structure and function to see what happens when people make decisions ranging from the most trivial to the complex.

Perhaps most curious have been the perspectives on decision making arising in the arena of the philosophy of science. Linking philosophy of science to decision-making theory and practice may seem to be a bit of a stretch, but consider how all scientists who are engaged in serious research face profound questions in determining what is true and what is not. For one thing, they want to know whether the findings emerging from their experiments are true or whether they are artifacts of sampling bias, faulty equipment, or flawed measurement. Concern with truth goes beyond questions of experimental method: their experiments and analyses of data enable them to generate multiple hypotheses to explain the phenomena they investigate. Which explanation is true? Interestingly, scientists seldom face a paucity of explanations; instead, they suffer from a surfeit, and they must sort through multiple explanations in order to arrive at what is called IBE—inference to the best explanation. You can argue convincingly that ultimately, the most significant chore scientists carry out is determining how to decide which hypotheses should be supported and which rejected.

Over two years, I immersed myself in reading whatever I could that looked at decision making from a non–decision science viewpoint. When I began this effort, I was well versed in pertinent decision-making perspectives in the behavioral sciences (particularly economics) and philosophy of science, so most of my attention was directed at getting up to speed in social psychology, neuroscience, ophthalmology, and cognitive psychology. I was delighted to discover that the neuroscience, ophthalmological, and cognitive psychology literatures are accessible to anyone with a modest background in biology, chemistry, and experimental design. While I would be fortunate to understand the content of the first paragraph of an article written in *Physics Review*, I had no problem reading medical and psychological papers. I was also helped in this effort by my thirty-five-year background in research design and methodology.

A reading of the original scientific papers was important in helping me to understand the achievements and limitations of research and thinking in non–decision science disciplines. There's a lot of interesting stuff going on, and a goal of this book is to cover the new material. But my investigation also revealed substantial weaknesses in the studies I encountered, particularly methodological ones. One thing that was surprising was to see that the actual outcomes of experiments reported in scientific articles were far humbler than what popularizers report in best-selling books, such as Malcolm Gladwell's *Blink* (2005), Jonah Lehrer's *How We Decide* (2009), Cordelia Fine's *A Mind of Its Own* (2006), and most recently, Daniel Kahneman's *Thinking, Fast and Slow* (2011). (Fine's *Delusions of Gender* (2011), on the other hand, is a very good book.) These authors play fast and loose with tentative findings reported in the scientific literature. What they present as breakthrough discoveries about clever psychology experiments or the role of the brain in decision making are in fact tentative hypotheses that are barely supported by the data reported in the published studies. Something I emphasize in this book is that while attention to the biology of decision making is growing rapidly, scientists are only at the earliest stages of understanding the brain's role in decision making, and firm conclusions to date are few while exciting hypotheses are abundant.

Because the methodological deficiencies of several highly acclaimed studies are so pronounced, I touch on the methodological weakness of the research efforts in Chapter Nine.

I have criticized the decision science discipline as being insular several times in this Preface. I now direct the same criticism at other disciplines that are investigating decision making. (That's one of the consequences of being looked at by skeptics: no one is sheltered from their captious habits.) Neuroscientists, cognitive psychologists, social psychologists, and political scientists seldom look beyond the boundaries of their disciplines. To their credit, experimental psychologists have taken a stab at being interdisciplinary by establishing a behavioral economics subdiscipline, but as I discuss later in this book, behavioral economists devote too much energy to demonstrating through experiments that humans do not behave rationally—as if we did not already know this! Researchers and thinkers in these disciplines can learn much from decision science; after all, the sole focus of decision science is on decision making, and despite my call for a broader outlook on the domain of the discipline, I believe that decision science practitioners have significant insights that are lacking in other disciplines.

An improved understanding of what it takes to strengthen decision-making theory and practice will require substantial interdisciplinary cooperation.

In my readings, I have come across several books that step a bit outside the traditional decision science box and present different perspectives from those we normally encounter. They are Jonathan Baron's *Thinking and Deciding* (2007), Bazerman and Moore's *Judgment in Managerial Decision Making* (2008), David Hardman's *Judgment and Decision Making* (2009), Hastie and Dawes's *Rational Choice in an Uncertain World: The Psychology of Judgment and Decision Making* (2010), Newell, Lagnado, and Shanks's *Straight Choices: The Psychology of Decision Making* (2007), and Scott Plous's still relevant *The Psychology of Judgment and Decision Making* (1993).

ORGANIZATION OF THE BOOK

Chapter One argues that recent high-impact decision failures in the public and private sectors, epitomized by the economic collapse of 2008–2009, make it clear that despite increased access to information and the growing sophistication of information-handling capabilities, decision making at the level of individuals, organizations, communities, and nations is often ineffective and needs to be viewed with fresh eyes. Decision-making theory and practice need to reach beyond the traditional, narrow purview of decision science, with its focus on heuristics, modeling, and decision tools, such as linear programming, decision tree analysis, and Bayesian statistics. A big step toward broadening the purview of decision making is to recognize that consequential decisions are made in a social context with psychological, economic, political, moral, and cognitive dimensions that need to be addressed.

Chapter Two introduces readers to the nature of decisions and decision making. It distinguishes between unconscious decisions that people routinely make without thinking and mindful decisions of consequence that are made consciously. It also looks at ways that decision scientists have tried to deal with the uncertainty inherent in decision making. Most important, it highlights the fact that concern with decision making lies beyond the provenance of decision science alone. It examines approaches taken to decision making in different disciplines—decision science, economics, public policy, social psychology, psychology, law, neuroscience, and philosophy—and argues that a robust approach to decision making should accommodate the best features of these different disciplines.

Decisions of consequence should not be approached mechanically. The launching point for considering decisions should be people, because decisions occur in a social context and therefore have social, psychological, economic, political, organizational, and moral implications. While a traditional benefit-cost ratio may provide an optimal solution that suggests taking certain steps to address a problem (for example, closing a factory), the purportedly optimal solution may be politically, socially, and economically unacceptable. When social factors come up against technically optimal solutions to problems, the social factors generally prevail. Chapter Three examines the social context of decision making, demonstrating how technically optimal solutions can be derailed by the contending interests of a wide range of stakeholders, both within and outside the organization in which decision-makers function. It emphasizes that a key consideration in making good decisions is to take stock of the decision's social space. It also looks at the moral dimension of decision making, pointing out that problems of principal-agency, moral hazard, self-dealing, and prevarication are ubiquitous and must be recognized as such by decision-makers who make decisions of consequence.

Decisions of consequence are usually carried out in organizational contexts. Chapter Four looks at four aspects of organizational context: organization structure, organizational process, people in organizations, and organizational culture. It introduces organizational architecture as a technique to predict the management consequences emerging from organizational structure. When covering culture, it compares Athenian and Spartan cultures, risk-taking versus risk-averse cultures, and cultures that promote innovation versus those that cherish legacy. The goal of this chapter is to discuss how these organizational issues have a bearing on decision making.

A sad reality of decision making is that decision-makers often come across people who lie, cheat, break the law, engage in self-serving activities, and cut corners. Chapter Five reviews the full array of moral problems decision-makers may encounter while doing their jobs. It pays special attention to two major problems that contributed substantially to the economic collapse of 2008–2009: moral hazard and the principal-agent problem.

Chapter Six addresses a number of important issues about people as decision-makers. It promotes the view that the decision-making efficacy of people is determined situationally. It examines several factors that reflect the decision-making proclivities of people, including personality, creative capacity, intelligence, and competence.

In decision making, there is a constant tension between the need to get insights from a diversity of experts and stakeholders and the views of one or two highly perceptive, independent-thinking people who consistently outperform the crowd. Chapter Seven examines situations where individual decisions outperform group decisions and where group decisions offer superior results. It looks at how to obtain meaningful inputs from diverse sources, how to assess the degree of consensus among them, and how to capitalize on the unique insights of a handful of visionaries. It explores James Surowiecki's assertion that large groups have a wisdom that enables them to outperform experts. It examines new perspectives on group decision making, where we encounter decision successes among leaderless groups where decision making is completely decentralized, as reflected in the open source. It even looks at the phenomenal decision-making capabilities of bees, which make astonishing collective decisions that benefit the community, and suggests ways that their approach to decision making might be adapted to human groups.

Everything humans perceive is intermediated by the brain. Chapter Eight examines developments in neuroscience, psychology, and ophthalmology since the mid-1990s that enable scientists to understand how the brain supports decision making in humans. It highlights recent findings on brain research that have practical implications for the theory and practice of decision making. For example, it discusses how the brain does not stop its development until people reach their mid- to late twenties. As the brain develops, the last capability it achieves is the ability to make mature decisions. Another example is that the brain is a lazy organ, consuming only 10 watts of power. To conserve energy, it works from stored templates that come from past memories. When it encounters new experiences, it resists them, preferring to stick with tried-and-true templates. Thus, thinking out of the box requires people to break through the brain's comfort zone.

With the rise of behavioral economics in the 1970s, studies of decision making began to be carried out using systematic experimental methods heavily employed in experimental psychology. Chapter Nine looks at two categories of empirical studies that contribute to an improved understanding of how decision making works. One is based on empirical studies typically carried out by experimental psychologists. It contains an in-depth study of the evolution of empirical research on the question of whether unconscious deliberation of the brain yields better decisions than conscious deliberation. That is, is it better to make a quick decision or to sleep on it?

The second category of empirical studies is tied to research in neuroscience and ophthalmology. These studies attempt to map human behavior to activity in different areas of the brain. Some of the significant issues they have addressed include the role of emotion in rational decision making, the extent to which human perceptions are "fabricated" by the brain in an attempt to conserve energy, and the link between the maturity of humans—as defined by the changes of wiring of the brain that occur up through the late twenties—and their capacity to make effective judgments.

In closing, the last chapter distills the principal lessons offered in this book. Seven lessons emerge:

Lesson 1: Decisions of consequence occur in a social environment that strongly affects decision outcomes. These decisions should always accommodate social space.

Lesson 2: Decisions of consequence entail dealing with aggregates of people who have contending interests. Frequently the decision-makers' primary job is to work through these contending interests.

Lesson 3: An emphasis on tools often distracts us from effective decision making. To the four-year-old boy with a hammer, all the world is a nail.

Lesson 4: The idea of rational decision making is largely chimerical when dealing with decisions of consequence.

Lesson 5: Take heed of the moral dimension of decision making. Don't be duped by scalawags.

Lesson 6: Our perceptions of the world are intermediated by the brain: what we see, hear, and feel is not what we get.

Lesson 7: We can learn a lot from honeybees, including that leaderless distributed decision making is here to stay.

CONCLUSION

While this book assumes a skeptical mien, I believe its message is positive. I hope the skepticism I employ is not viewed as mean-spirited. The goal is to be skeptical in order to see things with fresh eyes. It is evident in retrospect that the economic and social turmoil that emerged from the Great Recession of 2008–2009 requires society to rethink how it goes about its business. To the extent the crisis was rooted in bad decision making, it behooves decision-making theorists and practitioners to learn lessons from the calamity. The key lessons I promote are captured in the book's subtitle: *decision making that accounts for irrationality, people, and constraints.* We must go beyond the traditional perspective that decision making can be handled mechanically, with a view to promoting rationality, logic, and optimal results. The reality is that when dealing with poorly defined, nontrivial decisions, which characterize decisions of consequence, we must roll up our sleeves and prepare to get dirty. My intent here is to prepare you for the muss.

September 2012   J. Davidson Frame
Arlington, Virginia

An Evolving Decision-Making Paradigm

Books, and the ideas they contain, are products of their time. As an author, it is easy to believe you are writing enduring truths for posterity. But the piece you have written, like the banana you buy at the supermarket, has a limited shelf life. Today's enduring truth is tomorrow's quaint whimsy.

You would think that a book about decision making would be enduring, since it is dealing with a timeless topic: making choices from among alternatives. Clearly, after decades of refining decision-making processes and tools, the experts have figured it out, right? Here is how it works. In making choices, smart decision-makers gather pertinent information, use this information to assess different alternatives, rank the alternatives according to their appeal, then select the alternative that rises to the top of the list. This is the refrain that decision-making books and courses preach to us. Isn't this how smart decisions are made? In this book, the answer is: "Sometimes yes, and sometimes no."

Like all other books, this one is a product of its time. It has emerged from reflections on a three-decade string of ever-growing economic disturbances, culminating in the economic crisis of 2008–2009. Yet it is not an economics or finance book. It is a book about decision making written for individuals who face choices and must decide what to do. The choices they address may entail Big Decisions—the kinds of choices department heads, chief financial and chief executive officers, and government leaders make. Or they may entail smaller decisions that managers and employees routinely face in their jobs: selecting a project, reconfiguring business operations, or hiring a new employee.

What is the link between the recent economic turmoil and the focus of this book? Answer: The economic crises we have been facing arose because a lot of people made a lot of truly awful decisions. Consider the 2008–2009 economic and financial meltdown that nearly plunged the world economy into an economic depression to rival the Great Depression of the 1930s.

Highly educated people in high-impact positions made bad decisions. Sadly for Alan Greenspan, chairman of the Federal Reserve from 1987 to 2006, this will likely be his enduring legacy.

Political power brokers made bad decisions. Beginning with Jimmy Carter in 1977 and Ronald Reagan in 1981, national political leaders were tripping over themselves to dismantle the federal government and its regulatory infrastructure in order to unleash markets to work their magic. As a result, government's regulatory efficacy dropped substantially. It is clear in retrospect that inadequate regulatory oversight contributed strongly to the economic crisis.

Business leaders made bad decisions. Taking advantage of deregulation, bankers, insurers, and Wall Street technocrats put aside their fiduciary responsibilities and began looking more like weekend gamblers in Las Vegas than guardians of depositors' and investors' funds.

And large segments of the general public made bad decisions: given a choice between saving money and spending it, they elected to spend. With an abundance of cheap debt, savings never had a chance. Personal savings plunged and debt skyrocketed.

The prevalence of bad decisions has been so substantial that thoughtful people must ask: What's going on here? Given unprecedented access to data, the existence of highly sophisticated decision support systems, steady methodological advances in the decision sciences, and guidance from highly experienced experts, how could we get things so wrong?

The economic crisis of 2008–2009 was a transformational event. It demonstrated that smart people aren't as smart as they and the public think. The elaborate economic and financial models developed with input from Nobel laureates didn't work as advertised. The long-held assumption that people make rational choices for the most part was debunked. Confidence in the value of the bell-shaped curve as a predictive tool was overshadowed by worries about fat tails and black swans—low-probability events that have devastating consequences.

Faith in free market capitalism was greatly shaken, and people turned to government as savior (a disturbing prospect to many).

The decision-making implications of the economic crisis of 2008–2009 go beyond decision making in business and public policy. They pertain to the full range of decisions people make, from the small to the grand, from social to technical. They bear as much on engineers deciding what design to implement for a technical product as on senior business managers deciding how to allocate their investment budget. Although the economic crisis of 2008–2009 highlighted decision-making inadequacies within a narrow band of economic activity, its lessons are far-reaching.

Transformational events cause people to rethink their assumptions about how things work. Thomas Kuhn wrote about transformational events in science in his classic book, *The Structure of Scientific Revolutions* (1996). He referred to them as *paradigm shifts*, where the old framework governing a world outlook is supplanted by a new one. In view of the contribution of bad decisions to the crisis of 2008–2009, now is a good time to reflect on the inadequacies of the traditional decision-making paradigm.

THE TRADITIONAL PARADIGM

In academia, the decision-making discipline goes under various titles: *decision science, management science*, and *operations research* are frequently used terms. For the most part, it focuses on quantitative techniques to help people make choices from among various alternatives. This orientation is captured in the articulated goal of the journal *Decision Sciences*: "*Decision Sciences* . . . is a quarterly, professional journal that uses the latest computer technology, mathematical and statistical techniques, and behavioral science." The awkward inclusion of ". . . and behavioral science" sounds like an afterthought, and probably it is. The journal's principal focus is on quantitative methods.

Many of these techniques are geared toward prioritizing alternatives, where the most attractive alternatives go to the top of the list and the least attractive drop to the bottom. They are covered by a plethora of names, including *multiattribute decision modeling, benefit-cost analysis,* and *analytical hierarchy process*.

The techniques associated with classical operations research deal with constrained optimization. They address questions such as: "In producing a given level of manufactured goods, what is the best arrangement of people, equipment, and materials to minimize costs?" Other techniques concentrate on generating data to help in decision making. For example, forecasting tools project future states of affairs based on past history and assumptions about evolving conditions. Their crystal ball glimpses of the future help decision-makers make informed choices today. Still other techniques simulate alternative outcomes associated with different actions: if you increase spending, the economy will go one way; if you decrease it, it will go another.

The traditional paradigm sees effective decision making as grounded in the employment of rigorous decision-making techniques. Students taking decision-making courses in universities spend much of their time studying a bevy of quantitative methods. I have firsthand experience of this because I have been teaching decision-making subjects at universities for some thirty years.

The old paradigm also views good decision making as a rational process. It holds that one way to demarcate good from bad decision making is to determine how logical and objective the decision-making process is. Good decisions require logic and objectivity. Although there is no guarantee that logic and objectivity will yield desired results owing to a range of uncontrollable factors, they are seen to be a necessary condition for establishing good decisions. Whimsical decisions rooted in emotion generally yield bad results. If satisfactory outcomes emerge from whimsy and emotion, it is by accident.

Economists capture the ideal of the rational decision-maker in their construct of *Homo economicus*, economic man. Adam Smith's invisible hand was built on the premise that individual decision-makers in the market operate on the basis of self-interest in a competitive environment. The combination of self-interest and competition ultimately yields efficient market behavior. As economists such as France's Leon Walras, England's Francis Edgeworth, and Italy's Vilfredo Pareto began employing rigorous mathematical economic models at the end of the nineteenth century, *Homo economicus* came to play a central role in economic theory. In its most robust embodiment, *Homo economicus* pictures economic decision-makers as rational players who possess perfect information to make decisions that maximize utility.

THE REAL WORLD

This book disputes three premises of the traditional paradigm. First, it takes a skeptical view of the idea that good decision making is rooted in the systematic process articulated at the outset of this chapter: gather information pertinent to the decision, use this information to assess alternatives, and so on. This is the abstract framework underlying most decision-making books and courses. It has commonsense appeal, but it places too much emphasis on employing a detached logical process, thereby addressing only a slice of what effective decision making really entails. A review of the academically oriented decision-making books published in the past three decades shows that in striving to promote objectivity, few make more than passing reference to the human and social elements of decision making, including biological constraints, and fewer still address important epistemological and metaphysical issues concerning the nature and value of the knowledge we gather for decision making and the limits of the models we use.

Second, this book rejects the idea that mastery of key techniques lies at the heart of effective decision making. The heavy emphasis on employing decision-making techniques distracts decision-makers from the real issues. At best, it can waste the time of countless men and women who spend incalculable hours studying diligently to become good decision-makers. How many great decisions owe their success to mastery of integer programming? For that matter, how many small decisions do? In spite of the fact that the value of integer programming is questionable for 99 percent of decision-makers, it is regularly taught in basic quantitative decision-making courses. And what holds for integer programming holds true for most of the other quantitative techniques that comprise the core of decision-making books and courses.

At worst, this emphasis puts the decision-making effort onto the wrong track. The old adage stands true here: to the four-year-old boy with a hammer, the world is a nail. When decision-makers define the decision-making process as centered on identifying the right tools, the decision-making effort has gone astray.

Third, this book rejects the assumption of rationality. On this point, it has plenty of good company. In 1957, Herbert Simon (1997) developed the concept of bounded rationality to challenge the notion that *Homo economicus* reflects real-world decision-makers. His well-known concept of satisficing avers that when searching for solutions, real-world decision-makers typically stop the search when they come across solutions that are good enough; in other words, they aren't looking for optimal solutions. In the 1970s, two psychologists, Amos Tversky and Daniel Kahneman (1974), began conducting psychological experiments that tested the rationality of decision-makers. They became preeminent figures in what was dubbed behavioral economics. Not surprisingly, they found that real-world decision making is seldom a rational process, something that just about everybody but economists recognized. Simon and Kahneman received Nobel Prizes in economics for their work in 1978 and 2002, respectively.

In this book, I go further than Simon and the behavioral economists in questioning the rational basis of decision making. For his part, Simon did not devote much attention to how people really make decisions. His principal concern was to identify the impact of satisficing behaviors on economic modeling. Kahneman and Tversky present a different story. Being psychologists, they were seriously interested in the behavioral component of decision making, but they were not wide-ranging in their investigations. They focused on how decision-makers in a laboratory setting rely on decision-making heuristics and are often unable to assay risk properly. Their experimental subjects were often undergraduate students at elite universities, a disturbing fact that has implications for the external validity of their findings. (How representative are the decision-making capabilities of inexperienced though conscientious nineteen-year-old with IQs typically greater than 120?)

Kahneman and Tversky's mission was to surface and understand the non-rational aspects of human decision making in order to help people function more rationally. Their approach was hardly revolutionary. They supported the existing paradigm by extending its coverage to nonrational behavior. An underlying premise of their research is, "If people have better information, they will use it to make better decisions." Although this assertion holds true in many cases, this book argues that it does not hold true in many others—which brings us back to the economic churning of the past two or three decades. A careful examination of events in business during this time makes it clear that the damaging decisions that business leaders and government policymakers made were driven largely by forces that economists in general—including behavioral economists—have ignored, and these include forces of pride, ideology, greed, and corruption, forces that hide incompetence and promote self-dealing and disloyalty.

Interestingly, this view closely echoes the views articulated a century ago by the American economist Thorstein Veblen (2007). Veblen had a front-row seat in the economic and social drama that starred the rapacious robber barons of American industry. To him, the free market was not a finely tuned watch that miraculously yielded optimal results; rather, it was a back-alley dog-fighting pit that favored opportunistic and merciless curs. Veblen would not be surprised by how events have unfolded in recent years.

This book investigates the moral dimension of decision making. It embraces the perspective articulated by Nobel laureate Paul Krugman (2009). When looking at the many finance debacles of recent years, Krugman identifies moral hazard as a major contributor to disasters and near-disasters. Here is the essence of moral hazard: financial decision-makers assume enormous risks, knowing that if their investments go sour, government will save the day. When their risks pay off, they generate substantial wealth for themselves and their clients; when they don't, the public foots the bill. Heads I win, tails you lose. Moral hazard is a subset of the larger issue of the principal-agent problem, where you find that people hired to do a job (agents) pursue their personal interests at the expense of the interests of their clients (principals). The principal-agent problem goes a long way in explaining why decisions in organizations go awry, and I discuss it in detail later in this book.

This book explores a host of additional factors that are embedded in real-world decision making. Included here are the competence and commitment of the players, the constraints of legacy, the reality of asymmetric access to information, the influence of politics, the pervasiveness of culture—and the ever-present temptations of greed.

The bottom line is that something that is usually viewed as invariant—the basic process of making choices—has undergone significant change. The economic crises we have encountered since the 1980s support this view. Advances in computers, communications, economic and financial theory, and decision-making techniques, coupled with extraordinary access to information through the Internet, fooled us into believing that we were on the road to achieving mastery over the decision-making process. Although we did not expect to hit the target all the time owing to uncontrolled uncertainties, we should usually get things right with due diligence and the application of disciplined methodology.

The precipitous fall into an economic abyss in 2008–2009 woke us from our dream world. What an ugly awakening! We now see that the decision-making premises we had been following since World War II were questionable. What is especially frightening is the realization that high-impact decision making is not a clean, rational undertaking, as advertised by the conventional wisdom, but is buffeted by nonrational elements, including moral failings, greed, outright corruption, stupidity, politics, black swans, human whimsy, failed models, hubris, and acts of God.

RETHINKING DECISION MAKING

As we rethink decision making, our attention should focus on two realities. First, it is important to recognize that decision making is a social activity. It is rooted in people and should not be approached as an objective process detached from human factors. People have personal perspectives and agendas and possess dramatic variations in capabilities. Quite often a decision is made by one set of people, executed by another set, is beneficial to yet another set, and is resisted by still another set. The constituent members of each set of people vary in their levels of competence, commitment to a solution, knowledge of the facts, moral outlook, and opinions about how given decisions should be handled. Decisions that are reached reflect the interplay of these people. The idea of attaining objective decisions that remove human subjectivity from the equation is silly. Making decisions outside a social context can yield unpleasant surprises and curve balls.

Second, decision-makers must recognize that decisions are the end product of wrestling with constraints: constraints of knowledge, time, resources, skills, political forces, legacy, laws of nature, human laws, ethics, personalities, and more. Effective decision making requires decision-makers to surface these constraints and figure out how to craft workable decisions that accommodate them. More often than not, they find themselves fitting square pegs into round holes. The common wisdom holds: "You can't fit square pegs into round holes." Actually, you can—if you possess a sharp pocket knife and good whittling skills. In real-world decision making, people fit square pegs into round holes all the time. Certainly this can lead to bad decisions, but sometimes decision-makers have little choice and the results of the whittling yield good-enough decisions.

Just about everyone agrees that constraints can color decisions. Even strong adherents of objective decision making grudgingly agree with this. However, the constraints are often treated as nuisances that distract from the real decision-making effort. The view taken in this book is that these constraints are central to the decision-making process, not secondary forces. Rather than distract from real decision making, they often drive it. They should be examined carefully and should not be brushed aside.

Social Context

When decision making is viewed as a social activity, it is clear that to understand it, you need to comprehend its human context. For example, people make decisions to achieve both selfish and altruistic ends. Or a decision may be wise, but the people implementing it foolish and incompetent. Or a decision may be foolish, putting wise people into the difficult position of trying to make it work. In articulating needs, some people may be insightful and clear thinking, so that they capture needs effectively; others may be dull and generally clueless, promoting nonsense needs.

To make this point concrete, consider a hypothetical example. When a publicly traded company shuts down a factory, the decision to do so incorporates inputs from a broad array of people, including senior executives, members of the board of directors, labor union leaders, consultants, plant managers, market analysts (if the decision will have an impact on stock price), and possibly political leaders in the affected community. The decision will have an impact on many people, including employees (who stand to lose their jobs), shareholders (who can expect either a rise or fall of stock price), vendors (who may experience lost business), local political leaders (who may face loss of employment in their districts), and the public (whose negative views may harm the company's reputation). Each of these players constitutes a stakeholder group in the decision process. Each stakeholder group will have a different perspective on the question of shutting down the factory, and those most heavily affected by the decision may strive mightily to influence the outcome of the decision process. As Miles's law perceptively observes, "Where you stand depends on where you sit" (Miles, 1978).

When considering stakeholder views, we often unconsciously hold that the constituent members of each stakeholder group possess a monolithic perspective.

We say things like, "This is what the public wants," or "This is the implementers' interpretation of the requirements," or "Senior management has determined that this is what needs to happen." In reality, the perspectives of individual stakeholder members vary. Consider the principal decision-makers. In getting to a final decision, members of this group will argue diverse views on what should be done. Once the decision is made, there will be varying degrees of agreement with and support for it. Even after a decision has been made, it may be misleading to offer a blanket statement suggesting that the decision-makers agree on the outcome. Some may; some may not. There will be differing degrees of agreement among those who support the outcome. Some decision-makers might be so hostile to the outcome that they strive to nullify it—if not now, then later. Of course, this hostile response might be offset by fervent champions of the decision who will do all they can to make sure it is carried out properly—at any cost.

The motivations underlying their positions vary. Some will be heavily influenced by selfish concerns; for example, if a decision leads to a drop in stock price, their personal wealth will also drop. Others will function altruistically, supporting a position that will strengthen the long-term health of the organization even if it yields short-term pain. Still others will strike a position reflecting their whimsical preferences of the moment.

Consider also the people charged with executing the decision. They are usually a different set of people from the decision-makers, and they too are not a monolithic body. When they are commanded to implement the decision, some may disagree with it, in which case their commitment to doing a good job is questionable. Their degrees of competence will vary: the highly competent will help deliver the desired solution effectively, while the incompetent will thwart its achievement—not through evil intent, but through incompetence. Their interpretation of the terms of the decision may not match the intended requirements of the decision-maker. This happens all the time. It is rooted in communication failure. The decision-makers say, "Do X." The implementers hear, "Do Y." In this case, the actions carried out to implement a decision do not reflect the intent of the formulated decision.

The point is that decision making is rooted in people who have diverse values and capabilities that affect the choices they make. Even when there is a sole decision-maker and the decision entails narrow technical choices, it occurs in a social context. The social aspect of decision making should not be considered an afterthought, something to be looked at once data have been collected and prioritization tools identified. It is in fact the launching point for crafting good decisions.

Constraints

In addressing the constraints decision-makers face, this book adopts a Stoic perspective. Stoicism as a philosophy emerged in Greece in the third century B.C.E. However, its most influential proponent was a freed Roman slave named Epictetus, born circa 50 C.E. Like Socrates, Epictetus never wrote down his ideas. However, one of his students, Arrian, took extensive notes of his discourses and compiled them in the *Enchiridion*. Our knowledge of Epictetus's teachings comes from the *Enchiridion* (Epictetus, 1991).

The principal Stoic lesson arises from a statement that appears early in the *Enchiridion*, where Epictetus notes: "In life, there are things you control, and things you do not control. Focus on the things you control." Sancho Panza showed Stoic proclivities when he cautioned Don Quixote, "Don't tilt against windmills."

To most people, the term *stoic* is associated with the ability to face adversity with a stiff upper lip. Stoics are seen to be people who accept tribulations without complaint. This interpretation, however, does not actually reflect the Stoic perspective. The interpretation arose because Stoics did not express strong grief when family or friends died. Their phlegmatic bearing was not tied to a stay-tough attitude but reflected their view that death was something over which they had no control. Since death is inevitable and uncontrollable, it doesn't make sense to wallow in grief when you lose a loved one.

This perspective has a bearing on decision making. Decisions are crafted in a context of limits. Limits constrain action. Decision-makers are like the artist who is given a No. 10 sable hair paint brush and a palette containing one color, prussian blue: there is only so much he can do with these materials. Effective decision making requires people to understand the limits constraining them.

The following sections consider some important limits.

Limited Information. This is a favorite topic among decision-making experts and is covered in many decision-making books. It has a name: *decision making with uncertainty.* In the effort of trying to make a decision, a universal frustration facing decision-makers is the absence of crucial information on how things now stand, as well as on the consequences associated with pursuing different decision-making alternatives. For example, when thinking about developing a new product that will entail a substantial investment, senior managers may be thwarted from making an informed judgment because they lack information on the product development challenges they will face, the array of competing products that will be in the market at the time the new product is rolled out, and the future state of the economy. Conventional decision-making perspectives deal with risk and uncertainty by factoring probabilities into the decision-making process.

Limited Capabilities. A decision is no better than the capacity of people to implement it. What's the point of deciding to make an omelet if you don't have eggs, or to enter a singing contest if you are tone deaf? There is often a gap between an ideal image of how a decision will be implemented and reality. While decision X may in theory appear to be a great one, in practice it will be flawed if no one is able to implement it effectively.

Limited Commitment. Everything that pertains to limited capabilities pertains equally to commitment. If the people responsible for executing a decision have little commitment to implementing it aggressively, it is unlikely that the decision will be actionable. Commitment can be low for various reasons. As a general rule, people who are consistently indifferent to their job responsibilities are not likely to be diligent in fulfilling requirements to implement any decision. Those who are hostile to the decision may implement it grudgingly or may actually work to sabotage it. Those who are normally diligent in doing their jobs may be so overwhelmed with other chores that they do not have the time to do what needs to be done. When commitment to implement a decision is low, the fate of the decision is jeopardized.

Limited Imagination. When making decisions, decision-makers must be able to envision a wide range of scenarios, addressing a variety of questions such as these: What great things can we do? What are our adversaries doing? What crazy alternatives can we visualize, and what are their likely consequences? When we face difficult challenges, what creative approaches can we take to execute our decisions? The answers to these and other pertinent questions will vary dramatically from person to person and group to group. Individuals and groups blessed with a rich imagination will likely generate superior decisions to those who possess limited imaginations.

Legacy-Rooted Limitations. Sometimes decision-makers find themselves in the position of mastodons trapped in a tar pit: they have a good sense of what actions they should take, but they are unable to shake free of the sticky strands of legacy that bog them down. Legacy can constrain decision making in many ways. The best known is revealed in the statement: "We've never done things this way before." This outlook forces people to follow deeply rutted paths that have been traveled many times. Legacy also may be rooted in operating rules that are obsolete, sales commission regimes that distort behavior, peer pressure that discourages risk taking, and so on. In one of the most insightful management books written in recent years, *The Innovator's Dilemma* (1997), Clayton Christensen points out that a company's customers may be the primary culprits killing initiatives that promote innovation. This is a fascinating finding in view of the universal mantra offered at business schools: "Always listen to your customer." It suggests that listening to your customer too attentively can lead to your demise. The important point here is that legacy can prevent people from deciding what needs to be decided.

Psychological Limitations. History and literature are filled with stories of people whose downfall was rooted in psychological limitations. Hitler's megalomania caused him to deny the possibility of a Normandy landing by the allies. Digital Equipment Corporation's downfall was rooted in its prideful CEO's refusal to pursue what he perceived to be the second-rate technology of personal computers. Psychologically unable to bite the bullet to deal with the Nazi threat, Neville Chamberlain's appeasement policies provided Hitler the time he needed to strengthen Germany's military might. In *Crime and Punishment*, Raskolnikov's obsession with the theory of the extraordinary man leads him to believe he can commit murder without consequence. What holds true for these specific examples applies universally in the arena of decision making. People are a product of their psychological makeup, which limits the range of actions they are capable of envisioning and pursuing.

Biological Limitations. Ultimately all decisions trace back to electrical and chemical activity that occurs within a sponge-like organ that resides inside the skulls of humans. In the final analysis, how people perceive and respond to events is determined by the way their brain functions. The brain is the most complex thing we are aware of, and we have only a rudimentary grasp of how it works. Thanks to the brain's filtering activity, no two people perceive reality in exactly the same way. This means that even the clearest facts are subject to multiple interpretations, which has big implications for decision making.

Limited Time. Decision-makers rarely have the time they need to be thorough in reaching decisions. This situation arises for a number of reasons. For example, they often do not have enough time to collect the information needed to make an informed decision. Or if they are unable to achieve quick consensus on a decision, they may find deliberations extended indefinitely. Or if they are required to make spot decisions, they need to respond instantly, in which case there is no option to spend time reviewing alternatives carefully.

Moral Limitations. Decisions are colored by values, which vary substantially among cultures, and within a culture they vary from individual to individual. Historically, values and their moral implications have not been consciously addressed in traditional decision-making theory and practice, where it has been assumed that people obey the law and generally behave in accordance with accepted moral practice. Of course, decision scientists recognize that moral shortcomings exist in humans, but these have not been viewed as central determinants of how decisions are made and consequently have not been incorporated into decision-making theory and practice. I confess that in most of my thirty years of teaching decision making, I stuck with the party line and treated decision making as morally neutral. Today, I believe this is a naive perspective. It took the likes of Michael Milken, Ivan Boesky, Nick Leeson, Bernie Madoff, the traders at AIG's Financial Products division, and countless men and women selling subprime loans to unqualified buyers to wake me to the real impact of moral factors on decision making. These individuals are the big players. Their questionable moral practices that have been carried out on a grand scale also exist on a microlevel among people making everyday decisions.

Limits Rooted in the Power and Political Actions of the Players. In some cases, the most significant limit constraining decision making is tied to the power status and political actions of key players. When Joseph Stalin said, "This is my decision," the search for optimal alternatives would stop. In this scenario, the decision-making process was easy: implement whatever decision Stalin dictated. When power issues are more complex, entailing two or more players, and entail influencing decisions through political action, the decision-making process becomes more difficult. However, as the players jockey to gain advantage, there is an opportunity to see to it that decision making accommodates merit as a decision criterion.

Limits Imposed by External Forces. Some constraints lie completely out of the control of decision-makers—for example, economic downturns, actions of competitors, the sudden rise and fall of new fads, force majeure (hurricanes, fires, tsunamis, and so forth), and government regulations. In the risk management arena, various strategies are employed to deal with these external sources of risk, including establishing contingency reserves (a risk-acceptance strategy), making decisions that steer you away from potentially bad events (a risk-avoidance strategy), and purchasing insurance and entering into contracts (risk-transfer strategies).

THE COGNITIVE CHALLENGE

The biggest limit of all is the cognitive limit: that is, the limit of what humans are capable of knowing. Because it is pervasive and governs all aspects of human perception, I am treating it separately from the other constraints.

The cognitive limit has two components. One is the limit of what we can know imposed on us by the structure and operation of the brain. Every sensation we experience is intermediated by the brain. Every idea we hold is a product of the brain's interpretation of the data it processes: 1,400 grams of wet meat, 100 billion neurons, trillions of neuronal pathways, 11.2 million bits of information processed per second! The role of the brain in decision making is becoming a hot topic, thanks in large measure to advances in technology that enable scientists to track brain activity, particularly fMRI (functional magnetic resonance imaging) technology. One of the most significant findings of recent brain studies is recognition that in its search for efficiency, the brain is constantly taking shortcuts to conserve energy. For example, when it experiences an event, it stores the experience in a virtual storage bin of reusable templates that define human perceptions of future experiences. What you see is not what you get—literally. What you see is the brain's best guess of what you are actually experiencing. This book dedicates two chapters to covering the emerging area of the biology of decision making.

The second component is philosophical, falling in the domains of epistemology and ontology. Epistemology is concerned with how we acquire, interpret, and disseminate knowledge. Ontology is concerned with what is real. What this second component addresses is the notion that facts are determined contextually— they are not objective truths—and do not speak for themselves. There is only so much humans can know.

ADJUSTING TO THE NEW PARADIGM

In *The Structure of Scientific Revolutions* (1996), Thomas Kuhn notes that paradigm shifts occur when the prevailing paradigm is unable to resolve troubling puzzles. For example, in the late nineteenth century, James Clerk Maxwell developed four equations that together constituted a comprehensive theory of electrodynamics. These equations treated light as an electromagnetic wave and became the mainstay of beliefs regarding electromagnetic phenomena. However, in examining what was called the photoelectric effect, where certain metals emit electrons when exposed to light, Einstein discovered that Maxwell's equations did not work. In 1905, he argued convincingly that light possessed the properties of particles, which he called photons and whose name was ultimately changed to quanta. He won the 1921 Nobel Prize for this insight (not for his theory of relativity). Thus began the quantum physics revolution that overturned the classical treatment of electromagnetic phenomena and opened the door to explaining how atoms work.

When paradigm shifts occur, the old paradigm often is not jettisoned in its entirety, though there are well-known cases where this has happened (for example, the rejection of the Ptolemaic view of an earth-centric solar system, phlogiston theory explaining how things ignite, and the concept of a pervasive ether through which electromagnetic waves travel). In its time, the old paradigm was successful because it supported workable predictions of phenomena. To the extent that components of the old paradigm still allow successful predictions, they are kept. For example, Einstein's general theory of relativity demonstrates that gravity does not really exist as a force; what appears to be the mutual attraction of objects is caused by the curvature of space-time, not a force of gravity. However, scientists continue to use equations based on Newton's theory of gravity because they work nicely for most of the phenomena we encounter. However, they cease to work effectively when dealing with super-massive and very small objects or when dealing with objects traveling at near light speed.

In this book, I maintain that we are undergoing a paradigm shift in our approach to decision making. The economic collapse of 2008–2009 cannot be adequately explained by the traditional paradigm's argument that people make bad decisions owing to uncertainty and imperfect information. Many of the players who contributed to the crisis knew exactly what they were doing. A better explanation is that owing to a host of social and moral factors, including deregulation, moral hazard, greed, hubris, and the principal-agent problem, key players in society made self-serving decisions that undermined good economic principles. This interpretation is in line with the emerging paradigm showcased in this book.

Having said this, I believe that much of the old paradigm has value, but its purview needs to be broadened. Despite my criticism of the premises of traditional approaches to decision making, I do not propose to throw out the baby with the bathwater. My principal criticism of the traditional decision-making perspective is that in its pursuit of the employment of quantitative tools and its single-minded drive to promote models based on rational behavior, it is too narrowly focused. It does not effectively deal with decision-making constraints and understates the social dimension of decision making.

Nonetheless, many of its techniques are valuable when dealing with structured, well-defined situations. Any operation built on well-defined processes can benefit mightily from the implementation of decision science tools. Manufacturing and logistics stand out here. In manufacturing, it is impossible to conceive of a profitable player being able to maintain profitability without using standard decision science tools such as linear programming. In logistics, we see that the miraculous growth of FedEx was tied to the employment of advanced algorithms that worked out the most efficient route to get package X from Selma, Alabama, to Fort Wayne, Indiana.

For example, regardless of its underlying premises, decision making entails prioritization among alternatives, and the traditional prioritization techniques are useful. Similarly, decisions are made under conditions of uncertainty, and many traditional insights regarding uncertainty are helpful.

CONCLUSION: IT ISN'T EASY GETTING IT RIGHT

From January 2008 through midsummer 2008, crude oil prices increased by nearly 50 percent. I initially watched the price rise with curiosity, and then with alarm. At the outset of the year, the price was steady and below $100 per barrel, which was hardly a bargain considering that crude was selling in the range of $60 per barrel one year earlier. In February, the price of crude broke through the $100 per barrel mark. Then it rose steadily and peaked at $145 per barrel in July, by far the highest price in history.

As the price climbed to unprecedented levels, I expected this to be headline news in newspapers and on television broadcasts, particularly in view of the fact that this oil shock was occurring at the same time frightening stories were surfacing about horrific problems with subprime loans. Instead, while the record oil prices were nonchalantly reported as records, most commentary focused on the impacts of the price hikes on the summer driving habits of Americans! Here we faced the most massive and speediest transfer of wealth in the history of the world, chiefly from industrialized countries to oil-producing countries, and the American press and public were worried about what it would cost to run behemoth SUVs during the summer vacation.

There was something unreal about all of this.

Two months after crude oil prices peaked, the fourth largest investment bank in the United States, Lehman Brothers, went bankrupt, an event that helped trigger the onset of the world's worst recession since the Great Depression.

Fast-forward one month after the collapse of Lehman Brothers. In October 2008, I facilitated a one-week off-site executive training program directed at upper-level managers being groomed to run a large shipping company. The managers were bright young men and women from Europe, North Africa, Asia, and the United States. Some of them were destined to be the leaders of their substantial shipping enterprise. This was a high-status, high-impact management development program. The participants were smart, dedicated people who were willing to work sixty-hour weeks year after year in order to serve their company.

During the week, participants steadily produced presentations describing their perception of the greatest challenge their company faced: managing success. Participant after participant provided trend data on the growth of their business in this port and that, and talked about the challenges of managing this growth effectively. Port facilities needed to be expanded. Information systems needed to be upgraded to handle the increased scale of business. The human resource departments at different ports needed to hire more people.

As the participants described the challenges their company faced, I grew increasingly uncomfortable. Although I was no expert on international shipping, my understanding of the current unraveling of the global financial system made it clear to me that these bright men and women were living in a fantasy world. To them, the big challenge they faced was how to manage effectively the buckets of money they would continue to be making. It was common wisdom among prominent government officials, economists, and business players that international trade would grow explosively. But this isn't what I saw. If we were lucky, we were on the verge of a serious recession; if unlucky, we faced a reprise of the Great Depression. One thing was clear: given current economic trends, global trade would slow down or grind to a halt. Participants deflected all of my efforts to shift the discussion to the possibility of a business slowdown. In fact, a senior manager attending the session took me aside and told me to stick to the script and stop politicizing the event.

It was unreal.

The global economy imploded within weeks of this management development session. Two months after the managers returned to their jobs, the *Washington Post* pictured a photo of empty container ships moored in a mile-long line outside Singapore. For the next year, global shipping ground to a halt.

The fact that the key decision-makers of a large shipping company were so wrong about their business prospects at a time when there were many signs indicating an imminent global economic implosion is disturbing. But these players reflected the rule, not the exception. Few business and government leaders saw what was coming, even though the evidence that things were amiss was abundant. The most convincing explanation of the collective blindness to the impending disaster is that business and government leaders were convinced of the efficacy of finely tuned economic and financial policy. The fact that business and government working together managed to minimize economic troubles for some forty years led to a feeling that financial crises were a thing of the past. The possibility of economic Armageddon was inconceivable.

In a word, the implosion was rooted in hubris.

This experience offers a lesson for decision-makers: they need to be humble. They need to recognize the limits of their ability to fully understand and handle the challenges they face. They need to expand their perspectives and start thinking about the unthinkable, because the unthinkable occurs more often than they would suspect.

2 Decisions and Decision Making

It is easy to argue that decision making is no big deal. Everyone does it, and they do it every day.

To support this point, consider some decisions I made this morning before leaving for work:

- I *decided* to take a shower.
- I *decided* to cook two eggs and two pieces of bacon for breakfast.
- I *decided* what to wear.
- I *decided* what route to take to work after hearing the morning traffic report.

During the morning, I also carried out routine actions automatically, including these:

- I took out the trash, because it is trash collection day.
- I drank two cups of strong coffee (this routine hasn't changed in twenty years).
- I fetched the morning newspaper from the driveway.

These morning choices entail routine decisions that I make with little or no thought. As the day progresses and I engage in management decisions at the office, the decision-making effort becomes more explicit:

- I *decide* on an approach to take to craft a lecture I will deliver next week.
- When reading student papers, I *decide* what grades to give.

- In my capacity as academic dean, I *decide* how the university policy on academic dishonesty should be reframed.

- In conjunction with the curriculum committee, which I head, I *decide* to support the expansion of our engineering management curriculum.

When the workday is done, and after I have returned home, I continue the decision-making effort, but in a more relaxed vein:

- I *select* a menu for dinner.

- I *decide* to drink a glass of merlot wine.

- I *decide* how I want to spend the evening. Television? Reading? Writing?

The happy fact is that on a typical day, I make many decisions without exertion. By the time I turn off the bedside lamp at 11:00 P.M., I am hardly aware that I have made any decisions at all.

The lesson here is that decision making is an integral part of life. Everyone is a decision-maker, and during the course of a day we make innumerable decisions without conscious effort.

Given this fact, it may seem pointless to write a book on decision making, since we all have expertise in this area through our life experiences. Why would you educate people on a topic they already know? You wouldn't teach a chef how to boil an egg, so why teach natural decision-makers how to decide things?

The answer is simple. When it comes to *unconscious decisions*—the scores of decisions people make each day, without paying attention—people do a pretty good job, and there isn't much to discuss that will enlighten them on what decision making entails. Their responses are determined automatically in accordance with context and experience. A key point is that the consequences of the decision are small. Should a decision turn out to be wrong, the impact is inconsequential. For example, if I routinely elect to have two cups of coffee each day, that reflects my personal preference and is a matter of little consequence. It may be that one morning I drink my two cups of coffee and suffer acid reflux. So what? If acid reflux persists, I will cut back to one cup a day. The point is that I don't need a decision-making expert to offer me insights on coffee drinking consequences and alternatives.

However, when it comes to *mindful decisions*—consequential decisions that require a measure of reflection—we move beyond the natural decision-making capabilities of most people. Mindful decisions have consequences that register above some invisible critical threshold. Let's say a recent research breakthrough shows that people who drink two or more cups of coffee each day encounter an increased likelihood of developing a large wart on the tip of their nose. When I read about this finding in the morning newspaper (which I have unconsciously retrieved from the driveway), I sense what feels like a jolt of electricity pass through my body. This information has direct bearing on my life. The decision to drink two cups of coffee a day is no longer inconsequential: I don't want a large wart on my nose. At the same time, I don't want to give up my cherished two cups of coffee per day. What had been an unconscious decision that served me well for twenty years morphs into a mindful decision requiring study and conscious prioritization.

The principal feature of mindful decisions is the existence of nontrivial decision-making consequences. There is no need to linger over decisions with minuscule consequences. Consider the following scenario: As I approach a McDonald's outlet at the airport, I am debating whether to order a Big Mac or Quarter Pounder. The difference between the two is of little consequence. Certainly one isn't healthier than the other, because each is chock full of calories, salt, fat, and carbohydrates. They taste pretty much the same, since they have the same core ingredients. When I reach the counter, an employee asks: "What can I get you, sir?" Without thinking, I blurt out "A Quarter Pounder, please." I could have just as well said, "A Big Mac, please." It really makes little difference.

Contrast the purchase of a hamburger with the purchase of a new automobile. Buying a new car is highly consequential. To begin with, it entails a substantial investment: for most people, the purchase of a car is the second largest purchase they make, second only to the purchase of a house. It also has psychological importance, because buyers realize that whatever car they buy projects an image of who they are. Beyond this, it will be a cash flow drain into the foreseeable future, with monthly loan payouts, insurance expenses, maintenance costs, and gasoline expenses. Clearly there are additional consequences that car buyers think about beyond the short list offered here.

This book focuses on mindful decisions—those with nontrivial consequences. Mindful decisions are not made using autonomic responses. They require conscious reflection. In thinking about an impending decision, decision-makers sort through many considerations. Of course, one of the most important is the consequence of the decision. What is its nature? Will it be big or little? Who will it affect? Many decision-makers carry their reflections forward at least one more step, and look at WIIFM: What's in it for me? Other considerations are revealed in the questions: What will it cost to pursue different alternatives? What effort will it take? Am I qualified to pursue the alternatives? Will benefits outweigh costs? And so on.

This chapter aims to do two things. First, it highlights contributions to the theory and practice of decision making that come from a range of disciplines. Anyone who has read about decision making from the perspective of public policy will confirm that public policy writings make no reference to work done in decision science and other disciplines. By the same token, decision scientists appear vaguely aware of important insights that social psychologists and neuroscientists have developed. For their part, social psychologists and neuroscientists function in isolation from other disciplines. I hope that the effort to explore what's going on in a handful of key disciplines in this chapter can contribute to expanding the domain of decision-making theory and practice.

Second, the chapter highlights two important issues that color our approach to decision making, whether we are decision scientists, social psychologists, philosophers, or members of some other discipline. One is the issue of the degree to which decision making is or should be focused on pursuing rationality. Certainly traditional views on decision making make the achievement of rationality a top priority. But it is not clear that such an aspiration is either achievable or desirable. This chapter offers preliminary coverage of this issue, which I explore in more depth in later chapters.

A second issue goes to the heart of the biggest problem facing decision-makers: they operate in a world of unknowns and seldom have all the information they need to make the best decisions. Ironically, they often have good-enough information to guide them on routine decisions but lack critical information on truly significant, high-impact decisions. Again, the coverage of this issue here is brief; I offer no more than a thumbnail sketch. The challenge of handling unknowns will be treated more fully in later chapters.

DIFFERENT PERSPECTIVES ON DECISION MAKING

Because decision making is a universal activity, it should not be surprising to learn that it is a component of several disciplines and that some of these disciplines have their own particular spin on it. While the decision science discipline is dedicated entirely to the making of decisions, its perspectives do not cover everything there is to know about decision making. In fact, when considering the full realm of decision-making possibilities, it is clear that decision science holds a decidedly narrow outlook on what decision making entails.

This section looks at different perspectives on decision making associated with different disciplines. Even here, I focus only on the disciplines that deal with decision making explicitly. For example, I do not look at decision making in the natural sciences—physics, astronomy, earth science, chemistry, or biology—because the decision-making process is incidental (though important) to their core rationale. What may surprise readers is that I do look at neuroscience (this book dedicates a full chapter to it) since all decisions that people make—100 percent of them—are ultimately tied to the firing of synapses in the brain. Everything that people perceive, every opinion they hold, is intermediated by the brain. As scientists develop greater insights into the structure and functioning of the brain and its intermediating role in decision making, it becomes clear that treatises on decision making will need to accommodate the new knowledge.

Looking at different approaches to decision making offers a fuller view of what it entails, enabling us to go beyond the insights that are treated in traditional approaches to covering this topic.

Disciplines that play big roles in understanding decision making are decision science, economics, public policy, social psychology, psychology, law, neuroscience, and philosophy.

Decision Science

I start with a review of the discipline that deals with decision making most explicitly: decision science, dedicated to exploring the theory and practice of decision making. It also goes by the name of management science and, in a narrower context, operations research. There is no firm agreement on the extent of its purview. As we saw in Chapter One, the journal *Decision Sciences* sees the discipline as focused on "the latest computer technology, mathematical and statistical techniques, and behavioral science" as they pertain to decision making. This is the prevailing perspective among most of its practitioners, but not all. The Decision Sciences Institute (DSI), a leading professional society, identifies its mission as follows: "**Mission:** The Decision Sciences Institute advances the science and practice of decision making." Its vision is stated as follows: "**Vision:** The Decision Sciences Institute is dedicated to excellence in fostering and disseminating knowledge pertinent to decision making." This is pretty all-encompassing. Actually, DSI shows its true colors in the opening statement on its Web site: "The Decision Sciences Institute (DSI) is a professional organization of academicians and practitioners interested in the application of quantitative and behavioral methods to the problems of society." Despite the sweeping purview articulated in its mission and vision statements, its principal concern is with quantitative approaches.

The decision science discipline is often closely associated with a set of decision-making tools that it promotes. Three categories of tools are prominent: tools that address optimization, systems analysis, and model building.

In some circles, decision science is viewed more expansively as the systematic approach to understanding the decision-making effort in its broadest context. This is how we viewed it during my nineteen years at the Department of Management Science at George Washington University. Certainly a cornerstone of our program addressed quantitative techniques, information systems, and decision support systems, but we also included organizational behavior, leadership, and technology management in our domain. However, our approach reflects the exception and not the rule.

Economics

When approached formally, economics is defined as the study of the allocation of resources under conditions of scarcity. On a practical level, economics is concerned with people buying and selling things in the market. Because economic activity lends itself to quantitative analysis, the discipline has become strongly quantified over the past century and a half, beginning with the work of Leon Walras (1834–1910). The pages of leading economics journals are often packed with more mathematical symbols and equations than you would find in leading physics journals. A substantial portion of the time economists spend in doing their jobs is developing mathematical and statistical models describing economic activity.

These models play an important role in decision making. Governments use them to understand and handle the complexities of the national and global economy. The models enable them to test and execute monetary policies, provide them with guidance on pursuing fiscal policies, offer a view of the future of the economy through what-if analyses, and so on. Financial companies use economic models to provide them guidance on buying and selling financial assets. One of the best-known (and most notorious) economics-rooted financial models was the one built in accordance with the efficient market orientation of Myron Scholes and Robert Merton (future Nobel laureates) for Long Term Capital Management (LTCM), a hedge fund that began operations in 1994. Employing the model to guide investments enabled it to experience fantastic initial returns of 40 percent a year for a few years. But excessive confidence in the model's magic led LTCM's leaders to overleverage themselves. The Russian default crisis of August–September 1998 caused bond prices to move in directions contrary to the model's predicted behavior, leading to losses of billions of dollars and triggering an emergency bailout of LTCM by other Wall Street players (Lowenstein, 2000).

Economists and others debate whether the discipline depends too heavily on its models to explain economic activity and provide decision-making guidance. It is easy to become seduced by the sophistication and predictive capabilities of these models, particularly since many of the most significant models are grounded in solid economic theory that has withstood the test of time. Their weak underbelly is their assumptions. This was Herbert Simon's concern when he questioned the assumption of rationality built into many models. As the models grow in complexity and sophistication, they incorporate an ever-expanding list of assumptions. What LTCM experienced with its model's costly hiccup showed us that if just one of these assumptions is violated, it can introduce unexpected volatility that has disastrous consequences.

What I have described here can be roughly categorized as the traditional economics perspective—what students in typical university economic programs can expect to study as they work toward their degrees. Within economics, however, prominent schools of thought stand outside the traditional sphere and offer differing perspectives on decision making. Practitioners of behavioral economics focus on how the peculiarities of human cognitive processes play a role in economic decision making. They reject key assumptions that underlie most economic models, particularly those that hold that decision-makers are rational and focused entirely on maximizing their gain. A large portion of their scholarly effort is based on experiments they carry out on how people really make decisions.

Another prominent school focuses on public goods, which contrasts with the attention offered private goods by traditional economists. Public goods have two distinguishing traits: nonrivalry and nonexcludability. Nonrivalry means that your consumption of a good does not keep others from consuming it as well. For example, when I breathe air, I am not depriving others of access to air themselves. Contrast this to private goods, which are rivalrous: when I buy a ticket to a concert, that leaves one fewer ticket for others to purchase. Nonexcludability means that everyone has access to the good. Public parks offer access to everyone. Country clubs, in contrast, restrict access to members. An example of a public good is national defense: one individual's coverage does not deprive coverage of others, and it extends to all people residing within the boundaries of a country (even traitors).

Yet another school of economics focuses on game theory. The game-theoretic perspective sees people's behavior as being responsive to actual and anticipated actions undertaken by others. John's decision on the price to sell his antique dresser is determined by his perception of Mary's desire to acquire it. For her part, Mary feigns disinterest in the antique dresser, knowing that John will charge more if she appears eager to purchase it. The microscale game that John and Mary are playing can be extended to cover national economic strategies pursued by governments and military strategies between countries and can be used to explain a range of human behaviors, including altruism.

Public Policy

Decision making is a key component of public policy. In fact, public policy can be defined entirely in decision-making terms as follows: *the principal concern of public policy is for government to make and implement decisions that serve the public good.*

All high-level decision making in government can be subsumed under public policy, including, for example, decisions on tax levies, road construction, sewage treatment, education outlays, immigration laws, and defense spending.

What distinguishes decision making when viewed from a public policy perspective is that it is carried out by public servants and is directed at serving the public good. The biggest decision-making challenge facing public servants is determining what the public good is. The source of this challenge is that *the public* is not a homogeneous entity. The public comprises many players—individual citizens, businesses, political groups, ethnic groups, the powerful, the disenfranchised, and many more—who have different views on the policies that government should pursue. Despite the well-intentioned imprecations of pundits who maintain that proper public policy can be devised to yield win-win solutions to problems, the reality is that public policy decisions cannot escape the zero-sum nature of many problems: it often happens that constituent A's interests can be served only at the expense of constituent B's.

Public policy decisions face significant pitfalls. The most obvious is that these decisions are made by politicians who find it difficult to ignore serving the special interests of their constituents. You could argue that serving constituents is hardly a pitfall, because that's the politicians' principal charge. Problems arise, however, when politicians address the wants of one set of constituents at the expense of others and, when serving these interests, do not serve broader societal interests. In recent years, leaders of the two major political parties in the United States have found themselves captives of their party's political base, which comprises a minority of party members: antigovernment conservatives in the case of Republicans and left-wing liberals in the case of Democrats. Party leaders find that whatever decisions they make are framed in such a way as to pass the litmus tests that their party's base has established, no matter how contrary to the broader public good.

Another significant decision-making challenge associated with public policy is dealing with the ever-lurking possibility of moral hazard—the situation that arises when people who have fiduciary responsibility for a client's assets take risks that they would not take had they been dealing with their own money. We saw that prior to the financial implosion of 2008–2009, traders on Wall Street took irresponsible risks with investors' money, knowing that they would benefit handsomely if the investments paid off and that they faced no personal loss if the investments failed. By the same token, in the public sector there are politicians who are profligate in spending taxpayer money if it enables them to curry favor with their constituents, even if such spending damages the interests of the public at large. Like Wall Street traders, they have no personal stake in spending other people's money.

Social Psychology

Social psychology is a discipline that bridges two much larger disciplines: psychology and sociology. Whereas psychology investigates the behavior of individuals and sociology examines the behavior of human collectives such as small groups, large groups, and communities, social psychology addresses the effects of social forces on individuals.

Social psychology got its start in the mid-twentieth century with the work of Muzafer Sherif and Solomon Asch. Both of these men were interested in devising experiments to see how individual decision making was affected in group settings. In his 1935 doctoral dissertation, Sherif studied the autokinetic effect. In his experiments, a small group of subjects sat in a darkened room with a small light spot projected on a screen before them. While sitting in the darkened room, each subject experienced the autokinetic effect: the spot appeared to move, although it was in fact stationary. While individuals sitting alone in the room would report many variations on the distance traveled by the spot, when people observed the spot as a group, they achieved a consensus on the distance traveled. When they were individually brought back to the darkened room one week later, they continued to assess the distance traveled as they had when in a group, leading Sherif to conclude that when dealing with events collectively, groups can achieve consensus on their meaning, even if there is no objective basis for this consensus. And after groups disband, their members persist in maintaining the norms they establish through their group-based decisions.

Asch's (1955) most famous experiment entailed bringing together a group of five to seven people. Only one was a true experimental subject; the others were actors pretending to be subjects. Asch showed the group an image of a line segment. Then he showed them three additional line segments of different lengths and asked them to identify which of the three line segments matched the original one. At the outset of the experiment, the actors would identify the correct line segment and the subject would concur. But after a small number of trials, each of the actors would begin selecting a line segment that was clearly wrong. By the time the true subjects were asked to identify the correct line segment, 37 percent of the time they conformed to the conclusion of the majority, even though it was clearly wrong. Only 25 percent stuck by their guns and gave the correct answer 100 percent of the time. This study demonstrated that the power of conformity could cause people to make incorrect judgments, owing to people's fear of going against the crowd.

The best-known social psychology study on social pressure for conformity in decision making was Milgram's 1961 experiment, where subjects were placed in a room and could observe other subjects (who were actually actors) through a glass pane in an adjacent room (Milgram, 1963). The true subjects were called teachers, and what turned out to be fake subjects were called learners. The teachers would ask the learners simple questions. If the learners got them wrong, the teachers were required to turn a dial that would shock the learners. Each time a learner made an error, the intensity of the shock would be increased by 15 volts. As the shocks appeared to increase in intensity, the learners (actors) would feign more and more discomfort. What was alarming was that in one set of experiments, two-thirds of the teachers continued ratcheting up to the point where the voltage reached 450 volts. Early in the trials, many of the teachers expressed misgivings about the pain they were inflicting on the learners but were urged to continue by the experiment's facilitator (an authority figure), which they did. Milgram's conclusion is that people will engage in behaviors they believe to be wrong if pressured to do so by authority figures.

Psychology

Psychology is a broad discipline that looks at all aspects of human mental processes and states. It comprises many subdisciplines, including perception (how humans collect data from the world around them), cognition (how humans process and interpret the perceived data), personality (how humans function in their daily lives), development (how humans develop psychologically beginning in the womb), and abnormal psychology (human dysfunctionality). The areas of psychology with the strongest ties to decision making are personality, cognition, and perception. Cognition and perception are closely linked to the functioning of the brain, and in this book they are addressed in the two chapters dealing with what I call the biology of decision making.

Personality is important in decision making because it colors an individual's decision-making practices. Psychologists have addressed this fact for many years, and their insights are well known among students of management. For example, the psychologist Abraham Maslow (1954) developed his hierarchy-of-needs concept based on the premise that people's approach to dealing with the world (including making decisions) is tied to their way of handling the challenges they face. If they are struggling to get by during bad times, their primary concern is survival, and this is reflected in simple decisions to do what is necessary to survive. If they have reached a point in life where their physical and social needs are adequately met, their life choices reflect a self-actualization outlook, where they make decisions to support their growth as individuals.

There are other well-known decision-related psychological perspectives applied to the practice of management. Robert R. Blake and Jane Mouton's (1964) concept of the managerial grid focuses on a manager's preference to make decisions that provide employees with a comfortable life versus one that has them producing as much as possible, regardless of personal consequences. David McClelland's (1961) concepts of need to achieve (N-Ach) and need for affiliation (N-Aff) hold that personality factors play a significant role in determining the choices people make. With N-Ach, their decisions are guided by a strong desire to make an impact and get ahead in life, while with N-Aff, their decisions reflect their desire to please others and not rock the boat. Carl Jung's (1971) theory of psychological types examines how people's personality makeup affects their approach to life. Jung addressed three dimensions of personality: preferences for extraversion versus introversion, for sensing versus intuition, and for thinking versus feeling. Katherine Briggs and Isabel Briggs Myers later added a fourth dimension, judging versus perceiving, when creating the Myers-Briggs psychological type framework (Myers, 1990).

Law: Adjudication

A legal system can be conceptualized as having three components: articulation of laws, adjudication, and enforcement, each requiring substantial decision making. Of these three, adjudication is the most interesting from a decision-making perspective, because the ultimate outcome of adjudication, whether through a jury trial or the verdict of one or more judges, is a decision of major consequence: the defendant is guilty or not guilty.

Viewing the adjudication process from a decision-making perspective highlights a problem all decision-makers face: how to identify what constitutes the best decision. Consider how the great majority of U.S. Supreme Court decisions are split decisions. Here we have nine presumably wise, well-educated, experienced men and women positioned at the pinnacle of the American legal system, and they almost never achieve full consensus on legal judgments. Ultimately the best decision is defined as the one made by the majority, whether the voting split is five judges ruling in the affirmative and four dissenting or all nine voting together.

Looking at adjudication from a decision-making perspective also provides another significant insight that the broad population of decision-makers wrestle with: the final decision—that is, the jury or judge's verdict—is sensitive to the standards of guilt that are established. Consider how O. J. Simpson was acquitted in a criminal trial but found guilty in a civil trial. The split decision can be explained in part by the different standards applied in the two trials. In the criminal trial, a standard of reasonable doubt prevailed. The judge instructed the jury that if there was room to doubt O. J. Simpson's guilt, then jurors should vote to acquit him. In the civil trial, a standard of preponderance of evidence prevailed. In this case, the judge instructed the jury that if the overall weight of evidence suggested O. J. Simpson's guilt, then jurors should find him guilty.

On the surface, it may appear that the two juries arrived at contradictory conclusions, and perhaps they did. But after considering the different standards of guilt that applied in the two trials, the contradictory verdicts can be explained as different results reflecting different standards.

Neuroscience

Few decision-making books address the biology of decision making, clearly a shortcoming of our orientation toward decision making. Because all human experience is intermediated by the brain, the operation of the brain has an impact on all human actions, including decision making. Until recently, decision-making experts in the decision science and economics disciplines have not directed much attention to the neurological aspects of decision making.

While traditional decision scientists do not study neuroscience, a growing coterie of neuroscientists is looking into the brain's role in decision making. They have begun applying their knowledge of the anatomy and functioning of the brain to understanding how decisions are made. Recent advances in brain mapping technology, particularly the introduction of fMRI (functional magnetic resonance imaging), enable scientists to correlate different types of decision-making chores with activity in different parts of the brain. Prominent neuroscientists and neuropsychologists are involved in this area of research, including Antonio Damasio, A. P. Dijksterhuis, Cordelia Fine, Robert Alan Burton, Jay Giedd, Deborah Yurgelun-Todd, Gregory Burns, Mark Changizi, and Timothy Wilson. Empirical studies carried out by these scientists address questions such as these: When making decisions, is it good practice to sleep on the problem before committing to a decision? Do women's brains function differently from men's when making choices? To what extent is objective decision making rooted in emotional responses of the brain?

Recent insights into the functioning of the brain challenge the widely held belief that problems can be resolved if we are able to master the facts. One of the key rules of effective decision making is: "Make sure you've got the facts straight. Do not make uninformed decisions." An understanding of how the brain functions suggests that facts cannot be objectively determined. In a sense, all decisions are uninformed in some measure. One thing that is certain is that two people looking at the same physical object, say a pencil, will have different visions of it because their brains process the stimulus differently. After the object's photons strike the observers' retinas, the data will travel down different paths to the occipital lobe for each observer and from there down different paths to the frontal cortex. Each of the brain's 100 billion neurons has links to 10,000 neurons (more than 1 trillion potential neural pathways can be traversed and the likelihood that the data will travel down identical paths for two people is effectively zero).

I would guess that some critics will ask: "Isn't delving into the functioning of the brain going overboard? Does somebody really need to know what's happening under a car's hood in order to drive the car?" I think the engine-under-the-hood metaphor is a good one. My answer to the car driving question is: "The more you know about how your car functions, the better able you are to deal with unanticipated contingencies that might arise while you are driving." We saw a good example of this in September 2009 when an off-duty highway patrol officer's Lexus sped out of control and ultimately crashed and killed its four occupants. What made the incident particularly horrifying was that we have the voice transcripts of a passenger's last words, since he was describing the incident in a phone call, even as the driver was trying to slow down his car. Maintaining a cool head and using basic knowledge of how cars work could have enabled the officer to stop his car. For example, an informed driver could (1) put the car in neutral, thereby disengaging the drive train; (2) turn the ignition key one click in the off direction, thereby turning off engine power without locking the steering wheel; and (3) recognize that the accelerator pedal might be jammed by the floor mat and dislodge the floor mat from the pedal.

Basic knowledge of the biology of decision making yields better insights into the decision-making process. For example, knowledge of the brain's workings will transform decision-makers' attitudes regarding the sanctity of facts. They will recognize that even allegedly unassailable facts may not be as solid as they think because all facts are artifacts of the brain's intervention. As Descartes (1965) pointed out long before the invention of fMRI, objective reality is elusive. The only certainty he was comfortable with was captured in his statement: "I think, therefore I am."

The idea that even the most solid facts can be shaky is buttressed by neuroscience research that examines visual illusions. By showing us images that do not actually exist, visual illusions demonstrate the brain's ability to be tricked. It is disconcerting to see how easy it is to fool the brain.

An understanding of brain functioning also provides decision-makers with a skeptical outlook on people's certainty about being correct on issues, including their own sense of certainty. The fact that someone feels absolutely certain that he or she is correct in understanding a problem and its solution does not necessarily have much meaning. Research suggests that feelings of absolute certainty are tied to a particular emotional state, which may not reflect truth. Recall Hitler's total feeling of certainty that the Allies would invade France at Calais, which led him to disregard the general staff's assessment that the invasion would be at Normandy beach (Burton, 2008).

Knowledge of the function and anatomy of the brain offers us many other insights. For example, in order to conserve energy, the brain constantly engages in predictive behavior: what a baseball batter sees traveling toward him at ninety miles an hour is not the actual baseball but the brain's projected image of the ball. With predictive behavior, what we see isn't necessarily what we get. Another example: in order to function efficiently, the brain depends heavily on templates drawn from experience. Consider that while you are walking on an ice-covered sidewalk, your brain does not carefully analyze how you should deal with this particular situation; rather, it guides your muscles and balance system by drawing on "slippery ice" templates that capture your prior experience walking on slippery surfaces.

Given the rapid advances neuroscientists are making in understanding how the brain contributes to decision making, it is certain that in the foreseeable future, standard decision-making texts will incorporate these new findings.

Philosophy

Philosophy seems so far afield of practical decision making that it is difficult to see how it can have a bearing on decision-making theory and practice. But it does. Several branches of philosophy have pursued lines of thought that are strongly pertinent. Four stand out:

- *Epistemology*, which focuses on how we gather, process, and interpret knowledge

- *Ontology*, a branch of metaphysics whose central concern revolves around looking at a fact or phenomenon and asking: Is it real?

- *Scientific reasoning*, which looks at examining problems from either an inductive or deductive perspective, recognizing the strengths and weaknesses of each approach

- *Explanation*, which examines how we can muster the data we have gathered, apply scientific reasoning, and develop solid explanations of why things happen the way they do

Together these philosophical perspectives cast light on the challenges that decision-makers face when making mindful decisions. *Epistemology* reminds us that "assembling the facts" is a nontrivial undertaking. Facts are not like fruit on a tree, waiting to be picked. Some have true substance; many do not. Furthermore, how you select your facts has a big impact on the facts available to you for decisions. In selecting facts, decision-makers often unconsciously choose those that buttress their personal biases so that their decisions are based on distorted reality.

Then we face the common situation where we are clueless as to what the facts are. Consider how government and industry decision-makers were paralyzed in determining how to react to the disastrous BP oil spill in the Gulf of Mexico in 2010 because they were overwhelmed in sorting through an avalanche of contradictory facts. For weeks, they had no idea of how much oil was gushing out of the well, this despite video images of the leak and decades of experience in dealing with malfunctioning wellheads.

Similarly, *ontology* reminds us that the facts and theories we develop that guide decisions are often shaky when examined carefully. Even facts backed by scientific research often turn out to be chimerical. The great eighteenth-century philosopher and skeptic David Hume (1988) offered convincing arguments demonstrating that we know far less than we think we do. This outlook is supported by David Freedman's powerful and meticulously documented book, *Wrong* (2010), demonstrating that a substantial portion of scientific findings headlined in the news today are without merit. Too often they reflect mere speculation based on flawed research methodologies. Because they provide findings that may intrigue the public, they are given substantial press coverage. A month or two later, they are yesterday's news, and follow-ups are seldom carried out to attest to their validity. Freedman's *Wrong* should be required reading for all decision-makers who claim to be intent on making fact-based decisions. By reading Freedman's book, they will learn that many of the facts that they employ to support their reasoning process are not facts at all.

Scientific reasoning addresses the logic people use to reach conclusions. There are two paths they can travel: deductive and inductive reasoning. As the Greeks recognized, deductive reasoning is unassailable. The conclusions are completely supported by the premises, as illustrated in the following example:

Premise A: Wang is Chinese.

Premise B: All Chinese use chopsticks.

Conclusion: Wang uses chopsticks.

If the premises are correct, then so are the conclusions that flow from them.

The big problem with deductive reasoning is that in the real world, few situations lend themselves to this way of explaining things. While deductive reasoning is employed heavily in mathematics, there are few other circumstances where it can be used effectively.

Inductive reasoning argues from specific observations to more general principles. All empirical science is built on inductive reasoning. Scientists observe phenomena through experiments or in their natural setting and then use the observed data to establish hypotheses and theories. When decision-makers ponder the logic of the circumstances they face in order to make decisions, they too operate inductively.

Philosophers have reflected on the implications of inductive reasoning for centuries and have established a large body of literature on this topic. Hume's well-known *problem of induction* provided the foundation for his skepticism. The induction problem holds that no matter how frequently you observe a phenomenon, you cannot say that the next observation will be in line with the previous ones. Philosophers of science like to illustrate this point with what they call the black swan story: if every swan an individual observes is white—let's say she has observed thousands—can she say with certainty that the next swan she observes will be white? The answer is no. Deductive reasoning can offer iron-clad logical conclusions, but inductive reasoning cannot.

As a historical aside, philosophers' use of the black swan example was an inside joke in the nineteenth century. Prior to the discovery of black swans in Australia in 1790, the only swans Europeans were acquainted with were white ones. Consequently, it could appear reasonable to speculate from observations of ten thousand swans, where each is white, that all swans are white. The sudden appearance of black swans provided a dramatic demonstration of the limits of inductive logic.

RATIONAL, IRRATIONAL, NONRATIONAL DECISIONS

When Herbert Simon introduced the concept of bounded rationality in the mid-1950s, he was addressing the assumption of traditional economic models that held that decision-makers function rationally (Simon, 1997). Rational behavior rests on meeting two requirements: (1) decision-makers have all the information they need to make decisions, and (2) in deciding among alternative courses of action, they select the choices that maximize utility. Utility is a concept introduced in 1738 by the Swiss-Dutch mathematician, Daniel Bernoulli (1954). Bernoulli recognized the limitations of assessing payoffs solely in monetary terms, noting, for example, that a 1,000 drachma prize is worth far more to a poor man than a rich one. Consequently, he posited an abstract payoff measure he titled utility, which would serve as a measure of the innate value of something to someone. It may be as simple as financial returns or more subtle, such as a sense of fulfillment of personal preferences.

Thus, the traditional perspective holds that by using perfect information and pursuing a drive to maximize utility, those who are buying goods and services in the market pay the "right" price, given the constraints that exist in the market. Rational decision making leads to optimal choices.

The problem is that in the real world, decision-makers seldom have access to all the information they need to make optimal decisions. The needed information may simply not exist. For example, when negotiating the purchase of a truly unique item, there may be no basis to estimate a reasonable market price for it. Even when good information exists, this information does not automatically yield decisions that optimize utility. The information may be employed in a poorly specified model. Or low-probability, high-impact events may dramatically alter the decision-making calculus. The bottom line is that lacking perfect information, decision-makers accept good-enough decisions. This is the essence of Simon's well-known concept of satisficing.

Another problem is information asymmetry. This arises when sellers withhold information that would affect the price buyers are willing to pay, and buyers withhold information that could drive up a seller's offer price. For example, in selling a used car, the seller may not inform the buyer that the car has had intermittent problems with its electrical system since the day it was purchased. Or in buying an old pen-and-ink sketch, the buyer does not tell the seller that the work likely came from the studio of Leonardo da Vinci.

Simon's bounded rationality argument was indisputable and unchallenged. Who would argue that people have adequate information to make perfectly rational choices? Nonetheless, mainstream economists continued to employ an assumption of rational decision making as a convenience that enabled them to build sophisticated economic models. Has this led to distorted results? Yes and no. The answer depends on the extent to which real-world decision-makers deviate from assumptions of rationality when they make actual decisions. If they deviate dramatically, then the models are obviously unrealistic and their value is questionable. If the deviation is small, then the models may be deemed sound, perhaps requiring modest tweaking to improve their accuracy.

The matter of rationality in decision making was addressed thoroughly by two psychologists from Hebrew University. Through their efforts, they helped bring attention to the emerging discipline of behavioral economics. Using their under-graduate students as subjects, Amos Tversky and Daniel Kahneman set up many experiments that examined the degree to which people are rational when making decisions. Tversky ultimately settled at Stanford University and Kahneman at Princeton University.

Tversky and Kahneman set out to demonstrate that when making decisions, most people do not employ perspectives or facts that lead to "correct" decisions, that is, decisions generated through a rational decision-making process. In 1973, their earliest high-impact paper, "Judgment Under Uncertainty: Heuristics and Biases," provided interesting insights into a range of practices and biases that lead decision-makers to deliver skewed assessments of circumstances. For example, in one experiment, subjects in a group were given five seconds to compute:

$$8 \times 7 \times 6 \times 5 \times 4 \times 3 \times 2 \times 1$$

Subjects in another group were given five seconds to compute:

$$1 \times 2 \times 3 \times 4 \times 5 \times 6 \times 7 \times 8$$

The median estimates of the product of these sets of numbers diverged dra-matically. It was 2,250 for the descending sequence and 512 for the ascending sequence. Neither answer came close to the correct answer, which is 40,320. One obvious conclusion is that people are unable to accurately assess data when given insufficient time to do so. Another is that people's interpretation of data is influenced by the way in which data are presented. No surprises or profound insights here.

Tversky and Kahneman, and battalions of their followers, offered strong empirical evidence that the assumption of rational decision making in economics does not hold water. These findings were widely promulgated. They eventually led to the Nobel Prize in economics for Kahneman in 2003. (Having died of cancer in 1996, Tversky was ineligible to receive the award.)

It would seem that such findings would lead to a serious reassessment of basic precepts in economic thinking. They did not. In a 2003 article, Kahneman admits that his work has not had a major impact on the prevailing approach economists take to doing their jobs. As he notes, they have invested so much intellectual capital in the existing paradigm that they are loathe to change it. While they may acknowledge that decision-makers are not fully rational, their models are nonetheless built on assumptions of rationality.

In theory, the work of Tversky, Kahneman, and other behavioral economists could be used to challenge the accepted economics paradigm as embodied in conventional microeconomic theory and practice. According to Thomas Kuhn's vision on how science moves forward, while the scientific community generally accepts the precepts of a prevailing paradigm, there remain annoying anomalies that the paradigm does not address adequately. What often happens is that newcomers tackle these questions and through their work expose weaknesses in the knowledge edifice. Further exploration on their evolving ideas then demonstrates that the prevailing paradigm needs to be replaced. Kuhn (1996) called this process a *scientific revolution*.

But this is not happening in the case of behavioral economics. In an indirect way, the work of behavioral economists appears to be geared toward supporting the prevailing paradigm, which is built on assumptions of rational decision making. Much of the work by behavioral economists directs most of their attention to discovering the myriad ways humans do not behave rationally. They do not say: "We should rethink our economic models to incorporate real behavior, given that the rational model of decision making does not accurately reflect how humans operate." Instead, they seem to be saying: "If only people acted more rationally, they would make better decisions," which reflects the premises of traditional economic thinking. Thus their findings can be taken to support, albeit indirectly, the prevailing paradigm.

During its heyday, prior to Kahneman and Tversky's earliest research, the Carnegie school of economics offered a serious challenge to the traditional economics perspective by investigating the organizational and behavioral roots of economic decision making. Key players at Carnegie University included Herbert Simon, Richard Cyert, James March, and Oliver Williamson. Cyert and March's groundbreaking 1963 book, *A Behavioral Theory of the Firm*, offered a concrete example of how microeconomics could be approached in a nontraditional, behavior-focused way. Despite the brain power and energy of these men, their focus on organizational and behavioral issues has not gained a big following among mainstream economists. We have seen no overturn of the dominant paradigm in economics. There has been no scientific revolution.

DEALING WITH UNKNOWNS

Perhaps the biggest challenge decision-makers face is making decisions with limited information. The extent of unknowns they face can vary dramatically, ranging from complete access to the needed facts to near-total ignorance. In the first case, they are walking along a sun-filled trail with twenty-twenty vision, viewing a crystal-clear panorama. In the second, they are hiking blindfolded on a mountain path on a moonless night!

There are many situations where decision-makers have plenty of information to guide them. With routine technical problems, such as configuring equipment on the factory floor to optimize throughput, they usually have ample information to make good choices. The capacities of the equipment they use are well defined, and the availability of materials employed in the production run is known. Furthermore, the production process is fully understood and can be broken down into clearly defined components. With linear programming, the optimal configuration of equipment and allocation of material flows can be determined once production constraints are identified.

In contrast, new product development projects are filled with unknowns. Decision-makers may have only the vaguest idea of the market segment they should address, the level of demand for the product once it is launched, the technical risks associated with developing something new, the actions of competitors, production challenges, supplier reliability, the propensity for the risk of the people within the enterprise who will make the final product launch decision, and the overall state of the economy at the time of product launch. With new product development, uncertainty is abundant. Consequently, deciding what features to include in the product and what market to target is tough. Often with projects that have so much uncertainty, the final decision on whether to proceed with the new product launch is determined by the willingness of senior managers to take risk.

In decision science, the question of dealing with unknowns has always been an important one, leading experts to talk about decision making under conditions of risk and decision making under conditions of uncertainty. Although the terms *risk* and *uncertainty* are often employed interchangeably in common use, they have distinct meanings in economics and decision science. With risk, you know the probability of an event, whereas with uncertainty you do not. This distinction makes a difference in how you approach making decisions. For example, if I look out the window and see dark clouds looming above, I predict that it will rain, so I decide to take my umbrella to the office with me. I have made a decision under the condition of uncertainty, with my decision informed by observation and judgment. Meanwhile, my neighbor Martha checks out the local weather forecast on weather.com and discovers that the probability of rain this morning is 85 percent, which leads her to take her umbrella to the office. She has made a decision under the condition of risk, with her decision informed by data.

The distinction between risk and uncertainty was first formulated by Frank H. Knight in his classic work, *Risk, Uncertainty, and Profit* (1921). Knight, incidentally, is best known as founder of the Chicago school of economics, spawning ground of the most vociferous proponents of free markets. Their ranks have included Ronald Coase, George Stigler, Milton Friedman, Gary Becker, and Friedrich von Hayek. All five economists won the Nobel Prize in economics. Free market proponents emerging from the Chicago school have had an enormous impact on U.S. economic policy since the 1950s.

Methods for dealing with decision making under conditions of risk and decision making under conditions of uncertainty have evolved. Because dealing with risk scenarios entails using probability estimates while handling uncertainty does not, the former generally yields more powerful insights than the latter. Still, a foundation for making solid decisions can be established even under conditions of uncertainty.

Handling Risk

There are well-established techniques for dealing with decision making under conditions of risk. Two are highlighted here for discussion purposes: expected value analysis and Monte Carlo simulation. Both are heavily used and yield good results.

With expected value analysis, you look at a set of values you encounter (say, different revenue-generating scenarios you can visualize by launching a business venture: revenues of $1 million, $3 million, or $5 million) and the likelihood of experiencing each of these values (say, 30 percent, 50 percent, or 20 percent, respectively). By multiplying each anticipated outcome by its likelihood and summing the results, you estimate what you would earn "on the average" if you were to launch this venture hypothetically an infinite number of times. This estimate is called *expected value.* In this case, you have:

$$\text{Expected value} = \$1,000,000 \times 0.3 + \$3,000,000 \times 0.5 + \$5,000,000 \times 0.2$$
$$= \$2,800,000$$

In other words, statistically, you would expect to earn $2.8 million in revenue on this business venture. Of course, this is simply a statistical average. Your actual revenue would be higher or lower than the expected value.

The worth of expected value analysis as a decision tool becomes evident when you assess the potential gains of a decision against the possible losses. For example, if you pay $2.00 to bet on a horse that has a 20 percent chance of earning you $12.00 in a horse race, you have:

$$\text{Expected value} = \$10.00 \times 0.2 - \$2.00 \times .8 = \$2.00 - \$1.60 = \$0.40$$

Note that if the likelihood of pocketing a winning of $10.00 is 20 percent, then the likelihood of losing $2.00 is 80 percent. Note also that the money you would pocket if you win is $10.00, and not $12.00, because you need to subtract the initial $2.00 payment you made on your bet. In this example, the fact that you have a positive expected value indicates that the odds of winning are in your favor, although not strongly so. You can justify making a bet on these grounds. Had the expected value been negative, this would indicate that the odds are against you and provide you with a rationale for foregoing the bet.

In business, the logic provided here with the betting example can be extended to examining expected revenue flows and cost flows. If the analysis shows expected revenues to be greater (or less) than expected costs, this provides you the basis of deciding whether to proceed with an investment.

Monte Carlo simulation is another popular tool frequently employed to handle risk. It offers decision-makers a way to model complex decision scenarios by using a random number generator to provide data to predict outcomes. Consider a simple scenario. The formula for profit is:

$$\text{Profit} = R - C,$$

where R = revenue and C = cost.

With Monte Carlo simulation, you run this "model" through a computer simulator many times—say ten thousand times—letting a random number generator randomly change values for revenue and cost in accordance with rules you define (for example, "Given historical experience in the business, let the random number generator create values for revenue based on a normal distribution where the mean is $1,400,000 and standard deviation $350,000 and create values for cost, using a normal distribution where the mean is $1,200,000 and the standard deviation $250,000"). The ten thousand computations of profit simulate different outcome scenarios that adhere to your assumptions and provide you with a quantitative sense of what the profit picture will be. There are many computerized Monte Carlo simulation packages available to run analyses.

Handling Uncertainty

When dealing with situations of uncertainty, you are operating at a higher level of ignorance than with risk scenarios because you do not know the probabilities of different events, so your analysis will be weaker. Still, strategies have emerged for guiding decisions intelligently. Let's say you want to estimate the profitability of selling a new line of T-shirts but lack hard data that would enable you to carry out an expected value or a Monte Carlo analysis. Without knowledge of the statistical distributions of revenues and costs, you can forecast sales and revenues based on what I call detective work. The forecasts may be rooted in previous experience in selling similar T-shirts. Or they may be developed by conducting a simple market research effort, where you survey potential customers to determine their buying preferences. Another commonly employed forecasting technique is to put together a panel of experts and see if they can establish a consensus on revenue and cost (in its most formal embodiment, this is called Delphi forecasting). As we will see in Chapter Seven, group decision making has its strengths and weaknesses. There are many approaches you can take to conducting your forecast. If you have carried it out effectively, you will find that you have generated insights that enable you to make an informed decision on how to proceed with the T-shirt venture.

Working with Risk and Uncertainty

In the real world, the most intractable unknowns that decision-makers encounter are those associated with human behavior. The concerns of the behavioral economists and Herbert Simon regarding the irrational behavior of decision-makers address the tip of the iceberg. A good understanding of effective decision making requires the investigation of a much wider range of behaviors, including those rooted in corruption, greed, incompetence, altruism, and politics. Beyond this, decision science needs to acknowledge what Nobel laureate Gary Becker demonstrated in his research: that unsavory behavior (for example, criminal behavior) is often rational! As Becker points out, when criminals opt to pursue lives of crime, they abide by the same laws of economics as conventional players in the market do. If the marginal return of criminal activity (ill-gotten gain) exceeds its marginal cost (jail time), they can establish a good economic argument justifying their criminal proclivities.

In the final analysis, we need to acknowledge that in dealing with risk and uncertainty, we face limits in what we can know. At the very best, we operate with probabilities and not certainties. Even these probabilities vary in the degree to which they are determined with great care, using good theory or empirical findings, or simply reflect our best guesses. With decisions of consequence that must take into account social context, we seldom operate under "at the very best" conditions. Instead, we function in the realm of uncertainty, depending on good sense and logic to guide us since we lack hard data, and recognizing that if nine Supreme Court justices seldom agree on what decisions to make, the idea of achieving a best decision may be chimerical.

3 The Social Context of Decision Making

On January 12, 2007, a young man dressed in blue jeans, a long-sleeved T-shirt, and baseball cap removed a violin from its case, placed the open case on the ground before him (and tossing in a few bills plus change), and began playing Bach's Partita No. 2 in D Minor. He set up just outside the turnstiles leading to Metro subway trains in a Washington, D.C., Metro station. Over the next forty-three minutes, 1,097 people, mostly federal government employees, passed him on their way to work. Fewer than thirty-five stopped to listen to him. When he finished playing after three-quarters of an hour, he had collected $32.17 in donations from the passersby.

What made this event interesting is that the young man was Joshua Bell, one of the world's leading violinists. The instrument he was playing was a $3.5 million Stradivarius violin, made in 1713. He plays to sell-out audiences in the world's major concert halls. A reasonably priced ticket at his concerts sells for about a hundred dollars. Yet on this Friday morning, this world-class violinist, playing world-class music, was invisible to the morning crowds. His Metro concert was videotaped and displayed on YouTube. As he plays his fiddle, you can see the crowds rush by. *Washington Post* writer Gene Weingarten (2007) set up this experiment and described it in a Pulitzer Prize–winning article. Of the $32.17 Bell earned, $25.00 came from a woman who recognized him.

This story highlights the importance of context. From the commuters' perspective, what they encountered was yet another struggling young musician trying to earn small change in the subway. Contextually he was a nobody. In another context, performing at a well-publicized concert at Carnegie Hall, he would be seen as a musical demigod. People would pay top dollar to see him and would wait in long lines to obtain concert tickets. But in the Metro station, he was just white noise.

Context frames our view of things. Human perception is defined contextually. We encounter this all the time. One community's hero is another's fool. One gardener's weed is another's ingredient for the evening salad. To Al Qaeda adherents, a woman who sets off a bomb in a market filled with women and children is a martyr who will enjoy the fruits of heaven; to the rest of the world, she is a deranged terrorist.

In his classic *Patterns of Discovery* (1958), the physicist-philosopher Norwood Russel Hanson noted that context is a key component of scientific theorizing and understanding. He emphasized that contrary to popular belief, scientific efforts are not objective but are defined by the context of discovery. To illustrate his point, he observed that when trained physicists look at an X-ray tube, they see it for what it is: a device employed in X-ray machines. When nonphysicists look at it, all they see is a glass tube containing wires. They have no idea of its use and value. Hanson gave this principle a name: he said that scientific discovery is *theory laden*, meaning that it is impossible for scientists to carry out research and articulate findings outside the context of discovery, which is defined by their knowledge, experiences, and values.

An important theme of this book is that context is king. Decisions that do not account for context will likely be bad ones. To people concerned with decision making, mindful decisions of consequence must be examined within their social context. To understand social context, decision-makers must look at who the stakeholders are, what the payoffs of a decision are, who the winners and losers are, and what the side impacts are (including collateral damage) for a wide range of players in the community. They must also account for broader socioeconomic and political forces that can affect the decision and in turn can be affected by it.

The points raised here should be self-evident, but in practice they are not because the rational part of many smart people says: "Decisions should be made on their merits. We should not become distracted by emotional side issues." However, for those who are making decisions carried out in social milieus, the so-called side issues often move to center stage despite decision-makers' attempts to keep them on the sidelines. That's how the world works.

THE SOCIAL CONTEXT

To appreciate the importance of social context when making mindful decisions of consequence, consider how these decisions are typically reached as the result of the give-and-take negotiations of different stakeholders involved in the decision process. Some of the stakeholders may be big players, others incidental. Some may have a big stake in the outcome of the decision process, while others may feel indifferent about the outcome.

Stakeholders in Decision Making

Ultimately the decision process creates winners and losers. For the losers, the perceived loss can yield neutral or negative feelings. If the stakes are small, the stakeholders function altruistically, and the final decision is reached amicably; decision-makers achieve decision-making nirvana, where nobody feels like a winner or loser. All stakeholders accept the decision and move on with their lives. But if the stakes are large and the decision process grows ugly, arrogant winners and truculent losers may emerge. In this case, while a decision may purportedly have been reached, the game is not really over. The losers may not be inclined to accept the decision passively. Distressed by the decision-making experience, they may feel moved to resist it.

If this is what you face, you must question whether a decision has truly been made. Clearly buy-in has not been achieved, and without it, it is not likely that the decision will be implemented as intended.

The uncertainty of the status of the decision is compounded when you consider that the people charged with implementing it are often different from those who made it. For example, consider what happens when, after much deliberation, senior managers decide to launch a business process reengineering (BPR) effort in their company. BPR efforts require enterprises to alter the organization's business processes radically in order to improve organizational efficiency. Such efforts are often chartered as projects that reside in the human resource department. Human resources may put together a steering committee of players from the company's different departments whose job is to guide the efforts of the project team. The project team members are usually younger and midlevel people several levels below the senior managers who launched the initiative. Typically at this stage in their careers, they have had little exposure to senior managers or their concerns.

What can happen in this situation—and it occurs frequently—is that there is a disconnect between what decision-makers intend and what actually transpires. While the implementers may be provided detailed instructions describing their chores, they may have only a vague idea of the context of the decision and the decision-makers' intent. Not surprisingly, they interpret their charter in the context of their prior experiences, which may or may not be relevant to the current situation. Problems are compounded if their charter is expressed vaguely, which often occurs. In this case, their interpretation of the work efforts may be wildly off the mark. We have here a classic problem of miscommunication: what the decision-makers say is not what the implementers hear.

The Community and Social Forces

What I have described here addresses just half the equation. It considers the players directly involved in the decision process: those who make the decisions and those who implement them. To accommodate the full social context, decision-makers should also look at players affected by the decision who played no role in formulating or implementing it—what I call *the community*. When decisions work out nicely, community members benefit; when they fail, they may see themselves as victims of the decision. For example, when a new shopping mall is proposed to be built in a neighborhood, it will have manifest impacts that need to be considered when the municipality makes a zoning decision on whether to approve or scuttle the project. During the one- or two-year construction phase, local residents face substantial disruptions to their lives: increased noise, altered traffic patterns, dust, ugly vistas, and so on. Once the mall is built, they experience increased traffic congestion. Their real estate values might go down because the community is now seen as being part of an unsightly commercial zone, or they might go up, owing to the convenience of being near a shopping outlet.

The response of these ancillary players to a decision is often crucial in determining whether a given decision can or cannot be implemented effectively. If the community feels threatened by an initiative and successfully musters resistance to it, the initiative—the outcome of a major decision process—may be rendered dead on arrival. The effort of achieving a decision may come to nothing.

Beyond this, broad socioeconomic, political, and natural forces can play a significant role in determining whether decisions that are reached are wise or foolish. Consider the shopping mall example again. If the mall is completed during recessionary times, the stores may remain empty and the mall developer unable to repay its loans. If the economy is burgeoning, business may boom, and the local press may declare the developer a business genius.

THE SOCIAL SPACE OF DECISION MAKING

The factors that contribute to the trials and tribulations of the social context of decision making are captured in Figure 3.1, which pictures the social space of decision making. The principal elements of the social space include a number of key players—stakeholders, decision-makers (DMs), decision-implementers (DIs), and the community—plus external forces.

Figure 3.1 shows that decision making goes beyond what I call the *Solomonaic norm*. The Hebrew Bible presents King David's son, Solomon, as an idealized decision-maker. When God asks what gift he can bestow on him, he chooses wisdom, and he becomes the wisest man on earth. One of his roles as king was to resolve disputes among his subjects. He would gather the facts from the testimony of the disputing parties, then apply his wisdom to resolve the issue. The

Figure 3.1 The Social Space of Decision Making

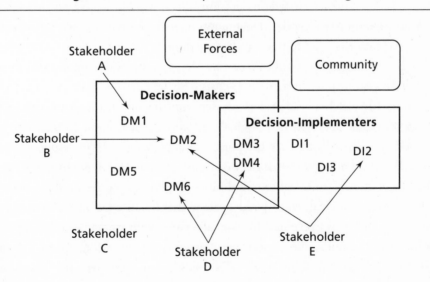

best-known case entailed deciding who was the real mother of a child. Solomon's decision was to use a sword to cut the child in two in order to split it among the two claimants. This decision led to well-known results, and the matter of the child's true mother was easily established.

Once a dispute was resolved, Solomon would move on to the next one. One king, one vote. There was no concern with achieving a consensus here. The king was the sole arbiter of decisions, big and little. That's one of the nice things about being an absolute monarch: you call the shots, resolve issues solo, then move on. From Solomon's perspective, another benefit was that as an absolute monarch, he was able to collect seven hundred wives and three hundred concubines! Of course, this created a host of nightly decision-making quandaries for him, because now he faced a superabundance of choices.

ALLISON'S MULTIPLE PERSPECTIVES ON DECISION MAKING

This presentation of the Solomonaic decision-making norm may look like a caricature of decision making, but it actually reflects the prevailing view of decision making—what Harvard's Graham Allison calls the rational-actor model in his classic work, *The Essence of Decision* (1971). The rational-actor model takes the stance that decision making is made in accordance with a single, rational, near-omniscient point of view where decisions are arrived at purely on their merits. Allison describes this model in the context of the Cuban missile crisis, a 1962 incident that nearly led to nuclear Armageddon.

In his book, he points out that one way to explain the dynamics of the missile crisis is to assume that the principal actors—Soviet decision-makers in the person of Nikita Khrushchev and American decision-makers in the person of John F. Kennedy—each operated in a logical and consistent fashion to pursue clearly defined objectives. They were the political equivalents of *Homo economicus*, the rational "economic man" whose decisions are based on maximizing utility. The Soviet attempt to install missiles just ninety miles off the U.S. coast was the consequence of a clear, considered strategy that balanced benefits against costs, as was the American response to blockade Cuba with warships. When thinking about Soviet actions, the Americans concentrated on the question: "What is Khrushchev's goal in doing what he is doing?" For their part, the Soviets were asking: "What will Kennedy's response be?" Of course, both sides recognized that decisions were being made by more than one person; Khrushchev and Kennedy were not operating alone. But in assuming that behavior was governed by rational actors pursuing defined goals, each side treated the collective decision-making effort of the opposing side as one generated by a single, rational player.

A big problem with the rational-actor perspective is its assumption that you can get people with divergent views to develop full agreement on the final formulation of a decision. The fact is that when decisions are made through the collective efforts of multiple players, as they invariably are when dealing with mindful decisions of consequence, they reflect an attempt to patch together the disparate views of stakeholders and decision-makers who possess different outlooks and to articulate them as if they are spoken with a single voice. But this is not realistic. The fact that members of a decision-making team acquiesce to a decision does not mean that the decision truly reflects their views and that they will support it.

For example, when a business analyst asks: "Why did the board of directors of Globus Enterprises decide to kill an outdated but nonetheless money-making product?" the implied assumption is that the multidimensional views of the board can be reduced to a single dimension, capturing the outlook of a theoretical, single, idealized decision-maker. The fact is that it is unlikely that the board members had full consensus on how to handle the money-making product. It is possible that some board members argued forcefully that because the product was generating revenue, it should continue to be supported, notwithstanding its obsolescence, while others countered by arguing that the short-term financial gains coming from obsolete products would be more than offset by damage to the company's reputation as a leading-edge enterprise. Ultimately the final decision on the matter would be determined by compromise and consensus. In many organizations, the majority view would prevail, where the majority would constitute anything greater than 50 percent of the vote, right up to 100 percent.

Note that the rational-actor model is not concerned with social context. With this model, it is assumed that decisions are made on the basis of their inherent merits, with social context playing a peripheral role.

Allison points out that while the rational-actor model can offer a plausible interpretation of what transpired during the Cuban missile crisis, there are convincing alternative interpretations as well. He presents two additional decision-making models as offering workable explanations, both of which accommodate elements of the social context of decision making. His *organizational-process model* is based on the proposition that decisions are made in accordance with the experiences decision-makers have gained in prior relevant situations. In handling different kinds of experiences, decision-makers create template approaches to dealing with them and apply the templates to future decision-making situations. These templates are incorporated into business processes. When facing problems, decision-makers routinely deal with them by employing business processes that have worked in the past. To the extent they can, they follow standard operating procedures. For example, when Soviet engineers began construction of the missile sites in Cuba, they employed the same configuration as they used in building missile sites along the Soviet Union's southern border, making it easy for U.S. analysts using spy plane photos to see what they were up to.

Allison's *governmental politics* model makes substantial use of social context. It addresses the fact that outcomes of making nontrivial decisions depend on accommodating inputs from a wide range of stakeholders. When viewed from the governmental politics perspective, Khrushchev's decision to emplace missiles in Cuba in 1962 resulted from balancing the conflicting interests of powerful stakeholders concerned with domestic issues in the Soviet Union, foreign policy issues, military issues, and ideological issues. Similarly, Kennedy's response was a product of debates carried out among his key military advisers, political advisers, and, most important, personal advisers, especially his brother Robert. In both the Soviet Union and the United States, the advisers to the leaders seldom saw eye-to-eye on matters.

In *The Essence of Decision*, Allison took a *Rashomon*-like approach to understanding what really happens when governments make significant decisions. As with Akira Kurosawa's 1950 movie, we see when looking at a real-world incident—the Cuban missile crisis—that an understanding of what actually transpires is elusive. No single model provides a complete answer. The truth is something that lies beyond a single viewpoint. From the perspective of this chapter, what is important to learn from Allison's book is recognition that the rational-player model by itself is not adequate to capture the full richness of the decision-making process. Implementing effective decision making requires an examination of social context.

THE LINK BETWEEN STAKEHOLDER AND DECISION-MAKER

Good decision making takes stakeholder interests into account. This becomes evident when we recast stakeholders as customers, where the customer is defined broadly as anyone who is affected by a decision or can affect it. Customer satisfaction stands at the center of business and government activity these days. In the case of business, companies that misread or ignore their customers' needs and wants over protracted periods of time struggle and ultimately go out of business. Those that delight their customers flourish. In the case of the public sector, the principal job of governments is to serve the people—their customers. In democracies, governments that address their constituents' needs and wants effectively enjoy longer, more stable tenures than those that do not. Because autocratic governments seldom serve the needs of their citizens meaningfully, their legitimacy is continually challenged. When they lose what the Chinese call "the mandate from heaven," they face serious societal disruption and may be overthrown.

When humans operate collectively, their differing desires and values surface. In fractious communities, the disparities in outlooks may be so great that they cannot be bridged, leading to an inability of the community to operate in a healthy way. Even with cohesive communities, you encounter a degree of heterogeneity in desires and values, but in this case, the differences are usually small and can be accommodated, enabling the community to carry out its business effectively. Given the reality of disparate desires and values among stakeholders, a big challenge facing decision-makers is to make decisions that sort through the contending perspectives of stakeholders to arrive at decisions that best satisfy the interests of both individuals and the community—what Jeremy Bentham referred to as "the greatest good for the greatest number."

A significant decision-making challenge is to establish a process to work through the contending needs of the stakeholders. Many approaches can be employed here. Most entail eliciting stakeholder interests in some way, providing an opportunity for the stakeholders to argue their points through some form of give-and-take process, prioritizing the articulated stakeholder desires, and "voting" on a solution that forms the basis of the ultimate decision that is achieved. This process is covered in more detail in Chapter Seven, "The Wisdom—and Foolishness—of Crowds," which explores the group dynamics of decision making. As the chapter title indicates, the effort to elicit, aggregate, articulate, and implement the interests of multiple stakeholders does not always yield good results. In decision making, there are no guarantees.

The bottom line here is to recognize that decision-makers must identify and weigh the contending needs of stakeholders affected by, or having an effect on, the impending decision. If they do this well, the odds of arriving at meaningful and workable decisions grow dramatically.

THE IMPLEMENTATION CHALLENGE

Mindful decisions of consequence typically entail implementations that require work effort by an implementation team. Quite often, the implementation effort is carried out as a project and is headed by a project manager. Thus, a decision to launch an advertising campaign might result in establishing a project to deliver the goods, or a decision to upgrade computer capabilities may trigger a contract with a company that will launch an information technology upgrade project.

The big challenge at this point is to get the implementation team to do what it is chartered to do: execute the decision as intended. This challenge is seldom covered in decision-making books and courses, where it appears that the authors and instructors assume that once a decision is made, its implementation will follow without a hitch. However, in practice, implementing a project that faithfully delivers a solution that corresponds closely with the decision's requirements requires substantial effort. Without conscious effort, it is likely that what the implementation team delivers is not what the decision-makers desire.

Disconnects can arise in a number of ways between a decision and its implementation. For example, to the extent that the project team members know little or nothing about the context of the decision, they may implement solutions that do not reflect the decision-makers' intent. This is illustrated in Figure 3.1, where we have decision-implementers 1, 2, and 3 (DI1, DI2, and DI3, respectively) who played no role in making the decision. Without knowing the key players and their perspectives, they may interpret the requirements provided to them in accordance with their personal experiences and preferences. However, as the figure suggests, their lack of insight into the history and intent of the decision can be offset by the presence of two decision-makers who played a role in making the decision being implemented: DM3 and DM4. If these two individuals serve as good mentors to DI1, DI2, and DI3, they can keep the implementation on track.

Figure 3.1 also shows that stakeholder interests can go beyond influencing a decision and can be carried forward into the decision implementation stage. In the figure, stakeholder D, for example, can exert influence on decision-maker 4 (DM4) and stakeholder E can exert influence on decision-implementer 2 (DI2), both of whom are actively engaged in implementing the decision that the decision-making body reached. By itself, this is neither good nor bad. However, it could undermine the decision if stakeholder D or E strives to encourage their proxies on the implementation team to pursue their special interests at the expense of implementing the decision agreed on during deliberations. This situation is not unusual. Stakeholders who have a big stake in a decision will certainly monitor developments during the implementation stage in order to safeguard their interests. They can be expected to offer the implementers "friendly guidance" on how best to execute the project. Stakeholder influence that can distort the implementation of an agreed-on decision can generally be handled by alert project managers who make sure the implementation team sticks to the implementation plan.

ACCOMMODATING EXTERNAL FORCES

As Figure 3.1 shows, external forces are a key component of the social space of decision making. These are major forces over which decision-makers have no control. They may be tied to a variety of events, including political actions, economic conditions, social turmoil, technological change, and acts of God, such as earthquakes, storms, fires, and other types of natural mayhem.

The possibility that these forces may arise and interfere with decisions needs to be addressed early in the decision-making process. This can be done by using a standard risk management procedure (Frame, 2003). For example, at the outset of the decision-making effort, decision-makers should conduct an environmental scan to identify consequential forces that currently exist or might arise. In doing this, they should explicitly address emerging political, economic, social, business, and government trends. Once they have identified possible environmental events, the impacts on the problem being addressed should be assessed, so that whatever decision is reached takes them into account.

The following example shows how these principles can be applied. Before expending substantial resources to bid on a major government infrastructure project (perhaps rehabilitating six aging bridges within the municipality), a company's decision-makers need to take stock of political conditions that can affect the bid process, the contract award, and the consequent project effort. Will the party in power, which is responsible for issuing the solicitation, likely be in power at the time the award is made? If not, will the new leadership still view infrastructure revitalization as a high-priority item? In looking at economic conditions, they need to ask: What is the likelihood that a poor economy will cause a budget crunch that leads to the cancellation of the initiative? An important business question to ask is: Where is the money for the program coming from? While the government assures them that funding for years 1 and 2 is available, where will funding for subsequent years come from? The answers to these and other questions will have a big impact on the approach the company takes to bid on the program. If the answers are not reassuring, the company may even decide to forgo bidding.

CONCLUSION

When dealing with decisions of consequence, decision-makers seldom are able to follow the guidance to base decisions on the merits. The basic premise of this chapter is that the merits of a decision should not be viewed in narrow, technical terms. They cannot be determined in isolation from social context because decision making does not occur in a vacuum. For one thing, it must take into account broad socioeconomic and political forces. Recessions, inflation, real estate bubbles, scandals, unemployment, regime change, revolution, cultural revivals, religious fundamentalism, and technology shifts have a significant impact on determining what decisions make sense in specific circumstances.

For another, it must accommodate the interests of a broad range of stakeholders who will be affected by the decision. Those who benefit from a decision will support it, and those who are net losers may not. It is dangerous to assume that the act of reaching a decision resolves the issue. Quite often it does not, and as a consequence, the decision is not implemented as intended. Effective decision-makers need to factor this reality into the decision process.

Three things may happen that disrupt realizing a decision's directives. First, through their actions (or absence of actions), unhappy stakeholders may sabotage the decision. Second, the people charged with implementing a decision may not do what is needed to effectuate it, perhaps owing to misunderstanding, incompetence, or a desire to pursue their personal interests. Third, even when decisions are executed exactly in accordance with the decision-makers' instructions and yield the intended results, the community that is affected by them may reject their outcomes, rendering them ineffectual in the final analysis.

The fact is that in work with decisions of consequence, the decision-making process is usually messy, particularly when stakeholders feel strongly about the issues being addressed. A thorough understanding of the decision space goes far in enabling decision-makers to reduce the messiness.

4 The Organizational Dimension

One of the most significant elements of social context is the organization in which decision-makers operate. Organizations are social systems, and they are not decision neutral. To appreciate this, let's carry out a thought experiment where you create a single challenge facing three organizations. To keep the experiment scientific, let's say that each organization is an oil company experiencing a serious petroleum leak in an offshore well in the Gulf of Mexico. (Sound familiar?) The conditions of the leak are identical for each company. Let's say the "challenge" each company faces is to decide the best approach to handle this emergency. Based on the experience of the 2010 BP oil spill, we know that managers have a range of options at the strategic and operations levels that they can pursue in a situation like this. A major factor determining how each company approaches the challenge is tied to organizational issues: organizational culture, structure, processes, and the caliber and outlook of its employees. Theoretically there should be an optimal technical solution to the problem that each company should follow in order to minimize damage and maximize long-term advantages, but in practice, we will surely see each company following its own course, one that reflects its organizational realities.

How decisions are made is affected by a number of organizational factors, each of which ties to social context. I look at four factors in this chapter:

- Organizational structure
- Organizational process

- People in organizations
- Organizational culture

ORGANIZATIONAL STRUCTURE

In the early 1990s, David Nadler and his coauthors at Delta Consulting (Nadler, Gerstein, and Shaw, 1992) coined the term *organizational architecture* in order to highlight the role of organizational design and structure in organizational performance. I liked the employment of the architecture metaphor and adopted it in my work on project teams in my book, *Managing Projects in Organizations* (2003). In playing with this metaphor, I linked it to the famous guiding principle of the Chicago school of architecture, which held that form follows function. This principle was first articulated at the end of the nineteenth century by the founder of the Chicago school, Louis Sullivan, and strongly influenced the work of his famous assistant, Frank Lloyd Wright (who later modified the principle to state "form and function are one"). Sullivan suggested that the design of structures should be derived from their function, or intended use. Basically, he was saying: "Tell me how you want to use a given space, and I will provide you with an attractive design for its best use." Sullivan was one of the first architects to design skyscrapers, and he used this principle to keep the new buildings lean, jettisoning designs that employed substantial ornamentation, the custom at the end of the nineteenth century.

In my writing on project teams, I stood the principle on its head and promoted the idea that function follows form. In other words, show me how a team is structured (including communication protocols and governing processes), and I will predict the managerial consequences emerging from the structure. For example, structuring a project team as a chain-of-command team has predictable consequences that are vastly different from the consequences of structuring it as a self-directed team. By literally sketching out team structure on a piece of paper and reflecting on the implications of the design, team leaders can predict many of the managerial challenges they will face.

Let's look at these two structures in more detail to see how organizational structure has significant managerial consequences and, as a result, implications for decision making.

Chain-of-Command Structure

This is the traditional military structure, where a corporal reports to a sergeant, who in turn reports to a lieutenant, who reports to a captain, and so on. With chain of command, final authority resides at the top of the chain: the general calls the shots. He or she issues orders to the colonel, who passes them to the lieutenant colonel, who issues them to the major, and so on (Figure 4.1). (In the real world, it is not quite this simple, but the basic principle still holds.)

Figure 4.1 Chain of Command

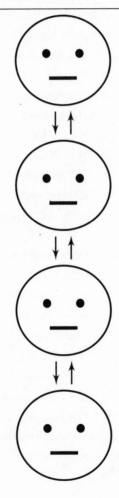

What are the managerial consequences of this structure? It has its pluses and minuses. If it didn't work, armies would not have employed it for the past four thousand or more years. From the 1890s through the post–World War II era, it was the dominant approach to managing the growing complexity of businesses and helped established the United States as the world's leading economic power. Still, in today's fast-pace world, where agility provides an advantage, it has plenty of drawbacks.

On the plus side, accountability is clear: managers are responsible for their own actions and the actions carried out by everyone under them. When a major snafu emerges in the military, there is a good chance that commandants will lose their jobs, because with the chain of command, the buck stops at the very top. In this environment, managers throughout the chain tend to be attentive to their responsibilities. Another plus is that in the chain of command, the orders that are ultimately executed will likely reflect those that were issued; because they are passed from one managerial level to another, there is no room to alter them. (Reality check: humans are astonishingly clever in figuring out ways to bypass rules, so there is no absolute guarantee that the initial orders will be implemented as intended; in addition, it is possible that as the orders are communicated from one level to another, they are misinterpreted along the lines of what we see in the kids' game Telephone.) Finally, if the orders are simple and clear, they can be implemented quickly, since time is not spent debating their merits and shortcomings.

On the minus side, the chain-of-command structure is rigid and does not lend itself to creative adjustments when they become necessary. In fact, it promotes risk aversion. If the players in the chain dare to adjust the orders, even if the change reflects manifest common sense, they can jeopardize their standing in the organization. Risk taking can be a career killer, particularly if a decision goes bad. Risk takers can easily become the scapegoat for failed decisions, even though their intervention made no contribution to the failure.

The chain of command can yield quick action in simple situations where orders are being issued in a top-down fashion, but it can lead to delays when managers need to respond to unanticipated situations. This arises because individuals in the chain are not able to make decisions without approval from above. Before action is taken, requests for approval to take action need to work their way up the chain until final authority for action is given; then the decision needs to work its way back down the chain so that it can be implemented.

With the chain of command, accountability is clear, but with a caveat: it is clear as long as the chain is short, with no more than four or five levels. But as the chain grows longer, accountability is attenuated. With long chains, incapable people can easily hide their incompetence. If something goes wrong, pinpointing where the problem arose is difficult. Studies of bureaucracy show that traditional bureaucracies with no more than four or five levels can function efficiently, whereas larger bureaucracies are plagued with inefficiency and incompetence. This illustrates the fact that operational effectiveness is in great part rooted in organizational structure.

Self-Directed Team Structure

The employment of self-directed teams became popular in the 1990s, although its origins hark back to the participative management initiatives of the 1960s. The idea underlying them was to push decision making down to the rank-and-file level. Instead of having higher-level managers call the shots from their Olympian heights (where they were far removed from day-to-day operations), operational decisions would now be made by the men and women who actually did the enterprise's work and were closest to customers.

With self-directed teams, team members are empowered to make decisions collectively. The level of empowerment can be modest or substantial. At the low end of empowerment, team members are authorized to arrange their affairs without direction from above. Thus, they can schedule meetings and tasks and coordinate work efforts without substantial management oversight. At the high end of empowerment, team members call the shots on many significant team-related decisions. Senior managers provide them with broad directives—technical requirements, budget targets, revenue targets, and a deadline date—and their job is to achieve the directives with little or no supervision. They may even be empowered to make basic human resource decisions, such as evaluating team member performance and hiring and firing team members. The decisions they make are typically arrived at collectively.

The architecture of the self-directed team differs substantially from the chain-of-command architecture as a comparison of the architectures pictured in Figures

Figure 4.2 Self-Directed Work Team

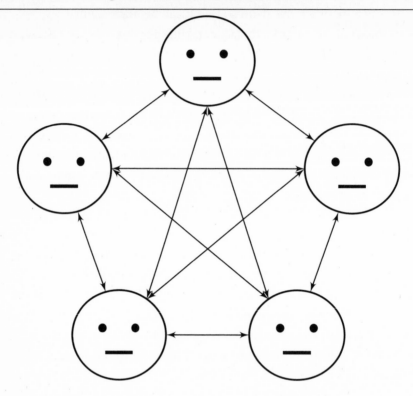

4.1 and 4.2 shows. The self-directed team employs a flat decision-making structure in contrast to the rigidly hierarchical structure of the chain of command.

As with the chain-of-command structure, self-directed teams have their pluses and minuses. On the plus side, the structure encourages inputs from all the players. If they have been selected wisely and reflect different points of view pertinent to the decision problem, this can lead to strong decisions that incorporate a wide range of perspectives, avoiding the tunnel vision characteristic of teams of like-minded individuals. Through discussions that strive to achieve consensus among the players, the players get to debate a full range of important issues that might not be covered with traditional structures that focus entirely on implementing management's solutions to problems. Ideally, the decisions that emerge are the result of thoughtful give-and-take negotiations among the players, with weak elements dropped and strong elements retained.

Another strength ties to the membership of the team. If its members adequately reflect different stakeholder interests within the organization, the likelihood of stakeholder buy-in to the team's decisions increases substantially. The team serves as a microcosm of the organization, and its deliberations reflect the organization's broader concerns. Thus, a decision focused on revamping an enterprise's inventory management system not only addresses narrow inventory acquisition and storage issues, but also takes into account the relevant concerns of the marketing, finance, and information technology departments. Because the decisions accommodate the different stakeholders' interests, they will be seen as being responsive to the organization's overall needs.

A final plus is that if capable team members become a decision-making unit within the organization over a period of time, they can evolve into a high-performing team in a matter of months. I have personal experience with this. In my early days as a research analyst and software developer, I was blessed to work project by project with a stable coterie of four colleagues over six years. When we were first brought together, we were five technically capable people possessing distinct skills. We were also strangers to each other, and our initial efforts at collaboration were friendly but awkward. By working together over a protracted period, we learned each other's strengths and weaknesses. After about six months, each player had earned the trust of colleagues. When a specific decision needed to be made, we would discuss it briefly, then defer to the judgments of the team members who were best suited to deal with it. We had gradually dispensed with formal team meetings and instead coordinated our efforts with hallway chats, short memos, and impromptu brainstorming sessions in the canteen. Through self-management that was nurtured over a period of years, we became a high-performing team. It was a great experience.

Self-directed teams also have their downside. I have worked with many such teams in different organizations since the early 1990s when they became popular. Most of the teams I encountered were not very effective. Typically they were an assemblage of well-meaning but confused men and women who were brought to together without much thought or guidance. They weren't sure what they should be doing. Quite often, they were told by a midlevel manager just one or two levels above them, "You are empowered to produce XYZ results. Senior management is watching your efforts. Get the job done!" That was the extent of the guidance they received.

Not surprisingly, their efforts were uninspiring. Team members tended to be long on talk, obsessed with defining what self-management procedures to follow, and short on results. They had trouble arriving at actionable decisions. My experience with such teams was not unique. Toward the end of the 1990s, criticisms of self-directed teams became pronounced. Following are some typical complaints that surfaced:

- With self-directed teams, it is easy to go adrift. When everyone is in charge, no one is in charge.

- If consensus on issues does not arise quickly, it is easy to experience decision-making gridlock, which slows the process.

- In order to get beyond the gridlock, eliminating contentious solutions (some of which may be innovative) and developing noncontroversial solutions that appeal to the lowest common denominator is tempting. This, however, contributes to groupthink.

- The larger the team is, the less effective it tends to be. Experience shows that once it grows beyond seven or eight people, handling the explosive growth of communication channels among team members interferes with the decision-making effort.

Problems on self-directed teams are often symptoms of inadequate team maturity. As I noted, too often self-directed teams are put together haphazardly, with the expectation that empowered, cross-functional team members can automatically harness their newly gained decision-making clout to treble their collective wisdom. By my reckoning, it takes at least six months for a team of carefully selected, capable people to develop a meaningful sense of teamness. The players need to arrive at an understanding of their individual capabilities by which they learn to trust their colleagues' judgments. They also learn how to work together smoothly, understanding what behaviors are appropriate and what are not.

Decision-Making Impact of Organizational Architecture

The discussion of the architectural consequences of the chain-of-command structure and self-managed team structure is used here for illustrative purposes. I am neither recommending nor criticizing their use. There are countless ways to structure decision-making efforts beyond what I have covered here, and each has its opportunities and pitfalls.

Consider the challenges facing contemporary decision-makers working with agile software development techniques. With Scrum, for example, decisions are made incrementally during team members' daily half-hour scrum sessions. During these sessions, the players address three questions: (1) What did we say we should achieve by today in yesterday's scrum session? (2) What have we done since then? (3) What should we do by tomorrow? Contrast this daily process learning approach with conventional decision-making wisdom that emphasizes the need to study the problem, develop solutions, and then implement them.

Or consider the challenges associated with serving on virtual teams, with team members scattered at different locations, possibly in a half-dozen different time zones. Some of the questions decision-makers face in these environments include: How should we schedule meetings? Should our colleagues in New York be expected to drag themselves out of bed at 4:00 A.M. to attend a 4:00 P.M. teleconference originating in Beijing? What vehicles should we employ to communicate our ideas? Skype videoconferences? Teleconferences? E-mail? When our virtual team spans national boundaries, how should we accommodate cultural and language differences?

The important lesson here is to recognize that organizational structure has a significant impact on how decisions are made. Structural issues should not be viewed as curious distractions handled on the sidelines. When examined carefully, they demonstrate that the view that decisions should be made on their merits is chimerical. Let's get it straight: chimerical decisions are those that ignore the implications of organizational architecture and other social context realities.

ORGANIZATIONAL PROCESS

I will keep this discussion of organizational process short, because this topic is a natural extension of the discussion of organizational structure. Process, like structure, defines clear boundaries that physically constrain the decision-making effort. Structure identifies the physical configuration of the system, and process defines the rules governing the functioning of the system and its components. So structure and process go hand-in-hand. For example, the chain of command is as much process as it is structure. The structure places the colonel over the lieutenant colonel, the lieutenant colonel over the major, and the major over the captain. Individuals in each position are accountable for their own actions and the actions of everyone beneath them in the chain. But the structure functions in accordance with an established process, which dictates rules of behavior. For example, to make an independent decision of consequence in the chain of command requires authorization from your superior, who in turn may need to gain authorization from the next level up, and so on.

In contrast to the hierarchical chain of command, the self-managed team structure is flat, with the players operating at the same level. While the chain-of-command structure can be visualized as a vertical decision-making structure, self-managed teams can be visualized as horizontal. As with the chain of command, structure and process are intertwined in self-management. To function effectively, this flat structure operates in accordance with a process that defines appropriate rules of behavior. For example, a key decision-making process for a self-directed team may require that decisions be based on principles of majority rule.

Of course, there are organizational process requirements that operate independent of structure. When I was working with a major Wall Street company whose primary source of income was tied to supporting investments that underlie pension plans, my clients implemented a process to establish work priorities by following a principle articulated in George Orwell's *Animal Farm*: "All animals are equal, but some animals are more equal than others." When prioritizing internal information technology project requirements, the highest priority went to requirements issued by the Internal Revenue Service (IRS). These requirements basically said: "If by October 15 you do not adjust your handling of the tax requirements for XYZ-type pension plans to reflect new tax policy, we will shut you down." In this organization, the Top Animal that was more equal than the others was the IRS.

The lesson here is that organizational processes, along with organizational structure, constitute an important element of the social context of decision making. They help determine how decisions are made. Once again, this perspective undermines the view that decisions should be based solely on their merits and decision-makers should ignore the distraction of so-called side issues.

PEOPLE IN ORGANIZATIONS

Decisions are made by people and for people. Clearly an inquiry on how mindful decisions of consequence are made and implemented that ignores the people element of decision making will be wildly off-target.

In discussing people in decision making, many issues need to be addressed, including these:

- *The capability of the decision-makers.* Are they qualified to address the issues being considered?

- *The capability of the implementers.* Are they qualified to implement the decision-makers' decisions?

- *The special interests of the stakeholders.* What are the vested interests of the different stakeholders in decision outcomes, and how far are they willing to go to make sure their interests prevail?

- *The knowledge of stakeholders and players regarding key issues.* Do they fully understand the issues and their implications?

- *The moral quality of the decision-makers and the key players working to influence the decision outcomes.* To what extent are their decisions and actions carried out to achieve selfish interests? In their dealings with others, are they honest?

- *The psychological traits of key decision-makers, stakeholders, and the public.* Are they willing to take risks, or are they risk averse? Do they behave in accordance with accepted norms, or do they display some measure of pathology?

Because people issues are so significant, they warrant detailed treatment that goes beyond what I cover in this chapter. Consequently, I defer a discussion of people issues to future chapters:

- Chapter Five looks at how the moral failings of individuals and institutions create decision-making challenges that are often overlooked.

- Chapter Six examines factors that affect how people make decisions, particularly those related to personality.

- Chapter Seven looks at the pluses and minuses of group decision making.

- Chapter Eight focuses on the physiological and perceptual foundations of decision making.

- Chapter Nine highlights empirical research carried out over the past two decades on how and why people make decisions.

ORGANIZATIONAL CULTURE

When I was in college, I often spent summers at my family's home on the Upper East Side of Manhattan. One of the classiest department stores in America was located just a few blocks from my parents' apartment: Bloomingdale's. One year, I was one of the lucky few college kids to get a summer job at Bloomingdale's. It was a good experience at a great store.

Bloomingdale's epitomized the intelligent nurturing of corporate culture. It regaled in it. My first two days on the job were spent in what the human resource department called orientation. I couldn't believe that the company was paying me a salary to sit in a classroom. More than half of the time in orientation was spent discussing Bloomingdale's special attributes and the Bloomingdale's Way. In other words, it entailed imbuing new employees with the Bloomingdale's culture.

Decades after attending the orientation, I vividly recall the message the trainers conveyed to those of us who were newly hired. First, although it had become a New York City icon, in fact, Bloomingdale's was world famous. Wealthy people would fly into New York simply to shop there. Nonetheless, despite its international renown, it was drilled into us that Bloomingdale's was a neighborhood store: two-thirds of its customers came from Manhattan's Upper East Side. We should always remember this and treat our customers as our neighbors. (This was before Bloomingdale's expanded to shopping malls in the 1970s.) Second, the quality of its products was second to none. Bloomingdale's buyers searched the globe for the best goods. A higher portion of its products was imported from overseas than any other department store in America. Third, the store's strength resided in the quality of its employees: it was ranked as New York's number one department store because its employees created a wonderful shopping experience for customers.

That was the principal message of the orientation session, and one I have never forgotten. The lessons on using cash registers, managing inventory, and using the punch clock were so much boilerplate. I recall nothing about their content.

Culture counts. It captures the abiding values of human collectives, ranging from small teams to tribes to enterprises to nations. The values guide attitudes and actions. Culture is to social groups what personality is to individuals. As with personality, it defines core behavior, prescribing what people can and cannot do.

The concept of culture arose in anthropology, where anthropologists set out to investigate and understand the rules, roles, and relationships governing social behavior in well-defined social communities. Lugging notebooks, sketchbooks, cameras, and sometimes pup tents, anthropologists traveled to all corners of the earth to observe in situ how different communities function. I experienced this life briefly at college living with the Shipibo Indians along the Ucayali River in the Amazon jungle. The Jivaro headhunters residing fifty miles north of my base had been pacified the year before my arrival, so I was reasonably confident I would not lose my head! Lizards, tarantulas, scorpions, army ants, alligators, sloths, and piranha fish were my local buddies.

When my missionary uncle introduced me to the local Shipibo Indians as his nephew (*inoynoy*), they burst out laughing, and one fell to the ground in a near convulsion. The actual Shipibo word for nephew is *inaynay*. *Inoynoy* translates into "diarrhea." When my uncle was introducing me to the Shipibo, he was saying, as he gestured toward me, "I want to introduce you to my diarrhea." Anthropologists face linguistic challenges in addition to threats to life and limb.

Anthropological revelations in the early to mid-twentieth century had an enormous impact on Western views of the non-Western world. Cultural studies by noted anthropologists such as Margaret Mead, whose book *Coming of Age in Samoa* (1928), with its revelation of unfettered teenage sex among Samoan youth, rattled Western concepts of proper sexual behavior. It opened the eyes of the public to the multiple ways communities go about their business. The term *cultural relativism* arose to capture the sentiment that there are no cultural absolutes and that what may be deemed proper behavior in one culture may be anathema in another. Ultimately the idea of cultural relativism became viewed as sordid among religious conservatives, who were convinced that there are moral absolutes that happened to correspond to their religion's dogma.

In the 1970s, it occurred to students of organizational behavior that organizations themselves can be viewed as possessing cultures that define their rules, roles, and relationships. It became clear that in many respects, even the largest high-tech enterprises of the time, such as IBM, Polaroid, and Xerox, looked something like the tribes in the Siberian tundra, the Negev of North Africa, or the jungles of the Amazon. Thus emerged the concept of *corporate culture.* The deeper that people looked into the workings of companies, the clearer it became that what distinguished a company like General Motors from Toyota was the culture of each company. Each manufactured automobiles. Each used similar equipment to cut and bend sheet metal. Each produced a product that reflected the principles of the dominant design of the automotive industry. What most distinguished the two companies was the attitude each possessed toward the act of producing cars and selling cars. Ultimately this attitude, reflecting the corporate culture of each company, governed how the companies pursued automobile production.

The literature on corporate culture is enormous. It appears that there are as many ways to explain it as there are people writing and talking about it. One of the earliest contributions was the 1982 book *Corporate Cultures: The Rites and Rituals of Corporate Life* by Terrence E. Deal and Allan A. Kennedy. These authors look at corporate culture along two dimensions: propensity to take risk and openness to meaningful feedback. A leading corporate culture luminary, Edgar Schein, looks at corporate culture according to three cognitive levels: artifacts, values, and tacit assumptions (Schein, 2010).

Plenty of other organizational behavior savants have tweaked the concept in their own way. I will contribute to the corporate culture tower of Babel by offering my own perspective here. My points are straightforward and capture the basic tenets of most commentators. I attempt to capture the essence of corporate culture by means of three behavioral dichotomies, outlooks which I label Athenian versus Spartan, risk taking versus risk avoiding, and innovative versus legacy.

Athenian Versus Spartan Outlooks

The fifth-century B.C.E. coexistence of Athens and Sparta on a tiny spit of land that projected into the Sea of Crete offers a fascinating historical study in contrasts. Sparta was possibly the most militaristic society that ever existed. All citizens served the state. Individuals had no rights. Young boys were taken from their families at the age of seven in order to receive military training, and they spent their days honing combat skills. Girls also received physical training to toughen them.

Athens was the antithesis of Sparta. In 507 B.C.E., the city became a democracy, when a group of five hundred citizens, whose composition changed monthly, were charged with governing the city-state on behalf of all citizens. In the West, it is viewed as the birthplace of democracy. The Athenians cherished art, litera-ture, and wisdom. During the fifth century B.C.E., Athens produced Socrates, Plato, Aeschylus, Sophocles, Euripides, and Aristophanes, the last of whom wrote comedies that poked fun at the ruling oligarchs. The development of rigorous logical thinking during this time established the foundation for future generations of scientists and mathematicians, including Euclid, Eratosthenes, and Archimedes.

When we talk about corporate cultures being characterized by Athenian-versus-Spartan outlooks, we are principally looking at the degree to which they promote or abjure openness, participation in organizational affairs, and tolerance of criticism of the powerful by ordinary members of the community. Companies with Athenian outlooks promote openness, employee participation, and critical views, while those with Spartan outlooks hold an opposing perspective. Sergey Brin and Larry Page, founders of Google, claim to promote an open culture that cherishes excellence. Their stated goal to employ Google resources to capture all the world's written knowledge would certainly have pleased the intellectual elite of Athens. By all accounts, morale at Google is high, with employees feeling pleased that they are empowered to do great things.

A good example of a company pursuing a Spartan culture was EDS during the time it was run by its founder, Ross Perot. It was as close to a paramilitary orga-nization that a large corporation can be. Hiring preference was given to employees who had served in the armed forces. Strict dress codes were enforced. On one occasion, after delivering a course to EDS project managers, I had to smile when I saw that one participant wrote on the course evaluation sheet: "I was disap-pointed to see that some of my colleagues were wearing fuzzy socks and loafers with tassels." Total allegiance to the company was demanded. The list of thou-shalt-nots was lengthy. For example, employees were prohibited from discussing their salaries with each other or outsiders; violation of this rule could lead to dismissal from the company. Salaries were reputed to be the lowest in the infor-mation technology sector. The term *Spartan conditions* suited EDS perfectly. While it is difficult to see Google employees functioning effectively in such a regime, EDS employees themselves were highly charged go-getters who thought nothing of sacrificing their personal desires to serve the needs of the company. The Spartan culture energized them.

What we see here is that there are no absolutes that define what constitutes a good culture. As anthropologists recognize, cultural relativism abounds. With corporate culture, what works and what does not depends on fit. An individual whose values cherish independent thinking and the right to express dissent will be miserable in a Spartan environment. By the same token, the individual whose values emphasize the need for discipline, loyalty, and group cohesion will not be happy in a freewheeling, chaotic Athenian environment.

Working in an Athenian or Spartan culture has decision-making implications that tie back to the discussion of chain-of-command versus self-management decision-making architectures. The Spartan environment employs a chain-of-command structure: superior-subordinate relations prevail, with superiors calling the shots and subordinates implementing the commands issued to them. This culture works in well-defined production environments.

In contrast to the hierarchical nature of the Spartan decision-making structure, the Athenian approach entails employees who are engaged in free-flowing ideas, discussion, argument, and then consensus. This culture works in environments where the past provides imperfect guidance for the future—that is, environments experiencing rapid change.

Risk-Taking Versus Risk-Avoiding Outlooks

Organizations display dramatic variations in their attitudes toward risk. In some enterprises, risk taking is encouraged, and in others it is discouraged. Businesses that encourage risk taking advertise this fact proudly and loudly, shouting it from the rooftops. Interestingly, in risk-averse organizations, managers and employees rarely articulate the view that risk taking is discouraged in their organization because this position would not make them look good. As a general principle in business, risk takers are admired, whereas risk avoiders are viewed as meek and possibly cowardly. Few business leaders would boast of being risk averse. Still, through overall business procedures, career advancement paths, reward mechanisms, and approaches to developing products, most enterprises follow well-trodden roads that eschew uncertainty, holding to the view that it is safer to stick with what has worked in the past than to blaze new trails. They live by the old aphorism, "If it ain't broke, don't fix it." In most organizations, risk avoidance prevails.

One force working against supporting risky decisions is the absence of methods to accurately assess potential risk events and their impacts. In traditional decision science, a common approach experts promote to handle risk is to employ expected monetary value analysis. As we saw in Chapter Two, it entails knowing the probability that an investment will pay off and estimating the value of the payoff. With this information, decision-makers can compute, on the average, what the payoff of the investment would be if they were able to pursue this investment an infinite number of times. Use of this approach works brilliantly in gambling casinos where the probability of winning a game can be determined precisely and the payoff for each play is known. Because each category of game is played an enormous number of times in a casino, the law of large numbers kicks in, and the house can accurately predict its overall winnings across many plays.

In assessing business risks, investors do not have the luxury of pursuing the same investment thousands of times. If they could, that would enable them to determine how much money would go into their pockets over the long run. They face different circumstances than do casino owners. They make the investment once, so they cannot count on wins offsetting losses in the long run. Also, the two ingredients of expected monetary value analysis, the likelihood probabilities and payoff values, are based on crude guesswork. Decision-makers do not really know what these values are. Expected monetary value analysis can give them a sense of whether the odds are in their favor and may even help them rank different investment alternatives. But that's it.

Fear of risk in business is understandable, particularly when doing something new. Managers who back a new product, propose new processes, or support the pursuit of new business strategies can harm their reputations and derail their careers if their choices do not pay off. The consequences of failure are especially significant when a decision leads to monetary losses. Such losses reduce profit, and profitability is the altar at which businesses worship. In business, when you stick out your neck, you may find your head being chopped off.

Here is where corporate culture makes a big difference in how employees behave. Cultures that punish managers whose initiatives do not pay off, demand that investments have short payback periods, do not permit the questioning of decisions pushed down from the top, and support only investments backed with rock-solid data create risk-averse environments. The organization does not need to post signs in the hallways that admonish, "Do not take risks!" because this perspective is embedded in its rules and processes, which yield risk-averse behavior without anyone overtly talking about risk taking.

Decision-makers in a risk-taking corporate culture recognize that the big payoffs come from taking intelligent, informed chances. They know that the achievers who make their way into history books are individuals, groups, and organizations that dared to follow Robert Frost's road less traveled, and "that made all the difference."

They are genuinely uncomfortable with consistently safe decisions. They recognize that if their organizations are going to have an impact, it won't come from doing what has been done successfully in the past and what everyone is doing today. Their models of high-performing organizations include Microsoft in its earliest days, Apple Computer under Steve Jobs's leadership, Walmart under Sam Walton's guidance, and Google. If they have knowledge of business history, they recognize that today's fabled entrepreneurs are descendants of a long line of risk takers, including John Bolton and James Watt, Alexander Bell, Thomas Edison, Guglielmo Marconi, and Thomas Watson. The link between risk taking and business success long predates the dot-com era.

A risk-taking culture has these basic elements:

- *"Think different."* This is the slogan Apple adopted in 1997. Great achievements require doing things that have not been done before. IBM's Thomas Watson urged employees to "reach for the stars." At Apple and IBM, these slogans truly reflected the corporate culture and helped create an environment that encouraged productive risk taking.

- *Conformity is a greater sin than iconoclasm.* The word *iconoclast* means "breaker of icons." Iconoclasts break traditional icons that root people and institutions to the past. Risk-taking cultures promote the idea that rocking the boat is good. By keeping the boat stable, conformity ensures the repression of creative insights.

- *Great success requires tolerance of failure.* Whether you are dealing in the realm of new products, ideas, or processes, great achievements always entail the risk of failure. Organizational cultures that prohibit actions that can lead to failure prevent their employees from doing great things. Ironically, even as this outlook can minimize short-term risk, it may contribute to catastrophic long-term failure, because the risk-averse organization does not adjust itself to the steady stream of changes needed to respond to environmental challenges.

- *Failure is a great teacher.* Winners learn from their mistakes. A review of history's great achievements shows that more often than not, they are built on lessons learned from failure. To the extent an organization's culture emphasizes the positive side of failure, it encourages productive risk taking.

The positive value of adopting a risk-taking corporate culture is well known and widely preached. Who dares publicly promote the virtues of risk aversion? However, it is difficult to adopt a risk-taking culture in practice, even while preaching its theoretical virtues. When someone throws a punch at your face, you flinch. It is an involuntary reflex. No matter how hard you try to keep from flinching, you still flinch when that fist approaches your face. So it is when trying to implement the risk-taking culture traits. While everyone may talk about the need to take risk, decision-makers flinch when it comes to making a decision that has an obvious downside risk. The theoretical prospects of major long-term gains are more than offset by the possibility of failure.

Consider the first item in the list above: *Think different.* What exactly does this mean? At Apple and IBM, it means that everyone from the floor sweeper to the CEO should strive to free themselves from conventional thinking. But how this translates to practice is vague. Certainly productive geniuses travel along their own distinct trails, but so do sociopaths. When employees insist on marching to the beat of a different drummer, how do we know whether they are in pursuit of a great idea or simply delusional?

Consider the third item: *Tolerate failure.* Really? This is easier said than done. For one thing, if the failure leads to substantial financial losses, the decision-makers who backed the initiative have a lot of explaining to do to senior managers, investors, and employees whose projects are cut because of cash flow shortages. Beyond this, how can we distinguish between well-intentioned failure and failure arising from poor performance rooted in poor planning, poor execution, and lack of commitment to achieving goals?

The point is that when looking at an organization's orientation toward risk, you are likely to find a gap between what Harvard's Chris Argyris (1993) calls *theories of action* and *theories in use.* Theories of action articulate the purported values and actions an organization possesses. It is what the organization advertises when it describes itself. Theories in use, in contrast, reflect the way the organization really works. They capture the organization's true values and actions, which often diverge substantially from what it advertises. Thus, we encounter many organizations purporting to support some measure of risk taking (even if modest) but few with corporate cultures such as Apple's and Google's that demand it or support it in any way.

In view of the fact that risk taking is so alien to the psychological makeup of a large portion of the general population, can organizations actually create a risk-taking culture? Can you change a leopard's spots? The answer is yes and no. When I say yes, it is clear that many things can be done to remove barriers to risk taking. For example, an organization's investment policies that require very short payback periods encourage risk-averse short-term thinking. If you want the big returns associated with risk taking, you need to encourage the pursuit of long-term visions and downplay the requirement for quick return on investment.

Here's another example. Demanding that business cases for new projects be supported with rock-solid data works against speculative projects that have substantial upside potential, because with new ventures, you are not sure of what is technically possible or whether a market exists for a new good or service. By removing demands for foolproof business cases, you open the door for the introduction of more speculative, high-payoff initiatives—and you also increase the possibility of experiencing failure! As Hamlet said, "There's the rub."

Organizations trying to strengthen the risk-taking component of their culture can also implement positive steps. In the 1980s, 3M Corporation impressed business analysts with its steady flow of innovative new products. Among the many explanations for 3M's innovative prowess, a significant one is the corporate policy that required that at any given moment, 25 percent of the company's revenue needed to be generated by products that did not exist five years earlier. Twenty-five percent! One-fourth of corporate revenue! The scientists, engineers, and floor sweepers at 3M loved it. They laughed at the challenge and eagerly responded to it.

This brings me to my "no" response to the question: Can organizations actually create a risk-taking culture? In the case of 3M, the enterprise has assumed a positive risk-taking orientation since its founding in 1902. Its culture has been pro-risk since Day One. No management luminary told its CEO, "You must adopt a risk-taking culture." When you know something about the history of 3M, you are not surprised by its edict requiring that 25 percent of revenues come from new products.

Innovative companies like 3M thrive on a self-generated willingness to take risks. What we see here is an inherent pro-risk orientation in highly innovative companies. It comes from their leaders, who are willing to bet the bank on great ideas. It comes from employees, who are nonconformist risk takers attracted to a free-wheeling organizational environment. It is embedded in policies that promote innovation and decry doing things the way they have always been done. In these organizations, taking risks comes naturally. The big challenge is to avoid implementing processes that subtly discourage risk taking. If employees are required to pursue initiatives with quick payback and offer business cases that promote sure-thing investments, a healthy risk-taking environment will be diminished in some measure.

Innovative Versus Legacy Outlooks

I mentioned that almost everyone supports the idea that businesses need to be willing to take risks. Similarly, almost everyone holds the view that businesses must encourage innovation in their ranks. I have never heard a responsible leader say, "You know, we would be better off if we discouraged innovation." Business leaders, government policymakers, and academics universally promote the idea that for organizations to survive and thrive in these turbulent times, they must promote innovative outlooks among their employees.

I have been involved in innovation studies all my professional life. Early in my career, I worked with a research enterprise dedicated to studying scientific and technological productivity. I published some twenty articles on this subject in refereed journals. In 1979, when I joined the faculty of the School of Government and Business Administration at George Washington University, I was made director of the program on science, technology, and innovation. Through research, consulting, and teaching, I immersed myself in the literature on innovation. Many good books, monographs, and articles have been written in this area. When I reflect on what I perceive to be the dozen most significant writings on innovation,

Clayton Christensen's book *The Innovator's Dilemma* (1997) ranks near the top of the list. (Max Weber, Joseph Schumpeter, and William Abernathy are other members of my small circle of big thinkers in the innovation arena.)

In *The Innovator's Dilemma*, Christensen demonstrates the dilemma corporate leaders encounter when facing choices that will guide the innovation strategy they pursue. They can play it safe and stick to developing low-risk, sustaining technologies. These are incremental improvements to existing technology. A camera manufacturer that figures out how to go from offering 12 megapixel cameras to 16 megapixel cameras is focused on promoting sustainable technology. Another option is to pursue disruptive technologies that radically alter products and markets, a path filled with risk. Here's the dilemma business leaders face: business history shows that companies that hold a leading position in their markets regularly lose their leadership, and some go out of business, when they play it safe and eschew risky strategies to promote radical innovation. They are overwhelmed by risk-taking competitors. Quite often, playing it safe is riskier than taking chances.

In his book, Christensen's principal concern is with the promotion of disruptive technologies in companies. Disruptive technologies are the spectacular breakthroughs that can propel companies to the top of their industry. They are high-risk technologies in two respects: they carry technical risk and, more significant, market risk as well. Technical risk is rooted in the possibility that pushing technology to new boundaries can lead to technical failure. Like Howard Hughes's gargantuan Spruce Goose aircraft, the technology simply cannot get off the ground. With market risk, it is not clear that the new technology will sell. As Christensen points out, disruptive technologies face special challenges in the marketplace. In their earliest stages, they underperform existing technologies, so current users of a given technology have no interest in adopting them because they perceive them to be second rate. If the disruptive technology is going to be successful, it needs to create an entirely new market.

Polaroid's instant photography, Sony's Walkman, the Apple II personal computer, digital cameras, and mini-mills are modern examples of enormously successful disruptive technologies. If you experienced instant photography in its earliest form, you would wonder why anyone would buy a Polaroid camera because the photographic images were so shabby. The same can be said for the other disruptive technologies on the list. At the outset, they underperform. What makes them disruptive is that they create new markets that ultimately swamp the market for prevailing technologies. When disruptive technologies succeed, dominant players can disappear overnight.

The key features of disruptive technologies are nicely captured in the story of the personal computer. When Steve Jobs and Steve Wozniak developed the Apple II personal computer in the late 1970s, the computer market was dominated by mainframe computers, chiefly produced by IBM, and minicomputers, produced by a handful of companies, such as Digital Equipment Corporation (DEC) and Data General. Computers were used solely in business and government. They were too expensive and complicated to be employed by ordinary people. Small businesses lacked the resources and technical know-how to use computers in their operations unless they accessed computers through time-sharing services.

So when the Apple II came out, existing computer users saw it as a cute toy. This image was reinforced by the primary use of early Apple IIs, which was playing computer games such as Pong, Pac-Man, and Donkey Kong. It was difficult for traditional computer users to take the Apple II seriously. Early on, some visionaries within IBM saw the personal computer's market potential, which led to launching the IBM PC project in the late 1970s. But even then, the mainframe culture of IBM was so hostile to the idea of taking personal computers seriously that the PC development team was set up in a leaky warehouse in Florida, fourteen hundred miles from IBM's Armonk, New York, headquarters. Only by distancing themselves from the meddling heavy-hitters at headquarters could the PC team develop a viable product.

Personal computers excited a new generation of software developers, who began developing business applications to run on the new devices. Of particular importance was the development of first-rate word processing and spreadsheet software applications. Small business owners immediately saw the emerging value of the PC to their operations, as did individuals working in professional services. With PCs, they did not need to invest tens of thousands of dollars in equipment, possess advanced computer skills, or hire an expensive computer systems staff.

Even as the Apple and IBM-style personal computers were taking off and developing ever more advanced processing capabilities and even as their prices were plummeting, traditional old-hand computer users, primarily engineers and mainframe programmers, persisted in viewing them as second-rate toys. To them, the weak performance of the new technology was obvious: when contrasted to an IBM 370 mainframe computer or Digital VAX minicomputer, its performance was pathetic. They were unable to see that personal computers served a different function and different audience than the computing behemoths they cherished.

This arrogant outlook ultimately led to the rapid collapse of the world's second-largest computer company, Digital Equipment Corporation. DEC produced the world's most advanced minicomputers, the VAX machines, which were the darling of engineers. Its founder and CEO, Ken Olsen, refused to believe that second-rate PCs were a threat to his first-rate VAX machines. So he persisted in building ever more advanced and more expensive minicomputers and avoided investing seriously in the development of PC products. In the 1990s, when PC manufacturers began offering thirty-two-bit computers for less than three thousand dollars a machine, DEC's demise was assured. It was bought by Compaq in 1998 and stopped doing business under the DEC name. In a matter of five years, DEC went from being the world's number two computer company to a nonplayer, taken down by a disruptive technology that its leaders would not view seriously. The irony here is that Olsen himself was the father of a disruptive technology when he and Harlan Anderson set up DEC and pioneered the development of minicomputers in the late 1950s and early 1960s. In the early days, their technology also appeared second rate to the mainstream. Yet Olsen was unable to link developments in the PC arena with his personal experience with the introduction of minicomputers.

Three lessons learned about disruptive technologies when looking at the evolution of PCs stand out. First, when disruptive technologies appear, their performance is inferior to what prevailing technologies offer. Users and producers of the prevailing technologies hardly give them a glance. Trying to sell them on the value of the new technology will fail.

Second, because buyers in the existing market show little interest in purchasing what they view as second-rate products, disruptive technologies grow by appealing to entirely new markets. As we saw in the case of PCs, the new market was composed of ordinary citizens—business owners, professionals, hobbyists, students—who viewed the capabilities of the new technology as matching their needs. These new users were not looking for more processing power. They were looking for user-friendly devices that enabled them to carry out basic business, professional, and personal functions efficiently. PCs fit the bill. Note that the size of the new market was much larger than the traditional computer market of engineers, scientists, and computer programmers.

Third, as the disruptive technology gains acceptance in the new market and the businesses that produce it experience dramatic revenue growth, they invest in technological advances. At some point, these advances enable the disruptive technology to outperform and replace traditional technology, and at a cheaper price. They offer substantially more value to buyers than the technology they replace. If you think about the early versions of the instant camera, transistor radio, personal computer, and digital camera, they were all substantially inferior to the existing products they ultimately replaced.

CONCLUSION

This book focuses on making mindful decisions of consequence. It is not concerned with what toothpaste you buy or the vacation package you select. Most decisions of consequence occur in some kind of organizational setting. They are often made inside an organization with a view to addressing organizational needs or the needs of players outside the organization. They often affect other organizations. For decision-makers engaged in making consequential decisions, it is valuable for them to understand the organizational context of the choices they intend to make. In this chapter, we examined organizational context along four dimensions: organizational structure, organizational process, people in organizations, and organizational culture. Effective decision making requires a good grasp of the impact of these dimensions on the decision-making process.

5   The Moral Dimension

Although it is seldom discussed in decision-making books, articles, or courses, decision making has a strong moral dimension to it. You could convincingly argue that the 2008–2009 global economic implosion was a disaster rooted in morally flawed decision making.

Here is some of what went on. Mortgage lending institutions ignored their fiduciary responsibility by offering home loans to unqualified buyers. Securities rating institutions such as Standard and Poor's and Moody's were remiss by rating subprime loan securities as AAA securities when they were clearly high-risk assets. Fannie Mae and Freddie Mac, which provided government-authorized mortgages, thought nothing of packaging and selling securities comprising subprime loans and labeling them as prime-grade securities. Meanwhile, banks, insurance companies, and institutional investors throughout the world gobbled up these shaky mortgage-backed securities because they were highly rated, had low margin requirements, and possessed high rates of return that exceeded what they could earn with the most prudent investments. This casino-like environment was abetted by the lack of government oversight of financial firms by government regulatory agencies, such as the Securities and Exchange Commission and the Federal Housing Authority, and Congress's obsession since the Reagan years with deregulating business. This was not a uniquely American phenomenon. As the European debt and bank crisis of 2011–2012 demonstrated, the same disregard for good financial practice and regulatory oversight prevailed across the Atlantic.

These reckless behaviors were largely the outcome of decisions made by people intent on promoting their own interests at the expense of the well-being of their employers, clients, investors, and the public. We know in retrospect that such reckless behaviors generated bad decisions that contributed to a global economic decline unparalleled since the Great Depression. At best, the decisions reflected poor judgment. At worst, they were morally reprehensible and sometimes illegal.

What occurred on a grand scale in these examples occurs routinely on a smaller scale. Consider some everyday examples. A salesperson knows that the transmission of a used car on the lot is about to blow but nevertheless tells prospective buyers that the car is in mint condition. Bidders on a contract fudge their qualifications by employing fake résumés. A city manager throws municipal business to a company in return for a tidy kickback. Senior executives exaggerate their companies' earnings reports in order to boost the price of stock. Candidates for public office hide their legal problems from voters. Safety managers at an industrial plant cover up a toxic spill that may ultimately leak into the groundwater. A manager's assistant insists that she has notified an important client about changes to a product's specification when she has not. Many of these tales bring to mind the old joke about scam artists selling shares of the Brooklyn Bridge to naive investors.

Each of these examples of small-scale moral failings has implications for people making decisions. The car buyer may decide to purchase a lemon based on the assurances of the used car salesperson. The bid review board may decide to award a contract to the contractor whose bid contains fake résumés because this contractor looks more capable than the others. Investors may decide to increase their holdings in the company with the inflated earnings report because the falsified good track record makes it appear to be an attractive investment.

The lesson here is obvious: when making decisions, decision-makers need to think consciously about moral issues. In this chapter, I first look at three broad categories of moral failings: deceit, illegal behavior, and negligence. I then look at two specific categories that are viewed as pervasive problems in organizations today and are much discussed in the business literature.

One is the moral hazard problem. In this case, people are using resources that are entrusted to them to make decisions that benefit them personally when the decisions work out nicely and do not harm them when the decisions yield bad results. With moral hazard, the unethical decision-maker assumes little or no risk for decision outcomes. The risk is borne entirely by the people providing the resources: business owners, investors, taxpayers, and pensioners. A simple example is the mortgage broker who provides loans to unqualified borrowers, knowing that each loan earns her a hefty commission even though it is likely that the borrowers will be unable to make their payments.

The second is the principal-agent problem. This is a universally encountered problem, where the people charged to do something on behalf of others—their bosses, clients, colleagues, or regulators, for example—do not execute their responsibilities as required. A simple example is the office administrator who spends most of his work time surfing the Web rather than carrying out his assigned chores. A more sinister example is a contractor who in working with your clients, adopts them as her own clients.

Clearly the categories of moral failings examined here overlap. Criminal acts often entail deception. Simple negligence can escalate to criminality. Negligence is also one of the manifestations of the principal-agent problem, when agents do not fulfill their responsibilities, yielding consequences that damage the organization. The exemplars of the evils of moral hazards, rogue mortgage brokers providing mortgages to struggling immigrants who are unable to read their contracts, may operate criminally, engage in deceit, and are negligent in fulfilling their fiduciary duties toward both their clients and their employers. Despite the overlap of the categories, it is nonetheless useful to look at each category separately in order to highlight its distinguishing characteristics.

BROAD CATEGORIES OF MORAL FAILINGS

This section examines three broad categories of moral failings: deceit, negligence, and outright illegal behavior.

Deceit

Both common sense and research studies offer strong evidence that people regularly tell lies—everyone does, including people of the highest moral stature. It would not be surprising to learn that Mother Teresa, when asked how she was feeling on a given morning, would answer, "Fine," although in truth she was feeling a shade peaked. Consider elementary school teachers working with kids who are earnestly struggling with their lessons and telling them, "You're doing a great job," when in fact they are performing below par. Mother Teresa and the school teachers are lying. However, their lies are understandable within context, and nearly everyone would consider them proper.

In the realm of dissimulation, we deal with shades of gray more than with blacks and whites. People routinely lie as a matter of social convenience. By lying on little things, they keep social relations on an even keel. If someone looks haggard, it's not smart to say, "Gee, you look terrible." If a friend performed poorly on an exam, you don't voice your inner thought that perhaps he isn't smart enough to handle the course material. The consequences of being scrupulously honest are pictured humorously in the 1997 comedy, *Liar Liar*, starring Jim Carrey. In this movie, a fast-talking lawyer has a spell cast on him where he becomes incapable of lying for a period of twenty-four hours; he cannot lie on even the smallest matters. The movie cleverly shows that during routine social interactions, it is nearly impossible to avoid distorting the truth. Most of the lead character's lies are small potatoes, issued to smooth social relations. In society, people recognize that there are acceptable lies, and they highlight their pristine nature by calling them *white lies*.

In their scholarly article, "Lying in Everyday Life," B. M. DePaulo and her colleagues (1996) divide lies into two broad categories: nondeceptive presentations and deceptive presentations. The first category serves an editing functioning. That is, through white lies, the liar is able to project an image that is convenient or otherwise desired. For example, when someone asks you how you are feeling and you respond, "Fine," your goal is to keep the chatter short. If you say, "Actually, I've had a headache for two days," the conversation on your health will be prolonged and move in an undesired direction. With nondeceptive presentations, the goal is not to deceive but to edit. The nondeceptive presentation covers most white lies.

The goal of a deceptive presentation is to deceive. When you pad your résumé, tell folks you are six feet tall (when you are five ten), assure a customer that a product is defect free (when it isn't), or demand that your accountant overstate your corporate earnings to make your company look good to investors, you are engaging in deceptive presentation. This category of lying can have strong implications for decision making. The liars lie to influence decision-makers to serve their needs. For their part, decision-makers must always question the veracity of the information they use to make decisions, so that their final choices are not based on misinformation. Informed decision making requires good information. Effective decision-makers strive to surface and discount the lies.

In their research article, DePaulo and her colleagues track the lying habits of seventy-seven college undergraduates and seventy adults attending community college. The participants are asked to keep a daily social diary for a week in which they describe the deceptive statements they make, including their context and consequence. The authors found that their undergraduate subjects lied an average of twice daily, while the adults in community college averaged one lie per day. In this study, a lie is defined as a conscious deception, whether of a nondeceptive or deceptive category. Studies that define lying more broadly to include the smallest white lies that serve the function of social convenience find lying to be practiced much more frequently than reported here.

Decision-makers should be concerned with the negative consequences of deceptive presentation lies. Lies distort the information decision-makers need to develop an understanding of what they face in their lives and business. To function effectively, they need reliable information. Lies deny them access to this information and portray a reality that is false and does not jibe with the real world. Decisions based on this false reality are ill informed and do not address the real issues. They result in actions that do not serve the interests of the decision-makers and may in fact harm them. The harm can assume different forms, ranging from loss of reputation to serious damage to business operations to bodily harm.

Surfacing lies can be tricky. One rule many people employ to circumvent lies is to deal only with trusted players who are well respected in the community and strive to maintain their good reputation. As an overall rubric, this is a good practice. But take care! As Bernard Madoff showed the world, it does not always work. Madoff was the respected chair of Bernard L. Madoff Investment Securities, LLC, which he founded in 1960. He played a significant role in the founding of the NASDAQ stock market and served as its chair, and he was a significant philanthropist as well. But as we learned in 2008, he is also one of the greatest con men in history, using his securities firm to bilk billions of dollars from investors (many his personal friends), resulting in investor losses of some $18 billion.

Madoff's enterprise was built on lies. The fabricated data on fake trades in his trading reports were concocted by an assistant to match a predetermined return on investment for each client that Madoff cooked up. In 2009, while serving jail time, Madoff expressed amazement that he was able to get away with such a major scam for so long, especially in view of Securities and Exchange Commission investigations of his activities over the years. Madoff was able to get away with his scam thanks to his impeccable reputation, the naiveté (and greed) of his investors, and the incompetence of government regulators.

Lying can take many forms. I highlight only a handful here with a view to illustrating the diversity of lies that decision-makers must be prepared to contend with. There are no obvious rules for dealing with liars and their lies. The best defense is vigilance and good sense.

Bald-Faced Lies. Bald-faced lies entail presenting an absolute untruth. When Kenneth Lay told Enron's shareholders and employees that the company was strong and that they should buy more Enron stock, even as he was dumping large amounts of his personal holdings, he was engaging in a bald-faced lie. Lay was a credible businessperson. He was the son of a Baptist preacher, held a Ph.D. in economics from the University of Houston, was a prominent philanthropist in Houston, and was CEO of one of the most powerful energy companies in the world. Yet he was a liar, and his lies did untold damage to people who believed in him and followed his advice.

When a realtor tells you that a house you are looking at has never experienced problems but knows otherwise, he is engaging in a bald-faced lie. When a company's bookkeeper cooks the books to portray the appearance of corporate strength, she has perpetrated a bald-faced lie.

A good antidote to bald-faced lies is skepticism. Many bald-faced lies do not make sense when looked at carefully. For example, one rule of thumb in buying houses is to go into the basement and see if you can detect the telltale stains of water damage. While you are at it, look for cracks in the foundation, which suggest that the house is not as stable as the realtor claims. No matter what the real estate agent tells you, the water stains and foundation cracks scream out: "Take care, take care."

Another cure is to get a second opinion. When smart home purchasers make an offer to buy a house, they include a contingency provision that states that the offer is good contingent on the house's passing an engineering inspection. One thing that keeps realtors honest is their recognition that their assurances of good quality can easily be overturned by a two hundred dollar engineering report.

A significant explanation of why bald-faced liars are able to get away with often implausible lies ties to the desire of their targets to believe that things are fine. I came across this recently when helping a friend find a location for a fashion boutique in Manhattan. After looking at attractive properties that would bust her budget, we came across a small property that was affordable and situated in a prime location on Second Avenue along the Upper East Side. It had previously been a newspaper stand that sold newspapers, hot coffee, doughnuts, magazines, bottled beverages, and packaged food. The lower portions of the walls were covered with black mold. What the realtor described as a charming mezzanine had a sagging floor. The ceiling was covered with cables that served the Internet needs of the tenants in the apartments upstairs. The basement was shared with a Vietnamese restaurant and offered no security for storing inventory. The real estate agent said, "I know this looks a bit shabby now, but everything will be fixed once you sign the lease agreement." After listening to the real estate agent and looking at this abomination, my friend said: "This is great. I will sign the lease." It took a while, but I ultimately convinced her that this was a truly bad decision.

Tell-the-Boss-What-She-or-He-Wants-to-Hear. I have been a professor of management for more than thirty years. To stay in touch with the latest management developments, I am constantly picking the brains of people I encounter: senior managers, middle managers, students, experts, taxi drivers, store clerks, waiters, and the cleaning staff at my office. One of my most significant sources of information on the mind-set of CEOs has been my sister, Sally Frame Kasaks. Over a twenty-five-year time span, she was CEO of Ann Taylor, Talbots, and Abercrombie and Fitch. Early in her career, *Business Week* identified her as one of the top female executives to watch.

A few years ago, I took advantage of being brother to a top executive and asked Sally: "How would you identify the single biggest problem you face as CEO of a significant company?" Her answer: "I think the biggest problem I face is that my deputies filter the information I receive. They tell me what they think I want to hear. Mostly this is news that confirms my predilections. That's not what I want. I know the limits of my insights. I can detect right away what they are doing, and it upsets me. I need to learn what's really going on so that I can make the right decisions." The way she handled this problem was to carry out spontaneous, unannounced visits to local stores.

Sam Walton's perspective was the same as Sally's. In order to bypass the filtered information he was getting from his lieutenants, he regularly ventured into the field to see things firsthand. He would climb into his personal airplane and show up unannounced at Walmart stores throughout the United States. When visiting these stores, he would play the role of a Walmart associate, stocking goods on the shelves occasionally and assisting customers. This is one way he monitored the pulse of his company.

Tell-the-boss-what-she/he-wants-to-hear may be done with good intentions. Why be a Gloomy Gus? Why not put a nice spin on things? Arab hospitality is famous for this practice. Westerners traveling and working in the Middle East learn quickly that in their desire to be polite, their Arab colleagues may prefer to gloss over bad news with encouraging reports in order to cheer them. In my trips to the Middle East, I learned to dread the word *malesh* ("don't worry"), because when a colleague, contractor, hotel clerk, or travel agent employed this word to comfort me, I grew convinced that things were worse than I thought. Pursuing good intentions can be kind, but there is truth in the old adage that the road to hell is paved with good intentions. In decision making, frankness consistently trumps good intentions.

Telling the boss what she or he wants to hear may also be carried out for nefarious reasons. When the second-tier leadership encounters serious problems, it is less painful (at the moment) to provide the boss with information that confirms her or his cheerful delusions. Besides, the bad news may reflect poorly on the performance of the second tier. Perhaps it is best to keep the boss in the dark.

Half-Truths. With half-truths, facts are presented with significant omissions. The individual relating the tale tells only part of the story. Consider the following example. Mom sees her son, ten-year-old Davey, playing a video game in his room. The house rules she established allow Davey to play on his PlayStation for an hour each day, but only after he has completed his homework. She asks her son, "Did you complete your history homework?" Davey answers truthfully, "Yes." Satisfied with this answer, Mom leaves Davey alone. What her son doesn't tell her is that although he finished the history homework, he hasn't worked on his math or English assignments. He has told a half-truth. (In his case, you can argue he told a one-third truth!)

As with all other forms of deceit, half-truths provide decision-makers with a distorted view of reality, impairing their ability to make informed decisions. Recently the washing machine in an apartment I rent out stopped functioning. Because my tenant was being inconvenienced every day the machine was out of order, an important criterion in purchasing a replacement was that it could be installed quickly. Two vendors I contacted told me that their inventory was depleted and would not be able to deliver the washer in less than three weeks. I explained the need for urgency for quick delivery to a third vendor, but rather than reassure me, his response put me on hyperalert: "I will place an order for it to be delivered to the apartment next Tuesday." Given my experience with the two prior vendors, I then asked: "Do you have the washer in stock?" After a moment's hesitation, he answered: "No, but it should be arriving any day, and I am sure I can get it to you by Tuesday." A half-truth. He truthfully would place an order for a Tuesday delivery, but he falsely implied that the washer could be delivered at that time. I did not place an order with him then and do not plan doing business with him in the future.

In business, the opportunities for encountering half-truths are limitless. The company CEO who goes on the road to sell her company's technology capabilities to investors, but neglects to tell them that an important patent application is likely to be rejected, is conveying a half-truth. The proposal writing team that assures top management that they will complete their proposal by the deadline date, knowing that crucial performance data were not collected or reported in the proposal, is conveying a half-truth. The software development team that reports that the new enhancement they are working on will be released on time, without informing management that their capabilities are much lower than those of competing products, is conveying a half-truth.

Half-truths can be hard to detect, because they contain elements of truth mixed with snippets of falsehood. In a spot check to validate a statement's veracity, the facts may play out correctly, so you may develop a false sense of confidence in its correctness. Even if you hit on something that does not ring true, the statement may contain enough truth to lead you to believe that the untrue element is a small, inconsequential error.

In trying to root out half-truths, you need to be careful how you phrase the questions you ask. For example, let's say you ask your project manager whether the information technology installation his team is working on at a client site is on schedule. The project manager might truthfully answer yes. What he doesn't tell you is that owing to anticipated quality problems, there is a good chance that delays will be encountered in the future. He is answering your question truthfully although not candidly. You are dealing with a half-truth here, although you do not know it. The question you should have asked is: "Will we meet the deadline in delivering the installation to the client?" Given what he knows about impending problems, the project manager will answer no if he is truthful.

Negligence

Negligence is the antithesis of diligence. Diligent people are individuals who pursue their chores with great care, intelligence, and energy and avoid making mistakes to the extent possible. They both follow the rules and employ good sense, because they recognize that mindless pursuit of a rule may lead to disaster. If necessary, they break the rules in order to achieve the underlying goal of the work effort.

Negligent people are the opposite of diligent people. Their approach to executing chores is sloppy. They eschew hard effort. They are indifferent to the outcome of their work effort. An abiding trait they possess is laziness. One dictionary definition in fact characterizes negligence as "lazily careless."

Negligence is categorized here as a moral problem because negligent people have little or no interest in meeting their obligations. Instead of pursuing their responsibilities with care, intelligence, and energy, they actively shirk their duty. The disregard for meeting their obligations can have consequences that harm the interests of others, including the public, as well as their colleagues, investors, customers, and employers. An egregious example of negligence would be aircraft maintenance personnel who do a sloppy job caring for the aircraft under their charge. Their slipshod ways can contribute to an aircraft crash with loss of lives. Legally they can be charged with negligent homicide.

Negligence becomes a decision-making problem when decisions are made based on the presumption of diligent work efforts. The hypothetical Globus Enterprises may win a contract to upgrade a client's customer relationship management system because its bid is well priced, the work plan intelligently laid out, and the implementation team presented as diligent. If the implementation team pursues its chores negligently—that is, without care, intelligence, and energy—what was initially viewed as a dream team may turn out to be the team from Dante's sixth ring of hell. Following are some likely traits of Globus's negligent team:

- Its members do not follow good practice in their development work.
- They are sloppy in maintaining documentation.
- Their testing procedures are flawed.
- They do not communicate effectively with the client.
- They project a sense of apathy rather than the can-do attitude needed to execute the project successfully.
- The final product they produce will be a disaster.

Anticipating the possibility of negligence requires decision-makers to surface its telltale signs during the due diligence phase of decision making. Negligent players have a tough time covering up their negligence. Discerning decision-makers should be on the lookout for subtle indications of sloppiness, disregard for procedures, and lack of commitment to executing chores diligently. If prospective players are late to meetings, get e-mail addresses wrong, write error-filled correspondence, and frequently draw from a deep well of excuses to cover their deficiencies, you have good cause to believe that they will behave negligently when carrying out the chores you need done. You should not be surprised if they do a substandard job. Here are some questions you can ask yourself to discern negligence:

- Do the players charged with implementing the decision have a track record of diligence and reliability?

- In your dealing with them, do they convey a sense of operating effectively? For example, do they respond quickly to phone messages? Are they energetic? Do they appear to be well organized? Do they take operational processes seriously?

- In your transactions with them, do you sense that they strive to produce error-free results, ranging from the simplest correspondence to complex chores?

If the answer to any of these questions is no, you need to pause before supporting them through your decisions.

In preparing for the possibility of negligence, decision-makers must also look to themselves. They should ask: Do we have processes in place to monitor the activities of the players we will be supporting? Do we have backup plans to handle the consequences of negligence? If the answer to either of these questions is no, then the decision-makers have not prepared for the possibility of negligence.

Illegal Behavior

There is bad news for the world's Pollyannas: it's a jungle out there. Plenty of predators are ready to pounce on unsuspecting prey in an attempt to separate their victims from their property. Evidence of the existence of miscreants intent on creating mischief lies no further than your e-mail inbox. Consider the following hypothetical scenario. When you open your e-mail account in the morning, you encounter an official-looking letter from your bank, complete with logo and all manner of bureaucratic babble and intimidating codes, warning you that your bank account has been compromised by hackers. To deal with this serious breach, you simply need to click on a link, which will direct you to a log-on page that requires you to enter your bank password and PIN.

Two items down the inbox list is another official-looking letter, this one from a banker in Nigeria telling you that for a small investment on your part, you can access millions of dollars of unclaimed assets sitting in a vault in Lagos. Simply click on the supplied link to begin the process.

A little further down the list of inbox messages you get a letter from PayPal indicating a serious mix-up in your eBay transaction yesterday. To deal with it, click on the supplied link and log onto your PayPal account—using, of course, your log-on code and password. This message actually alarms you, because you did indeed engage in a large eBay transaction yesterday evening and the message sounds credible.

Finally, you come across a don't-miss deal for purchasing Viagra and Cialis at super-low prices. Just fill out the attached electronic order form, and be sure to supply credit card information.

An amusing feature of many of these attempts to victimize you is their flawed grammar, spelling errors, and near-comical phrasing. Recently I received an "official" notice from Facebook, saying it was from the "Facebook Team," indicating that my account had been shut down. Following is the rationale the e-mail message offered for this action:

> Your account has been disabled. All of your ads have been stopped and should not be run again on the site under any circumstances. Generally, we disable an account if too many of its ads violate our **Terms of Use** or **Advertising Guidelines**. Unfortunately we cannot provide you with specific violations that have been deemed abusive. Please review our **Terms of Use** and **Advertising Guidelines** if you have further questions.

Of course, the message was a sham. Note that the phrasing of this passage reflects the misguided attempt of someone with no business or legal background to sound authoritative. The boldface links in this passage are hot links that, if clicked, would have put me into the hands of cybercriminals. Certainly, 99.9 percent of recipients of this message will see it for what it is and delete it. Where the criminals benefit is from the 0.1 percent of recipients who click on the hot links.

What you and I encounter in our e-mail inboxes on a daily basis occurs on a grander scale in larger enterprises. Decision-makers in these enterprises not only need to fend off scam artists but be alert to the possibility of ordering substandard, counterfeit inventory components from crooked vendors; entering into partnerships with crooked partners; investing money in crooked ventures; surfacing crooked employees involved in kickback schemes; and so on.

Illegal activity can affect decision making in two ways. First, your decisions may put you in the position of being a victim of illegal behavior. If you hire unscrupulous employees, expect trouble. For example, consider how in 1995, Nick Leeson's rogue trading activities brought down Barings Bank, one of the world's oldest and most venerable banks. More recently, in 2011, the UBS rogue trader Kweku Adoboli incurred $2.3 billion in losses to his Swiss employer.

Similarly, if you enter into contracts with unscrupulous vendors, expect trouble. The materials and services they provide will be substandard and may cost you lost business. In construction and manufacturing, the substandard components may lead to equipment and structural failures, and they may even create serious legal liabilities for you.

This gets us to the second point: your decisions may involve you with illegal activity that puts you and your organization in legal jeopardy. Consider the following true story. A few years ago, a travel and tourism company contracted a bus company to transport its clients for touristic travel. It turned out that the bus company employed unlicensed bus drivers and therefore was breaking the law. The bus company's illegal operations were revealed after a highway accident led to the deaths of three tourists. Because the travel and tourism company was responsible for organizing the ill-fated tour, including hiring transport, it was targeted in multimillion-dollar lawsuits and investigated by the state attorney general. Its existence was jeopardized by the illegal operations of a contractor.

The best defense against becoming victimized by illegal activities is, once again, vigilance. Business owners do not need to be told to be vigilant, because they recognize that the assets they own are constantly at risk. Savvy business owners continually assess the risk implications of their decisions. Their employees, however, are more susceptible to being victims of illegal activities, because they do not have a personal stake in the enterprise's assets. They do not have ingrained in them the natural caution and paranoia that a business owner has. The same can be said of employees in publicly owned companies. Even members of the executive suite of publicly traded companies will generally be more cavalier than business owners about the risks their decisions entail, because the negative consequences the enterprise may experience do not translate into personal losses.

This phenomenon has a name: moral hazard. Moral hazard arises when decision-makers do not have a personal stake in the consequences of their decisions. In his explanation of recent economic crises, culminating in the economic collapse of 2008, Nobel Prize winner Paul Krugman (2009) identifies it as the single most significant culprit leading to the troubles that trigger financial mayhem. It is a major problem associated with decision making, ranging from the smallest decision a drugstore clerk might make to billion-dollar decisions by the largest corporate players.

MORAL HAZARD

The concept of moral hazard arose originally in the insurance industry, where insurers were concerned that by underwriting risk, they could be encouraging risky behavior among their policyholders. For example, health insurance with no penalties for smoking could encourage smokers to continue smoking if they believe that the health consequences of their behavior are covered by insurance payments for medical expenses.

A little reflection suggests that moral hazard is tied to the links among risk apportionment, rewards, and accountability. From the decision-makers' perspective, if they face little or no personal risk in making a decision that can generate big benefits for them, what incentive do they have to behave accountably when others will pay the price for their reckless actions? From a purely financial point of view, the incentive is low in business organizations. They can take big risks and pocket the benefits if their decision pays off or suffer no financial consequences if it does not. The negative consequences will be borne by the players who foot the bill.

For people who personally practice high levels of accountability in their life transactions, their behavior is likely rooted in moral concerns: their personal system of values requires them to assume responsibility for their actions regardless of payoffs. If moral concerns play a small role in their thinking, they may still behave accountably because their sense of accountability is tied to enlightened self-interest: they recognize that their reckless behavior can earn them short-term gains but will damage their reputation in the long run.

Paul Krugman believes that the problem of moral hazard played a central role in the financial crises we have experienced in recent decades. To a large extent, the reckless behavior of large financial institutions was encouraged by a belief among their managers that if their enterprises got into trouble, they would be bailed out by the public on the grounds that their collapse would adversely affect the public good—the so-called too-big-to-fail concept. For example, when the LTCM hedge fund was about to go under in 1998, the Federal Reserve intervened and organized a bailout of $3.6 billion among large financial institutions. Roger Lowenstein's detailed accounting of the culture of LTCM in *When Genius Failed* (2000) shows it to have rested on a philosophy of gambling-makes-big-bucks when using other people's money. Many of the principals at LTCM lost millions of dollars of their questionable gains, but they remained multimillionaires after the debacle and none was held legally accountable. Many of their investors, however, took irrecoverable hits.

Sadly, the too-big-to-fail rationale appears to have merit. This was demonstrated in autumn 2008, when the Bush administration decided that the catastrophic problems facing Lehman Brothers Holdings should not be covered by a government bailout. Lehman should pay the price of its reckless behavior. Lehman's subsequent collapse and the signal that government would not bail out troubled companies triggered a global economic crisis that contributed significantly to the economic implosion of 2008–2009. Federal officials immediately recognized the deleterious impact of their decision and arranged for a $700 billion bailout of troubled financial and industrial companies through the Troubled Asset Relief Program. The too-big-to-fail argument won the day.

While the moral hazard problem is usually discussed in the context of large companies taking large risks and experiencing large losses, it is common in the everyday world. Consider the situation that employees who are compensated by sales commissions face. By its very nature, commission-based compensation is a breeding ground of moral hazard. Commissions are earned by success in selling a good or service. If you make the sale, you earn a commission. If you do not, you earn little or nothing. The incentive to make a sale by any means is substantial. Businesses that employ commission-based compensation successfully include safeguards to avoid egregious excesses associated with moral hazard. For example, they may carry out postsale surveys to determine customer satisfaction with the products they buy and their buying experience. Or they may pay employees decent base salaries, using commissions as an added bonus; in this case, salespeople can earn income even when they do not make a sale. But even here, there is no assurance that employees will behave as desired. Consider the waiter who provides a client with a second glass of 1990 Châteaux Margaux Bordeaux wine "gratis" (listed at $950 per bottle on the Internet) in an attempt to gain a large tip. The waiter and patron will do well in such an arrangement, but the restaurant owner loses.

Recently I bought a new car. While working with a car salesman, I decided to conduct an experiment to see what the commission-driven salesman was willing to say to make a sale. I showed great interest in a high-end German car but expressed disappointment that the only model his dealership had in inventory lacked GPS capabilities. The salesman immediately responded, "Do you know what? The capabilities of a $100 handheld Garmin GPS are superior to what the car offers. Just buy the car; then navigate with your handheld GPS."

I then turned my attention to a higher-end model that had GPS capabilities. It came with a highly rated 2.0 liter turbo engine that offers oomph yet has good gas mileage. The salesman said: "This is our most popular model. With it, you get great pickup as well as good fuel economy. It's a fantastic car." But I expressed reservations: the car being offered did not have a backup camera, which I wanted. The salesman asked: "Do you really need a backup camera? Haven't you driven successfully all your life without one?"

Because most of my driving would be in the West Virginia mountains, where oomph is more important than mileage, I finally settled on a yet higher-end model that possessed a 3.2 liter engine, GPS capabilities, and a backup camera. The salesman said: "You've made a great choice. Personally this is the car I would buy."

Once the sale was consummated, the salesman told me that I would be receiving an evaluation questionnaire in the mail. "You've got to give me all 10s," he said. "Anything less than 10 is considered failure."

This fellow had no shame.

In this story, I relate the most benign form of moral hazard. The salesman wasn't fooling anybody. He knew that I knew that he would say anything in order to close a deal. It's part of the car-buying game. No one was hurt in this game. All three of the cars I looked at were high-quality products, and I would have acquired a nice car no matter what decision I made. The reputation of the car brand and the salesman's dealership remained intact despite the salesman's near-humorous con game.

The salesman's manipulative pitch would be less benign had I been looking at used cars and followed his advice by settling on a car he "guaranteed" was excellent but that he knew to be defective. In this instance, he would collect a commission for the sale, and I would suffer. So would his company. I would grow unhappy when I discovered I had purchased a lemon. When the lemon broke down, a high-probability event, I would face inconvenience and out-of-pocket expenses. I might grow into a vengeful customer: if I suffer, I want the dealer to double-suffer. I would complain loudly to the dealership and would warn as many friends and acquaintances as possible to avoid doing business with the unprincipled company. I would expose the sham on the Internet. The salesman had earned his commission, but the dealer's reputation would be damaged.

How can decision-makers deal with the problem of moral hazard? I offer three suggestions here. First, as with other morally rooted problems, including lying, negligence, and illegal activities, they need to exercise vigilance. Moral hazard has its telltale signs that decision-makers need to spot by mulling over insightful questions—for example:

- What is the character of the people involved in the decision process, including decision-makers, stakeholders, decision-implementers, and members of the affected community? What decision-makers should look for here are signs that suggest weak moral character: lack of commitment to achieving goals, lack of diligence, a tendency to pursue shortcuts, and evidence of a weak ethical outlook.

- In reviewing the decision-making process in its entirety, what conflicts of interest surface, if any, for the highest-level executives to the humblest players? Conflict of interest and moral hazard go hand-in-hand.

- Are the purported benefits being relayed to the decision-makers too good to be true?

- Are the estimated costs and limitations provided to the decision-makers too low to be true?

Second, decision-makers should operate in an environment where performance monitoring is carried out thoroughly and routinely. Through performance monitoring, managers acquire feedback on their operations. This monitoring should address the performance of individuals and processes. The cases of rogue traders, such as Barings Bank's Nick Leeson and UBS's Kweku Adoboli, highlight the consequences of poor oversight. In both cases, we encounter relatively low-level traders making huge trades that never appear on their banks' radar screens. Why were their supervisors ignorant of their actions? Why didn't their banks' financial control systems pick up on their trading activities?

Third, decision-makers must recognize and acknowledge the link between organizational design (which includes the processes the organization implements) and the consequences that flow from the design. Businesses that thrive on commission-based sales must be especially sensitive to the perils of moral hazard. They should strive to establish processes that stimulate sales while minimizing the deleterious effects of moral hazard.

I illustrate this third point with an example from public policy: the 1999 recision of the Glass-Steagall Act of 1933.

As I mentioned in an earlier chapter, I am a fan of the concept of organizational architecture, which first surfaced in the book *Organizational Architecture* (Nadler and others, 1992). In my own work on organizational architecture (Frame, 2003), I have linked this concept to Louis Sullivan's famous architectural dictum, "Form follows function." However, I have reversed Sullivan's phrasing and focus on "Function follows form." In other words, "Describe to me the structure of a team [its form], or department or enterprise or procedure or law, and I can predict functional consequences emerging from the structure."

William D. Jackson, a researcher at the Congressional Research Service, pursued the "function follows form" principle in 1987, when Congress asked him to forecast the consequences of rescinding the Glass-Steagall Act of 1933. After the U.S. stock market collapse of 1929, Congress determined that a major cause of the crisis that led to the Great Depression was the mingling of commercial banking and investment banking functions in financial institutions. So in 1933, they passed the Glass-Steagall Act, which established a wall between commercial banking and investment banking. Commercial banks should function conservatively because they needed to protect the assets of depositors who placed their savings in the banks' care. Investment banks could assume greater risks, since they handled the money of risk-taking investors. Commercial banks were not permitted to gamble with depositors' funds, and investment banks were not permitted to carry out the functions of commercial banks.

The separation of the two types of banking worked fine until the 1980s when commercial bankers wanted to get involved in higher-risk transactions and investment bankers wanted to carry out profitable commercial banking functions, such as collecting depositors' funds and treating them like checking and savings accounts. At the time, they operated in a political environment that promoted the power of unfettered markets and supported deregulation. President Reagan made it clear that although he was the chief executive of the largest enterprise in the industrialized world, the U.S. federal government, he was no booster of government. He articulated this view when he declared in his 1981 inaugural address that "government is not the solution to our problem; government is the problem."

In a brief five-page analysis, Jackson (1987) listed the pros and cons of rescinding the Glass-Steagall Act. He was on target with his prognostication of the moral hazard problem. His report states:

> The case for preserving the Glass-Steagall Act includes the following arguments.
>
> - *Conflicts of interest characterize the granting of credit—lending—and use of credit—investing—by the same entity, which led to abuses that originally produced the Act.*
>
> - Depository institutions possess enormous financial power, *by virtue of their control of other people's money;* its extent must be limited to ensure soundness and competition in the market for funds, whether loans or investments.
>
> - *Securities activities can be risky, leading to enormous losses. Such losses could threaten the integrity of deposits. In turn, the government insures deposits and could be required to pay large sums if depository institutions were to collapse as a result of securities losses.*
>
> - *Depository institutions are supposed* to be managed to limit risk. Their managers thus may not be conditioned to operate prudently in more speculative securities businesses. An example is the crash of real estate investment trusts sponsored by bank holding companies a decade ago [in the 1980s].

The italics, which I added to this quotation, highlight moral hazard problems that would arise if the Glass-Steagall Act were to be rescinded. Twelve years later, in 1999, the Gramm-Leach-Bliley Act rescinded Glass-Steagall and freed commercial banks to gamble with their depositors' money. Nine years later, in 2008, many commercial banks were teetering on the brink of insolvency owing to their high-risk gambles. The federal government bailed out Bank of America, Citigroup, Wells Fargo, BB&T, and many other commercial banks to cover losses that were tied to their speculative investments, which would not have been permitted under Glass-Steagall. Jackson's 1987 prognostication got it right: by rescinding a law that was consciously crafted to reduce the problem of moral hazard, Congress contributed to the economic crisis of 2008. In Europe, the speculative activities of commercial banks put depositors' funds at great risk and threatened the viability of the European Union itself.

PRINCIPAL-AGENT DILEMMA

To a certain extent, the overriding theme of this chapter on the moral dimension of decision making has touched on what is known as the principal-agent dilemma. Anyone who counts on someone else to carry out some kind of work effort faces the principal-agent dilemma. It typically arises when one party pays another party to carry out a work effort. You—as the individual, group, or institution paying for a service—are *the principal*. The individual, group, or institution being paid to do a job is *the agent*. The dilemma can be captured in a simple question: Is the agent actually doing what he or she is being paid to do, and doing it effectively?

All serious managers worry about this issue. It ranks at the top of many bosses' list of concerns, and business owners may lose sleep over it. It boils down to the question: Are my employees or other agents, such as contractors, doing their jobs? When I walk through the office and see my employees glued to their computer monitors, are they doing company business or visiting social networking sites or purchasing birthday gifts on eBay? When it takes an information technology technician four days to carry out what I believe should be a two-day job, is she engaged in her best effort to serve the client, or is she goofing off?

There are many ways in which agents can fall short. For example, they may not be doing their jobs. Although they are being paid to work seven and a half hours a day, they put in only two or three hours of effort. This may become apparent by tracking their work hours: they arrive at the office late and leave early. Beyond this, they take two-hour lunch breaks and spend their time at their desks surfing the Web or chatting with colleagues at the watercooler rather than doing their assigned chores.

Another problem with agents arises when they do a bad job. This may be a consequence of the fact that they are unqualified to do the work they are being paid to do, or generally incompetent, or simply lack diligence. Doing a bad job can have many negative consequences. Poor work can damage a business's reputation. It must be remedied with rework, which encompasses delays and extra costs. If it leads to delivering systems that fail, the enterprise may face legal liabilities.

A third common problem arises when the agents work against the interests of the principal, which gets us back to the realm of moral hazard. What happens here is that while being paid to serve the principal's needs, the agents are primarily focused on promoting their personal interests. For example, the contractor you hire uses the knowledge and experience gained on the contracted work effort to set up a business that competes against you.

An interesting example of how convoluted the moral hazard/principal-agent relationship can be recently surfaced on Wall Street: Goldman Sachs's attempt to reap gains from a complex billion-dollar transaction by burning both ends of a candle. In April 2010, the Securities and Exchange Commission filed charges against Goldman Sachs for marketing a synthetic collateralized debt obligation, which it called ABACUS 2007-AC1 and claimed had been packaged by ACA Management LLC, a third-party entity with experience in assessing the risk of securitized mortgages. Goldman Sachs did not reveal that in fact, the hedge fund Paulson & Co. Inc. played a role in selecting the portfolio. The problem here is that Paulson was not a disinterested player and planned to assume a short position on the sale of the securities: it was betting that the value of the securities would decline. In selecting securities for ABACUS 2007-AC1, presumably it chose securities whose value it anticipated would decline. Meanwhile, Goldman Sachs was marketing ABACUS 2007-AC1 as a product whose value would increase. In the end, purchasers of the collateralized debt obligation lost $1 billion and Paulson gained $1 billion.

Goldman Sachs's ultimate winnings or losses on the deal are a matter of dispute and are a key component of ongoing litigation. What adds to the messiness of the case is that the deal was arranged by a thirty-one-year-old Goldman Sachs employee, Fabrice Tourre, which raises questions about his role as an agent.

This case illustrates the overlap between the principal-agent dilemma and moral hazard. From the principal-agent perspective, whose interest was Goldman Sachs serving? Buyers of the security it was marketing? Paulson & Co., which paid Goldman Sachs $15 million to put the package together? Itself? To what extent was Goldman Sachs a victim of its agent, Fabrice Tourre, setting up a deal that put the company's reputation in jeopardy—a classic example of the principal-agent dilemma?

People familiar with the case hold a broad array of opinions on the ethics, morality, and legality of Goldman Sachs's actions, ranging from the furor of the public, who see this case as the embodiment of Wall Street avarice, to conservative commentators, such as Rush Limbaugh, who believe that business is a rough-and-tumble adventure where anything goes, and caveat emptor. One thing most observers agree on: through the Goldman Sachs deal, Paulson & Co. became the single biggest winner of the economic disaster of 2008 and 2009, gaining $1 billion at a time when almost everyone else in the financial sector was losing fortunes.

MORALITY, ETHICS, AND LEGALITY: THEY ARE DIFFERENT

In this chapter, I have addressed the moral dimension of decision making without discussing a technical topic that is often raised in treatments about ethics. While using the words *ethical, moral,* and *legal* throughout the chapter, I have not defined how I am employing the terms and have not addressed the differences among them. The differences are real, and they are important. I did not raise this issue earlier because I viewed it as a didactic intrusion that did not contribute to the core points I am raising about the moral dimension of decision making. In fact, it would most likely serve as a distraction. Still, I am uncomfortable writing on this topic without addressing the differences among these three concepts. The point of this section is to highlight the differences. Readers should recognize that although a decision may violate an ethical code, it may be moral. And although a decision may be compliant with the law, it may not be moral.

The line separating ethics and morality is blurred. Both address the acceptability of behavior from a societal point of view. What distinguishes them is that ethics tend to focus on specific behaviors within specific contexts. These behaviors are often articulated in codes of conduct—rules—that clearly specify behaviors that are acceptable and unacceptable. For example, most professional societies have codes of conduct that do not allow their volunteer officers to engage in society-related activities that will benefit them or their employers financially. The codes may contain specific provisions prohibiting specific behaviors that are viewed as unethical. For example, an ethics code for a professional society might stipulate that officers are not permitted to hand out their personal business cards during official or unofficial society functions.

Morality addresses basic universal principles that reflect thinking on what is right and what is wrong by most people in most societies. It is not usually tied to specific rules in specific contexts. As a general principle, property theft is considered immoral. Murder and maiming are generally classified as immoral behavior. In business, misleading customers with false information is viewed as immoral. While a review of history reveals no shortage of societies that have countenanced theft, murder, and lying, none of these societies has earned admiration or respect for these behaviors—and many were short-lived, because the dog-eat-dog environment their immorality sustained did not provide the stability viable societies need.

To the extent a society has clearly articulated laws that are enforced, the distinction between legal and illegal behavior is reasonably clear—though not always. If the law states that you are not permitted to cross a street against a red light and you cross nonetheless, you are breaking the law. If caught by the police, you may be fined for your infraction. The law is clear, and so are actions associated with violating the law. All societies have laws prohibiting theft, murder, and misrepresentation. Of course, if these laws are not enforced effectively, and in many societies they are not, the laws have little effect on behavior.

One thing that makes the study of ethics, morality, and law interesting is the discovery that these three constructs do not necessarily overlap. To see this, consider the following scenarios:

• You can have laws that are immoral. The discriminatory Nazi laws imposed on Jews in the 1930s and 1940s were immoral, ultimately providing the foundation for genocide.

- You can hold moral positions that are illegal. Mahatma Gandhi's acts of civil disobedience entailed constant disregard for the laws colonial England imposed on its Indian colony.

- Your organization can have a code of ethics that prohibits behaviors that few people would consider immoral. Few people would view the distribution of personal business cards by society officers at professional society functions as inherently immoral.

- When you pay an intermediary to win business, this can be viewed as a legitimate commission in one ethical framework and as a bribe in another. Ultimately, its morality must be determined contextually (for example, did the payment bring you business that would have gone to other players based on merit?). Its legality is determined by the laws of a society. For example, in the United States, payoffs to win business overseas are viewed as illegal by the U.S. Foreign Corrupt Practices Act and could put businesspeople in jail. However, in other cultures, such behavior can be viewed as both ethical and moral.

LAST WORD

Decision making has always reflected societal and individual values, and it has always operated in a moral, ethical, and legal context. Of course, these values have varied across time and cultures, so that what was viewed as a wise decision in one context might be considered foolish in another. Consider the decision-making guidance offered by the world's oldest written legal code, formulated in cuneiform around 1700 B.C.E.: Hammurabi's Code. Law 2 of the code stipulates:

> If anyone bring an accusation against a man, and the accused go to the river and leap into the river, if he sink in the river his accuser shall take possession of his house. But if the river prove that the accused is not guilty, and he escape unhurt, then he who had brought the accusation shall be put to death, while he who leaped into the river shall take possession of the house that had belonged to his accuser [King, 1915].

Four thousand years ago, this was deemed a wise decision rule in Babylonia, although it does not meet decision-making standards employed today. (If I lived under the decision standard of Law 2, one decision I would make would be to take swimming lessons!)

Consider the precarious lives of Babylonian physicians. Today's physicians complain bitterly about malpractice lawsuits, but think about what they faced in Hammurabi's time, as described in the following medical malpractice prescription codified in Law 218:

> If a physician make a large incision with the operating knife, and kill
> [the patient], or open a tumor with the operating knife, and cut out
> the eye, his hands shall be cut off [King, 1915].

I wonder how many Babylonian parents encouraged their children to become doctors?

It is easy to see ancient laws as ludicrous when viewed from today's perspective, but it is instructive to reflect on their true value. They were not arbitrary. After stripping away the crude barbarity of Law 2, it is apparent that the signal provided to Babylonian citizens is to be sure of your facts before taking legal action against others. Unless you are 100 percent sure of winning your case, it is better to avoid litigation. With such a law, the level of frivolous lawsuits must have been much lower in Babylonia than in the United States today. By protecting citizens from unfounded malicious accusations, perhaps it contributed to a stronger sense of justice than we feel in the twenty-first century. Law 218 offers a similar signal: as a physician, be sure that you know what you are doing before slicing into a patient. If your medical procedures will harm your patients, then put them aside.

Effective decision-makers must take into account the moral dimension of decision making. As Hammurabi's Code illustrates, decisions reflect the values of their time and culture. They must also accommodate human frailty in its many avatars, including moral hazard, issues of principal-agency, outright criminality, and dissimulation. The idea that decisions can be made in accordance with some Platonic ideal of objectivity does not hold water. If they could, then the U.S. Supreme Court would have unanimous decisions in all of its rulings. But unanimous decisions are rare in the Supreme Court. The rulings of individual justices are often predictable, based on an understanding of their values as expressed in prior rulings. Conservative justices consistently rule one way, while liberal justices consistently rule another. What guides their rulings is not the employment of a linear programming algorithm or some other decision science optimization tool, but the values they hold, and these differ from justice to justice.

It is instructive to recall that in 1857, the U.S. Supreme Court, in a 7–2 decision, ruled that slaves from Africa and their descendants (whether free or not) were not entitled to constitutional protection. This was the *Dred Scott* decision. No doubt the justices who ruled affirmatively saw their ruling as fair and objective within the context of their time and culture. After all, slavery was legal in 1857, and it sustained the economy of the American South. Based on these facts, it was easy to formulate a logical argument that supported the majority ruling. By today's standards, the ruling was abhorrent. Even at the time, it was so controversial that it helped Abraham Lincoln gain the presidency in the election of 1860. The point is that *Dred Scott* affirms that even when decisions can be arrived at through logical thinking processes, they are not morally neutral.

6 People as Decision-Makers

This chapter looks at decision making from the perspective of individuals. The question it addresses is: When people make decisions, what is going through their heads? We have seen that the *Homo economicus* perspective offers a straight-forward answer. It holds that they balance possible choices with a view to selecting one that maximizes their gain. This is a convenient fiction that economists employ in building their models. However, it does not offer a serious explanation of how people actually make decisions.

In making decisions, people do not operate in a vacuum. Their decisions are made within a social space, as described in Chapter Three. The decisions are affected by a spectrum of social forces tied to an array of individuals, communities, politics, economics, and culture. These social forces impose constraints. Even the most independent decision-makers must contend with them.

Their decisions are also affected by the values they acquire as they move forward in their lives. There is no such thing as value-free judgment. Norwood Russell Hanson's (1958) concept of *theory ladenness* emphasizes that even the most objective decisions that scientists make are not value free, because scientists cannot escape the values they accumulate over their lives. On the sinister side, the previous chapter demonstrated that an examination of values brings us face-to-face with the prospect of immoral and possibly illegal acts associated with decision making.

Their decisions are also based on the perceptions of the world they gain through the intermediation of the brain and their senses. Because each brain functions differently, their views of the world vary, and the particular approach each takes to making decisions is unique. Beyond this, the structure and function of their brains, combined with their life experiences, put each person into a different cognitive and psychological state so that their decisions reflect their personality, level of creativity, intelligence, and general state of mind.

I make no attempt to be deep here. The points I raise are commonsensical ones that draw on well-established principles of psychology, perception, organizational behavior, creative practice, cognition, and competence. The goal of this chapter is simply to heighten readers' awareness of how different people approach decision making in different ways.

FACTORS THAT AFFECT HOW INDIVIDUALS MAKE DECISIONS

If someone asks you to reflect on all the factors that affect how you make decisions, you might be surprised at how long your list can grow. This would be a worthwhile assignment for readers of this book to pursue: take stock of and document what you believe guides your decision-making efforts. If you were to carry out the assignment, you might go through the following sequence of self-discovery.

At first you would focus on obvious factors. For example, you might start by asking yourself: "Will the decision benefit me in some way?" Raising this question may lead you to consider what you mean by *benefit*, so you will likely spend time sorting through the different kinds of benefits you could encounter, including material and psychic rewards that can accrue to you. While assaying possible benefits, it may dawn on you that equally important to you is avoiding disbenefits—things that displease, discomfort, or harm you. The length of the list of disbenefits would likely match that of benefits.

Ultimately this line of reasoning could lead you to formulate the following broad decision rule: "In making decisions, I should seek to increase the benefits I can realize and reduce disbenefits." This decision rule lies at the heart of the *Homo economicus* imperative: economic man is a benefit maximizer.

If you are a truly reflective thinker, the process of identifying factors that affect decision making does not stop here. After articulating the decision rule above, it may occur to you that the outlook you just crafted is too narrow. You should broaden the coverage of benefits and disbenefits to extend beyond yourself. In practice, many of the decisions you make accommodate the benefits and disbenefits that other people derive: your family and friends, coworkers, the tax collector, members of your community, and unfortunate people who are having a tough time in life—the uninsured, victims of famine, the homeless, and citizens caught up in civil wars. People with a social conscience find that they are willing to sacrifice their personal benefits to serve the good of others, in which case we say they behave altruistically.

Further reflection may take you down the path of exploring why you make the decisions you do. Traditional economists hold that you make decisions to maximize utility. The premise of Adam Smith's invisible hand is that when many buyers and sellers operate selfishly in the market, they create a viable market that sustains the economic underpinnings of society. In other words, the pursuit of individual selfish desires is beneficial to society in the aggregate. But you know from your personal experiences that other factors influence your decision-making behavior. For example, plenty of people make decisions in such a way as to win the approval of others. Harvard psychologist David McClelland (1985) explains that these individuals have a high need for affiliation. There are also ornery contrarians who automatically make decisions that go against the crowd. When the crowd cries "black," they go with white; when the crowd cries "white," they go with black. Another example: at times we feel compelled to make certain decisions we find unattractive owing to pressure from outside forces. When your boss asks, "You *will* do XYZ, won't you?" your decision is driven by external pressure rather than an objective effort to maximize utility or serve society. If you want to keep your job, you do XYZ as the boss suggested.

This kind of reasoning can go on indefinitely. Writing your list may release a torrent of what you perceive to be small but important factors touching on incidental things, such as the amount of sleep you get before making decisions, your familiarity with the issues, the amount of time you devote to coming to a decision, your religious creed, your state of mind after reading a moving novel, and so on. The point of this discussion is to highlight a commonsense lesson: the

Figure 6.1 Human Factors That Affect Decision Making

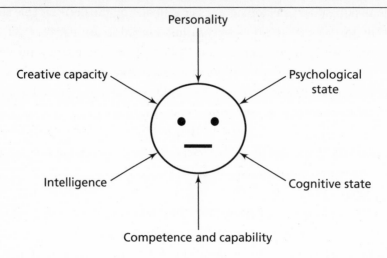

decisions people make are strongly influenced by factors that reflect their personal predilections, psychological state, physical state, and momentary distractions. Understanding how decisions are made requires that we take such factors into account.

Figure 6.1 offers a list of a handful of factors that I believe captures key human factors that affect decision making. Any listing of this kind will be arbitrary in some degree, and my list is no exception. A significant challenge is to avoid generating a list that is too short or too long. An overly short list, with only two or three factors, will miss important contributors to decision making in individuals. A list that contains an abundance of factors can be so focused on minutiae that it misses underlying patterns. I try to find a middle ground. I believe that there are six core factors that most thinkers and practitioners would highlight, and these are what I have included. Each is discussed briefly here.

Personality

The concept of personality is so central to literature, art, our daily experiences at the office, dealing with our in-laws, and determining whom we like and dislike that it would seem to be an idea whose development must have been refined and codified long ago. Certainly it has provided the stuff of good literature since the time of the Hebrew Bible with its profound exploration of the personality strengths and foibles of characters such as Jacob, David, Ruth, and Jezebel. It may come as a surprise to learn that the systematic approach to examining personality is a recent development, tied largely to the work of American psychologist Gordon Allport. His 1937 book, *Personality: A Psychological Interpretation*, is widely regarded as the first comprehensive academic treatment of the subject.

I am here defining personality as the expression of an individual's behavioral traits. When we say that people have a pleasant personality, we mean that they strive to accommodate the needs of those they encounter. They maintain a friendly demeanor, even when things go badly. These behaviors are inherent in their makeup. In contrast, people with a disagreeable personality generate a sense of ill will when dealing with others. They may be nasty, or pessimistic, or simply irritating. Their disposition is unpleasant, whether things are going well or not.

Later in this chapter, I look at three personality traits that play an important role in determining how people make decisions: one's propensity toward risk, openness to change, and judgment acumen.

The impact of personality on decision making is no mystery. It is often easy to predict people's approach to making decisions if you know their personality. Consider the situation where senior managers must decide whether they should invest substantial sums to expand their company's production capabilities. Focused on the prospect of generating increased revenue, the optimists among them will likely be more inclined to make the investment than the pessimists, who are worried about the possibility of losses. Each faces the same set of objective facts, but they decide differently owing to personality factors.

When looking at decision making from the perspective of personality, the question of whether people decide things rationally or irrationally becomes a side issue, and the idea of an external standard of optimal decision making becomes moot. What is deemed to be an optimal decision for one person is tempered by his values, as reflected in his personality, and this will differ from what is viewed as optimal by someone else. Chapter Seven points out that while it may be tractable to identify what constitutes rational decisions for individuals, determining the rationality of group decisions is problematic. In formal decision science terms, adding together the utility functions of two or more people does not yield an aggregate utility function that can be used to assess a decision's rationality. If the individual utility functions of group members differ substantially, their aggregated utility function is a hodgepodge that offers no insight on the rationality of the group decision.

Creative Capacity

The distinguishing feature of creative people is that they see things differently than most other people do. They have been viewed as special since prehistoric times. In an interesting article on the evolution of society's outlook on creativity, John Dacey (1999) points out that in the West, societal views of creativity evolved from the perspective that it was a gift of the gods bestowed on select individuals to the humanistic view of inherited genius to today's notion that it is a bio-psychosocial phenomenon. Today, creativity is viewed as closely tied to brain functioning. In order to conserve energy, human brains have their owners think according to reusable templates derived from prior experience. This modus operandi makes the great majority of people creatures of habit. They are most comfortable pursuing courses of action they have previously experienced and grow nervous when they are required to stretch themselves beyond what they know.

Creative people operate differently from other people. They reject the constraints imposed on them by their conformance-loving brains. When studying problems, they look at them from new perspectives. This is easy to see in the arts. In painting, what distinguished Delacroix, Monet, Van Gogh, and Picasso was their radically new way of seeing things. The same holds true in music: Mozart, Beethoven, Wagner, Richard Strauss, and Stravinsky deviated sharply from convention when composing music. This is why they are considered great.

Creativity applies to all endeavors. In the realm of physics, experts agree that Einstein's genius was tied less to a stratospheric IQ than to an astonishingly original view of the physical workings of the world. In business, Apple's Steve Jobs saw things differently than his competitors did, and he gave Apple an edge in the market.

Austrian sociologist Joseph Schumpeter was one of the first modern thinkers to examine the role of creativity outside the arts. He made two contributions that stand out. First, he saw creativity as rooted in new combinations of things (1934). His point is that creative insights do not arise out of a vacuum: they are rooted in familiar things that are seen through fresh eyes. Second, he viewed creativity as a process of brutally replacing old truths with new ones (1942). He termed this process *creative destruction*. An example of creative destruction that he touted is capitalism, with its continual economic churning, where old outlooks and institutions collapse under the forces of new ones.

As with Steve Jobs, decision-makers who have a high creative capacity are at an advantage over average decision-makers. If they are exceptionally creative, the range of options they face when making decisions is far greater than that encountered by ordinary people, whose vision is constrained by limited creative capacity. Creative decision-makers face a greater range of choices, whereas the decisions of most other people are tightly tied to prior experience. That is, they have difficulty going beyond what they know and have directly experienced, so their range of decision choices is small.

The neuroscientist Gregory Berns (2010) holds that we are not condemned to be prisoners of the constraints that our brain imposes on us. What we need to do is to make ourselves iconoclasts. We need to regularly carry out mental exercises that force us to see things from perspectives that differ from our usual outlook. I doubt that such exercises will significantly broaden the creative outlooks of most people, but I believe they are worthwhile: they can help us be open-minded in seeing the value of alternative approaches to solving problems when we make decisions.

Intelligence

The approach to intelligence taken here is a practical one. Whether you subscribe to Howard Gardner's view that there are eight intelligences (2011) or Daniel Goleman's perspectives on emotional intelligence (2006), or see IQ as the best measure of general intelligence, or adhere to some other perspective is immaterial, because I here employ an operational definition that holds that intelligence is simply a reflection of "smarts." In using this term, I am being vague intentionally. People possessing smarts are able to figure things out more readily than people lacking them. They can work easily with abstract concepts, understand causal links, and are mentally agile.

Possessing intelligence offers advantages when making decisions. One is rooted in the ability of smart people to calculate both positive and negative consequences of actions. This is important in decision making, because knowledge of consequences provides decision-makers with the information they need to distinguish good from bad choices. Consequences are seldom spelled out. It is up to decision-makers to figure them out. Here is where intelligence enters the picture. Identifying consequences often requires decision-makers to possess the ability to isolate and focus on relevant factors that lead to a predicted outcome, being sure not to get sidetracked by irrelevant factors. It also requires an appreciation of cause-effect relationships among the factors being examined, because the final outcomes are the end product of causal sequences.

Another advantage associated with intelligence is the capacity it bestows on smart people to frame problems in ways that are amenable to solutions. There is truth in the old wisdom that half the struggle in solving nontrivial problems is setting up the problems properly. Framing problems properly often requires higher-order thinking, because correct framing can entail dealing with subtle points. These subtleties are easily lost among average thinkers.

Competence and Capability

Competence and capability are related concepts that address being effective in getting things done. In my book on competence (1999), I summarize its principal feature in the following way: "The defining characteristic of competent individuals, teams, and organizations is that *they consistently produce desired results.* They deliver the goods—on time, within budget, and according to specifications—and they do this in such a way as to maximize customers' delight."

Competent people know their stuff. They don't make mistakes. They work efficiently. They get to the heart of a problem and eschew distractions. They understand the importance of being responsive to the external world. Employers love them because they can count on them to do what needs to be done.

The importance of competence and capability in decision making is clear when we recall that decisions are meaningless unless they are implementable. This knowledge is woven into the fabric of competent people, who are driven to produce actionable results. Throughout the decision-making process, they constantly ask themselves, "Are the options we are exploring implementable?"

In formulating decisions, competent players pursue what I call the three Ds: define, determine, and decide. First, they have the skills to *define* the scope of the decision problem clearly. When they face an abundance of data and issues to work through, they separate the wheat from the chaff. They zero in on what is important and discard irrelevancies. Second, they *determine* how the components of the decision problem fit together. This allows them to formulate the decision problem so that it is cohesive and actionable. Third, after studying the decision problem carefully—which entails collecting and analyzing data, taking stock of social space, and anticipating the consequences of different decisions—they are able to *decide* what choice to make.

The great value of competence and capability to decision making jumps out at us when we take a different tack in examining this matter and ask: "If we employ incompetent people to make decisions for us, how well will they do the job?" The answer is obvious: incompetent people make bad decisions. They have no mastery of the facts, are unable to focus on the real issues, and are easily led down blind alleys. Because they do not grasp the issues, they are unable to assess the consequences of different decision options intelligently. They are prone to make mistakes, and these require time-consuming and costly rework. Ultimately the bad decisions they make can lead to harmful consequences for our organization, our customers, and possibly the community.

In decision-making practice, we find that we contend with a spectrum of competence and capability in the people involved in the decision-making process. It would be great if we always had access to the reliable and on-target high performers. Typically the decision-makers we work with fall in a midrange of competence and capability. The hope is that we are able to avoid the truly incompetent.

Cognitive State

The brain intermediates all human perception so that no two people view the same set of "facts" in the same way. The information they use for making decisions can yield different decisions. Cognitive state refers to how brain activity affects the following cognitive processes:

- Perception
- Thinking
- Remembering
- Dealing with symbols
- Attention

- Handling information (gathering, storing, retrieving, and interpreting information)

- Problem solving

- Conceptualizing

How people perceive the information they review, how they recall past events, the degree of attention they devote to reflecting on an experience, and so on will have a significant impact on how they make decisions. Chapters Eight and Nine, which examine the biology of decision making, look at the link between cognitive state and the making of choices.

Psychological State

People's psychological state reflects their mental condition. In their pioneering exploration of human psychology, the early psychoanalysts, including Freud, Jung, and Adler, focused on describing and understanding their patients' mental condition. Because their patients came to them to resolve problems, early psychoanalysts directed much of their energy toward identifying and understanding psychological dysfunctionality, leading to the invention of psychology's most famous constructs, such as neuroses, psychoses, denial, paranoia, projection, and repression, each of which captures an element of psychological state.

Common nonpathological mental conditions we encounter when considering the effects of psychological state in decision making among individuals include:

- Anxiety

- Annoyance

- Identity crisis

- Morale

- Delusion

- Depression

- Elation

Each of these plays a role in how individuals approach making a decision.

That an individual's mental state can have a significant impact on his or her decision process is indisputable. If, when you are making a decision, you are overcome with anxiety, no one would be surprised if the choices you make differ from those you would have made had you been anxiety free. If a high level of self-confidence makes you delusional when assessing the challenges of pursuing a particular course of action, you may take risks that you would have avoided had you held a more realistic viewpoint. Depending on the intensity of your feelings, your mental state may have a small or great impact on your decisions.

Personality Factors of Particular Importance to Decision Making

When considering the impact of personality on decision making, it is easy to be overwhelmed by the range of traits that can play a role, losing sight of the forest through the trees. Most traits play an incidental role and do not warrant close attention. Three, however, stand out because they have an indisputable impact on decision making:

- Propensity toward risk
- Openness to change
- Judgment acumen

Propensity Toward Risk. I recently watched a television program highlighting the daredevil exploits of extreme rock climbers. Viewing them on a sixty-inch screen from the comfort of my family room caused my stomach to churn as if I were standing on a precipice instead of sitting on a couch. The program show-cased one rock climber who routinely climbed sheer rock faces without ropes. When the interviewer asked, "Do you get a rush when climbing rocks without ropes?" the climber answered, "Not really. If I feel a rush, I know I need to take it easy, because then I am in dangerous territory." Dangerous territory indeed! (To me, climbing a foot stool to fetch a can of chicken broth from my cupboard constitutes venturing into dangerous territory.)

The propensity toward risk varies substantially among people. This is easily seen when you consider the variety of sports activities that people undertake. They vary in riskiness from a low-risk half-mile jog in the woods to bungee jumping off tall bridges. While there is a tendency to focus on life-threatening activities when discussing the risk people are willing to take, all aspects of life present variations of the propensity toward risk. A fearless bungee jumper might

Figure 6.2 Risk Utility Function

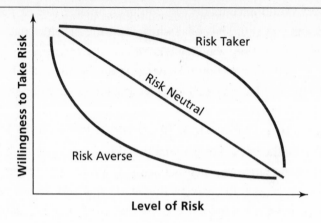

be terrified of committing herself to long-term romantic relationships. A Wall Street daredevil who regularly speculates on shaky start-ups might refuse to participate in any sports activity more dangerous than table tennis. While you may be a risk taker in one domain, you might be risk averse in another.

The risk propensity of decision-makers has a big impact on the kinds of decisions they make. Risk takers are willing to move forward with decisions where they see substantial rewards even though the possibility of loss can be substantial. Risk-averse decision-makers prefer to stick with sure things, knowing they may miss out on the possibility of large gains on slightly risky initiatives.

Three alternative approaches toward risk are illustrated in Figure 6.2, which displays a variant of a risk utility function. The horizontal axis measures the level of risk an individual faces, ranging from no risk on the left-hand side to high risk on the right. The vertical axis measures an individual's willingness to take a risk. The three curves portrayed in the figure picture an individual's willingness to assume risk for different orientations toward risk. The risk taker's profile is captured in the top curve. From the outset, she is highly willing to take risks. As the level of risk increases, the willingness to take a risk begins to decline slightly. Only when risk levels are quite high does the willingness to take risk drop significantly.

The profile of the risk-averse person is captured in the bottom curve. While he may be willing to assume moderate levels of risk, his willingness plummets and remains low as soon as the risk level begins to increase.

The profile of the risk-neutral person is captured by the straight, downward-sloping line. This individual has a high willingness to take risks when risk levels are low. As risk levels increase, her willingness to assume risks drops gradually in proportion to the increased level of risk.

Those who are staffing a position that entails making significant decisions must determine whether the candidates for the job have a propensity for risk that fits the requirements of the job. A high-tech venture capital company with a risk-averse CEO is going to have a tough time picking high-payoff winners. Similarly, one would hope the portfolio manager for a pension fund would be somewhat risk averse in selecting investments.

The consequences of having a mismatch between a decision-maker's risk propensity and the risk-taking requirements of a job can be substantial. This was illustrated with the earlier-mentioned 1999 repeal of a portion of the Glass-Steagall Act by the Gramm-Leach-Bliley Act, which removed the wall separating the kinds of activities that investment banks and commercial banks could engage in. It was not long before investment banks began taking on commercial bank functions (such as setting up money market deposits) and commercial banks began using depositor funds to engage in risky ventures (such as investing in sub-prime loans). Gramm-Leach-Bliley created an environment that encouraged the mismatch between a decision-maker's risk propensity and the risk-taking requirements of the job, which contributed to the economic meltdown of 2008–2009.

Openness to Change. The management literature, lectures by gurus, and chats in the corporate cafeteria often treat resistance to change as a behavioral pathology. Here is how the argument goes. A prevailing reality we encounter in today's world is that everything undergoes change, whether we like it or not. In the business arena, we encounter changes in technology, the economy, the fortunes of individual enterprises, the role of government, the introduction of new products, and so on. It has become an article of faith among progressive people to believe that organizations and individuals who resist change are doomed to failure. History is filled with stories that buttress this argument.

We encountered a dramatic example in the business arena in the case of Ken Olsen, game-changing founder and CEO of Digital Equipment Corporation (DEC) who led the team that introduced minicomputers as a powerful and affordable alternative to expensive and complex mainframe computers. But when personal computers came on the scene, he saw them as second-rate toys that posed no threat to his unbeatable machines. This inability to deal with change in the market led to DEC's demise. In a matter of a few years, the PC toys put DEC out of business.

We see this scenario playing out continually. For example, Nokia's dominance of the cell phone industry disappeared almost overnight with the introduction of Apple's iPhone. Nokia saw itself as a premier producer of telephones, while Apple presented the iPhone as a multifunctional entertainment and information center with panache. The public followed Apple's vision. As another example, video-renting supermarkets like Hollywood were knocked out of the ring by Netflix, which employed surprisingly low technology to deliver videos conveniently and cheaply to people's homes. But after several years of dominating the video rental market, Netflix lost market share to the large cable companies that could deliver videos to customers instantly by video streaming.

Arguments supporting the embrace of change are compelling in part because they have a scientific rationale, incorporating the essence of Darwin's natural selection process. Natural selection requires species to adjust to challenges posed by their environment. To survive, geckos living in a black lava field need to take on a black hue through natural selection, just as identical geckos living among tropical plants should take on a mottled green hue. Analogously, in order to survive, companies must be willing and able to adjust the way they do business to respond to emerging technologies, changing tastes, and evolving economic circumstances.

For all the talk about its evils, fighting change is the de facto modus operandi in most organizations and with most individuals. Hardly anyone notices when someone arguing passionately for the need to change switches gears in the next breath to defend the status quo by declaring, "If it ain't broke, don't fix it." The truth is that embracing change is not easy, and it can be dangerous. Extirpating resistance to change is difficult for two reasons. First, resistance to change is biologically rooted in humans, hardwired into the brain's neuronal pathways. Second, organizations resist change in order to define an acceptable status quo that enables them to function effectively; it is hard doing business if the modus operandi is shifting week by week.

Consider the biological roots of resistance to change. When you experience something new that warrants attention from the brain, the new experience is stored in the brain's labyrinth. (The most exciting investigations in brain research today are looking at how this happens.) It becomes your guide to truth and establishes the way your brain perceives reality. The more often this experience is reinforced, the more embedded it is in the brain's hidden layer. Artificial intelligence guru Marvin Minsky says that through experience, your brain establishes frames of thinking that establish stereotypes that guide your perceptions (Minsky, 1986). As you go about your daily life, your perceptions of the world are heavily colored by these frames, or templates. If a new experience contradicts a well-entrenched template, the brain's tendency is to go with the template in an effort to keep things simple and orderly and avoid being overwhelmed with the barrage of sensory inputs it receives each second. Overwriting the template consumes more energy than accepting it. Thus, in order to conserve energy, the brain resists change. If a new experience is sufficiently compelling, the brain ultimately overwrites the old template. This constitutes learning.

By understanding the biological origins of resistance to change, we see that the tendency of people to reject new ideas is not tied to a psychological deficiency that engenders pig-headed behavior. What actually transpires is that in order to conserve energy, the brain sticks to the script people have established through their life experiences. However, there are also significant variations in the degree to which people are able to handle their brain's inherent conservatism. Some people effortlessly digest new ideas, while some are unable to budge from legacy. Some of this variation has natural origins and derives from temperament, and some of it is learned. An important function of education is to program the brain to learn. Highly educated people effectively train their brains to seek out new perspectives on the world. When they achieve this goal, they become good at critical thinking and can overcome the brain's tendency to stick to template solutions.

Resistance to change also has institutional roots. It is not accidental that we refer to business and government enterprises as *organizations*—collective entities whose activities are coordinated by established rules. Consider that the antonym of organization is *disorganization*. We do not expect collective entities to achieve worthwhile outcomes if their operations are disorganized. Organizations are built on processes that are established in order to enable them to achieve desired outcomes. Their operations are governed by operating procedures, financial procedures, marketing and sales procedures, and so on. Max Weber (1947) recognized this when he defined bureaucracies as possessing a number of universal attributes:

- They are hierarchical: subordinates follow orders from superiors.
- They clearly specify jurisdictional areas and official duties.
- They are governed by rules.
- The property of the office is distinct from the personal property of individuals.
- They are impersonal.
- Employees are hired based on their qualifications.

A quick review of these attributes suggests that organizations that are capable of achieving worthwhile objectives are committed to sticking to established processes. They have trouble accommodating individuals or groups that do things in accordance with their own desires. They resist change.

The inclination of individuals and organizations to be open to change has enormous decision-making consequences. People who resist change have a tendency to offer a nearly automatic *no* to initiatives that entail wandering off the well-blazed trail, no matter what the merits. They may have trouble understanding the rationale for alternative courses of action because the alternatives do not match the template solutions held by their brains.

Organizational resistance to change manifests itself in many ways:

- An inordinate focus on past glories
- Hubris that leads to overconfidence
- A not-invented-here syndrome that rejects ideas and innovations from outside
- An organization that is entirely rules driven
- A culture that does not permit the questioning of decisions that have been made
- A hierarchical decision structure

By themselves, each of these traits is inimical to making decisions that incorporate change. Taken together, they make adopting decisions favoring change nearly impossible.

There is nothing abnormal about individuals and organizations resisting change. With humans, such resistance is hardwired into brains, and with organizations it is hardwired into business processes. Ironically, what may be considered abnormal in human nature is the eager embrace of change, because this goes against the natural order of things.

Even as I fully understand it is natural for the brain and organization to resist change, I confess to being a firm adherent of the principle of openness to change. The arguments of the progressive thinkers are on target. In a world of constant change, natural selection favors individuals and organizations that take stock of the full range of alternative solutions facing them and then select the one that increases their chances of survival. As in the natural world, this usually entails abandoning the status quo. Mottled green geckos that migrate to black lava fields will not survive long if they stick with their mottled green coloring. Their survival requires change.

Judgment Acumen. Newspapers are filled with stories of people exercising bad judgment. In June 2011, U.S. Congressman Anthony Weiner sent a lewd photo of himself to a twenty-one-year-old female college student through his Twitter account. What was he thinking? It cost him his job. When BP's CEO, Tony Hayward, decided to take a yachting vacation in the midst of the Gulf oil spill crisis in 2010, he created a public relations nightmare for BP and ultimately was removed as CEO. As he packed his bags for his yachting holiday during this time of crisis, what was he thinking? Also in 2010, the top U.S. commander in Afghanistan, General Stanley McChrystal, conducted an interview with *Rolling Stone* magazine in which he criticized the leadership of civilian U.S. officials in Afghanistan. When he was removed from his command, he publicly acknowledged that the interview reflected "poor judgment." As he sat with the *Rolling Stone* reporter and vented his frustration with the civilian leadership and the Obama administration, what was he thinking?

One of the most damning charges that can be leveled against managers and aspiring leaders is that they exercise bad judgment in doing their jobs. It can be a career killer. If you are accused of bad judgment, it means that your accusers believe you are likely to make decisions that are harmful to your own interests and the interests of other players, including your organization, customers, innocent bystanders, and the public at large.

The principal trait of people with bad judgment is the inability to assess the consequences of their words and actions. They are clueless decision-makers. Their cluelessness is often tied to one of three causes: inexperience, transitory lapse, or habitual cluelessness.

Clearly, inexperience can contribute to poor judgment. Each of us has had firsthand experience with this truth, because it is one of the rites of passage we encounter in moving from childhood to adolescence to adulthood. When we are young, our parents and teachers dedicate substantial energy to overcome our inexperience in life by instructing us on how to behave appropriately and function as productive citizens. They instill in us the values we use to guide our actions. Despite their best efforts, we stumble from time to time and speak inappropriately or engage in hurtful behavior. Over time, we learn lessons from our missteps (at least this is the hope). Through experience, we start seeing the connection between our words and actions and their consequences, and we adjust our behavior accordingly. To a large extent, this is what the maturing process is about: fashioning people so that they learn to exercise good judgment.

The perils of inexperience are not restricted to the young. Consider how we do not permit highly trained men and women with eight years of scientific education to practice medicine right out of medical school. Before they can practice medicine, they need to go through a period of residency that can last from two to five years, depending on their specialty. The point of residency is to enable them to gain substantial experience under the watchful eyes of physicians with ample expertise. Through this process, they develop judgment skills that allow them to practice medicine competently.

In the world of work, anyone who is new to a job faces the possibility of failure of judgment rooted in inexperience. We try to mitigate such failures through a variety of mechanisms, including training, employment of well-established processes, close supervision, and apprenticeship. Usually the attention we pay to the challenges facing inexperienced employees pays off as they move from being rank amateurs to experienced professionals. The test of their mettle is tied to the quality of decisions they make in carrying out their chores.

Transitory lapses of judgment are scary. They can be experienced by anyone, even capable, responsible, self-disciplined professionals who possess flawless track records of good judgment. General Stanley McChrystal is a case in point. A 1976 graduate of West Point, he was an exemplar of good judgment and self-discipline throughout his career, reaching the rank of four-star general. But in a brief moment during an interview with a magazine reporter, he let his guard down. Perhaps he was charmed by the reporter's demeanor. Perhaps he came to the interview smarting from an irksome telephone chat with an officious civilian. Perhaps he was momentarily suffering from hubris—a much revered commander who hitherto had received nothing but kudos from the press, strutting his stuff before a renowned reporter. Who knows? What is certain is that during his chat with the *Rolling Stone* reporter, he experienced a major breach of judgment that summarily ended his distinguished career.

Transitory lapses in judgment can be minimized and possibly avoided through steady vigilance. But as the old observation notes, even the most level-headed, highly disciplined people are "only human." There are times when they let down their guard. They may be with friends, or exhausted after fighting endless fires, or feeling a little daring after a glass of wine. They may feel compelled to share an honest thought with a sympathetic listener. It is at times like these that lapses in judgment occur. On most occasions, such lapses have no consequences. Whatever indiscretion that is committed is just so much noise. But sometimes it can have an impact with major consequences.

Of the three categories of poor judgment discussed here, the one that is of greatest concern to managers is habitual cluelessness. It characterizes people who are consistently unable to anticipate the consequences of their decisions. This does not stop them from making decisions. In fact, they don't dare not make decisions, because decision making is part of their job. Usually their poor judgment does not have major impacts because they are not making decisions of consequence. What often happens with these people is that they function as plodders, struggling to get things right. Often the action they take is inappropriate and needs to be undone and reworked. Supervisors find that they need to watch these people closely to keep them on track. After a while, supervisors may find that it is easier to do things themselves or shift work to other people than depend on the habitually clueless employee.

There are several possible explanations for the behavior of these people. One ties to Elliott Jaques's concepts of human capability and time span of discretion. As Jaques (1986) argues forcefully, when people are put into jobs that do not match their capability or time span of discretion, they perform poorly. The problems they encounter lie outside their ken, and so they cannot address them competently.

Another explanation is rooted in poor empathy skills. Empathy is the capacity of individuals to put themselves into the shoes of other people. If you have good empathy skills, it is fairly simple to figure out how others will respond to actions you take because you can see things through their eyes. For example, if you anticipate that an initiative you plan to undertake will delight the regulators who oversee your business, you can move forward with it. But if you anticipate that the initiative will launch them into a frenzy of disapproval, you are very careful before plunging ahead and confer with others first. In his best-selling book *Emotional Intelligence* (2006), Daniel Goleman reports on research he carried out that supports the view that the most significant psychological trait of people who make it to the top of their organizations is well-developed empathy skills.

Weak empathy explains why otherwise smart people can be habitually clueless. I have spent my entire professional life surrounded by highly educated, smart people and have found that a substantial portion of them struggle to function effectively in organizational contexts. The principal source of their problem is that they do not know how to read other people, including their bosses, employees, colleagues, and resource owners, so that they say things and take actions that work against them and their organization.

Neurological studies suggest a third explanation of habitual cluelessness: how the brain is wired. Research on people suffering brain damage has long led neurologists to hypothesize that the brain's prefrontal cortex controls certain executive functions, including the capacity to plan and to make decisions (Damasio, 1994). Just as IQ is distributed according to a normal distribution, it may be that variations in the performance of the prefrontal cortex generate a distribution of judgment acumen among people that is normally distributed. If this is true, then we can speculate that two-thirds of the population have judgment acumen that lies in a normal range of plus or minus one standard deviation, while 5 percent have exceptionally high judgment acumen and 5 percent exceptionally low judgment acumen.

A UNIQUE PERSPECTIVE ON PERSONALITY AND DECISION MAKING: ELLIOTT JAQUES, HUMAN CAPABILITY, AND TIME SPAN OF DISCRETION

For two years while serving on the faculty of the George Washington University's Department of Management Science, I had the privilege to occupy an office two doors down from visiting scholar Elliott Jaques. When I met him, I was unaware of who he was. I soon came to see our visitor as Dr. Dr. Jaques, since he possessed both an M.D. and a Ph.D. Regrettably, during his two years at GWU, we did not engage in deep conversation about his work and ideas, largely because each of us had busy schedules that seldom enabled us to be in the office at the same time. Still, we chatted from time to time, and I gradually became aware of his work. It was after he left us that as a matter of curiosity, I began collecting and reading his books and articles. I was impressed by what I encountered. He combined a background in psychoanalysis, behavioral science research, and organizational consulting to produce truly original ideas on human behavior in organizations.

Articles written about him and his work often raise the question: "In view of his highly original insights, why did Elliott Jaques not have a bigger impact on management thinking than he did?" The most frequent answer is that many scholars and management practitioners are uncomfortable with a key premise of his thinking: that there are substantial differences in human capability and vision that are inherent in people. To a degree, the work world he describes echoes the message of Aldous Huxley's *Brave New World*, which is that Alphas, Betas, Gammas, Deltas, and Epsilons each have clearly established capabilities that define what they can achieve. Alphas are programmed to run things, while Betas and Gammas implement and Deltas and Epsilons carry out the grunt work. Jaques's perspective fails the test of political correctness.

Beyond this, Jaques (1976) promoted the unpopular view that bureaucracy, when properly configured, offers the best organizational structure for employee satisfaction and enterprise productivity. He labeled the properly configured bureau-cratic organization the *requisite organization* (Jaques, 1986). Since the early 1980s, bureaucracy has been out of favor among most management thinkers and poli-cymakers, so individuals promoting its merits did not encounter a positive recep-tion of their ideas. However, in view of the fact that the economic problems beginning with the arrival of the new millennium have been tied to excessive deregulation of business activity and its attendant weakening of bureaucratic systems, both organizational thinkers and practitioners have been more open to rethinking the positive role of bureaucracy today than they have since the 1980s. The possible value of bureaucracy is now receiving positive scrutiny for the first time in decades.

In this section, I look at two pillars of Jaques's theory of organizational behav-ior that define his insights into how individuals make decisions in organizations: (1) an individual's effectiveness in the work world is inextricably tied to his or her human capability, and (2) an individual's effective decision-making capacity is tied to his or her time span of discretion (Jaques and Cason, 1994).

Jaques defines *human capability* as the level of work that a person can carry out, and he is referring to work that the individual values, not work that is imposed on him. By level of work, he is referring to such things as its degree of complexity, difficulty, significance to the organization, and sheer volume. In simple terms, deciding where to take an enterprise in order to strengthen its market presence entails a higher level of work than deciding what brand of mop to purchase to clean the corporate restrooms.

Jaques maintains that an individual's human capability is inborn, although he holds that through the maturation process, human capability can increase in discrete chunks over fifteen-year intervals. People with the capacity to deal with high-level, complex challenges are hardwired to do so. Similarly, those who can handle only the simplest chores have inherited this trait. As I noted, the notion that human capability is inborn has created difficulties for Jaques's theory since it goes against the prevailing view in liberal democracies that nurture trumps nature. That is, through proper socialization, orientation, stimulation, education, and child rearing, people can overcome limits imposed on them by their genes.

Jaques's best-known concept is his idea of *time span of discretion*. He defines it as the length of time it takes to carry out the longest-duration effort in a job assignment. Jaques is saying that in dealing with life's challenges, different people have different time horizons that they can work with. Some people can handle only short-term work efforts, ranging from, say, a day to several weeks. Others can easily handle one- or two-year time horizons, and still others—the most exceptional people—readily hold twenty-year visions.

Over the years, Jaques's research led him to conclude that different strata in organizational hierarchies correspond to different time spans of discretion. In his requisite organization, the stratum at which an employee can work effectively requires a good match between the work requirements of that stratum and her personal time span of discretion. Someone with a very short time span of discretion should carry out stratum I work efforts—for example, work on the shop floor, work as a checkout clerk, and low-level administrative chores. The boss of a stratum I employee occupies a stratum II job. He or she might be a foreman, shop floor supervisor, or small business owner running a simple business. The time horizon covered here is three months to one year. Stratum III jobs might be carried out by department managers (with a time horizon of one or two years), stratum IV jobs by a plant manager (with a time horizon of two to five years), and stratum V jobs by the CEO of an enterprise with five thousand employees (with a time horizon of five to ten years). Stratum VI and VII jobs would be carried out by CEOs of large companies and Fortune 500 companies, with time horizons of five to ten years and ten to twenty years, respectively. As with human capability, an individual's time span of discretion is inborn.

Although Jaques crafted this theory to explain human behavior in organizations, the theory has implications for decision making that are very different from what we encounter with more traditional decision-making, economic, and psychological perspectives. Whereas traditional approaches focus on, say, decision-makers as individuals attempting to satisfy personal wants and needs through optimization or satisficing, Jaques's requisite organization looks at the decision-making boundaries imposed on people rooted in their human capability and their time span of discretion. So-called high-level decision making can be made only by people with high-level human capability, while people with low-level human capability are restricted to making mundane decisions. Jaques is aware of people's need for the proper qualifications to make decisions and does not brush them away. The issue of qualifications is built into the definition of human capability, which is "the level of work a person *can carry out*." Implied in this definition is acknowledgment that a person must have the appropriate knowledge, skills, and abilities to carry out a work effort. Without them, the individual's human capability is discounted.

An individual's time span of discretion also defines the limits of his or her decision-making effort. Decision-makers with short time spans of discretion have difficulty visualizing the implications of their decisions, including their consequences, beyond short periods of time. They are qualified to make decisions for short-term work efforts that have limited long-term implications. The big decisions—strategic decisions, those involving serious forecasting efforts, decisions of major consequence—will be made by decision-makers with long time spans of discretion.

CONCLUSION

Many factors come into play when people make decisions. In this chapter, we have looked at six: personality, creative capacity, intelligence, competence and capability, cognitive state, and psychological state. Owing to the interplay of these factors, which varies from person to person, we find that people are like snowflakes, or fingerprints, in that they are unique: no two people approach making a decision in the same way, even when they face the same set of facts. This confirms the view that facts do not speak for themselves and explains why humans often have such a tough time agreeing on what course of action they should take. It also causes us to question whether the quest for rationality pursued by so many decision-making experts is a worthwhile inquiry. When considering the role of values, intelligence, personality, and other human traits, it is not clear what constitutes rational decisions. For example, if half of American voters decide to vote for Barack Obama in a presidential election, and half for Mitt Romney, can we say that one group of voters (decision-makers here) is behaving more rationally than the other? Is there an objective scientific test that can be carried out to demonstrate that one choice is more rational than the other? The voters' individual decisions are formed by their preferences, and these are rooted in the variety of human traits covered in this chapter. While supporters of each candidate might argue that their candidate offers the more rational choice, their arguments don't work, and the matter of rationality is a nonissue.

Understanding what influences individuals to make the decisions they do is interesting and provides us with insights that help us better comprehend what makes humans tick. But an important goal of this book is to explore decisions of consequence, and if we are concerned with such decisions, we need to go beyond looking at decision making from the perspective of individuals. We need to get back to our examination of the social space of decision making, which is populated by multiple decision-makers, decision-implementers, stakeholders, outside forces, and the public. The next chapter gets us back to decisions of consequence by looking at how the viewpoints of the multiple players in decision space function and are brought together to yield consequential collective decisions that affect how we live our lives.

The Wisdom–and Foolishness–of Crowds

Consequential decisions are seldom made by one person operating alone. Decision making occurs contextually. In particular, it occurs in a social space inhabited by decision-makers, stakeholders, decision-implementers, the community, and external forces. Although it is possible for decision-makers to make decisions based entirely on their own authority, without consulting anyone else, even the most autocratic individuals are influenced to some degree by the information and opinions they receive from the people surrounding them. One thing is certain: whether decisions are made by an individual or a group, they are colored by their social space.

This chapter examines group decision making. It looks at different degrees of involvement of groups in contributing to decisions; addresses the dynamics of group processes, showing how they have an impact on decision outcomes; and highlights both the strengths and weaknesses of group decisions. Once it has addressed the mechanical aspects of group decisions, it turns to the big question: Do groups outperform individuals in making decisions?

INDIVIDUAL VERSUS GROUP DECISION-PARTICIPATION SPECTRUM

As Figure 7.1 shows, there are varying degrees of group involvement in decision making, ranging from no group involvement, with decisions made by a single individual, to total involvement with what I call community-based decisions,

Figure 7.1 Degree of Group Involvement in Decision Making

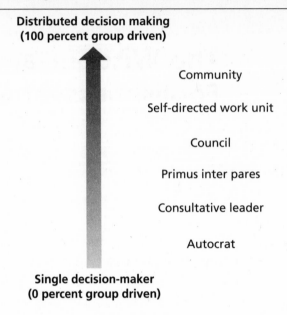

Distributed decision making
(100 percent group driven)

Community

Self-directed work unit

Council

Primus inter pares

Consultative leader

Autocrat

Single decision-maker
(0 percent group driven)

where distributed decision making reigns and no individual's contribution is evident. In discussing group decision making, we deal with a decision-participation spectrum. Each of the six categories of group decision making that constitute the spectrum's elements is covered briefly in the following sections.

Autocrat

In Greek, the word *autokrates* means self-rule (from *auto*, self, and *krat*, power). It is in the nature of autocrats to disregard the counsel of others. They go it alone. When assessed against the individual-versus-group decision-participation spectrum, they represent the extreme case of individualistic decision making. Adolph Hitler, Joseph Stalin, and Saddam Hussein were exemplars of the autocrat. They believed they had all the answers and were not concerned with feedback from anyone who did not agree with them.

In business and government today, you seldom encounter classic autocratic leaders. Business complexity, rapid change, and the expectations of knowledge worker employees work against the employment of autocratic management styles by senior managers. However, you can still encounter autocrats operating at the middle and lower levels of bureaucratic organizations who function as warlords overseeing their limited fiefdoms.

A decision-making advantage autocrats face is that they can decide things quickly because they do not spend time gathering information and building consensus among stakeholders. However, their disregard of views that vary from theirs often creates major problems for them, because their worldview is chimerical and does not reflect how things really work. They grow out of touch with reality.

Group decision making plays no role with autocrats.

Consultative Leader

Consultative leaders are decision-makers with substantial decision-making authority who seek counsel from their advisers, experts, and possibly adversaries. Although they solicit input from others, their decision-making style is not democratic: there is no voting on decisions and no requirement to seek or achieve consensus. They set the decision-making priorities. After seeking counsel from others, they decide whether they will heed it, ignore it, or adopt pieces of it. In the United States, presidents exercise this type of leadership. President Harry Truman's famous desk sign, "The buck stops here," captures the spirit of the consultative leader's decision-making orientation. It implies that while the leader is open to advice, decision-making authority ultimately rests entirely with him or her.

Powerful business leaders are often consultative leaders. By being open to counsel from all quarters, they are able to acquire a realistic sense of the business challenges and opportunities they face. However, they reserve the right to make the final decisions based on their personal judgment of what is best.

Decisions that consultative leaders make are distinct from those that entail active group decision making. However, unlike autocrats, consultative leaders can reach out to a wide range of individuals whose guidance materially affects their decisions. If outsiders want to influence decisions in this environment, they must consciously strive to catch the decision-maker's ear and articulate positions that will strike a responsive chord.

Primus Inter Pares

In Latin, *primus inter pares* means "first among equals." Decision-makers who fall into this category are men and women in leadership positions who need to accommodate the views of other powerful colleagues when making decisions. They have substantial decision-making authority but no blank check to make solo decisions. In the U.S. Congress, the Speaker of the House and the Senate majority leader are first among equals within their political parties. Because they occupy powerful positions in the legislature, their views can influence congressional decision making heavily. However, they operate within limits established by their colleagues. If they ignore these limits, they lose their legitimacy and may face a rebellion among the rank-and-file. A similar situation exists in parliamentary democracies, where prime ministers serve at the pleasure of their parties. Even the name *prime minister* captures the reality of primus inter pares: these men and women are first among equals.

Executive directors of professional societies often find themselves primus inter pares. They are the principal decision-makers of the professional societies they manage, but the range of their decision-making authority is constrained by the board of directors that they report to.

In the case of primus inter pares, the need for group decision-making skills can be significant, particularly when the colleagues that the primus works with hold differing views on important issues. If there is a serious split in the outlook of the colleagues, an important role the primus plays is to help them achieve a measure of agreement among themselves. When the split is rooted in ideological differences, guiding the contentious colleagues toward a position of agreement can be difficult. In order to avoid decision gridlock, the primus may need to side with one of the factions. At this point, she is vulnerable to accusations by the losing side that hold that she is adhering to the partisan interests of the opposing side.

In the United States, Speaker of the House John Boehner found himself in this position after the Tea Party election victories of 2010. The incoming Tea Party members were intent on changing the Republican Party's agenda and took positions opposed to those held by mainstream Republicans. Boehner attempted to straddle the two positions by promoting compromise, but his efforts failed because Tea Party members had no interest in compromise. Boehner's steps to travel a middle path weakened his standing as Speaker, resulting in decision gridlock and damage to the image of the Republican Party.

Primus inter pares reflects elements of both individual and group decision making. The relative role of each is often determined by the personality and communication skills of the primus. A charismatic or power-projecting primus is likely to have his will prevail; the weak primus will likely be reduced to being an order taker for his colleagues.

Council

Councils are composed of multiple players who represent the interests of an organization and its larger community of players. They appear in many forms: city councils whose elected officials oversee the governance and operations of a municipality, advisory councils whose experts provide information and guidance to decision-makers, and councils whose functions are to articulate the views and interests of a defined interest group.

A typical board of directors is the exemplar of a powerful council. The board of a corporation, for example, oversees the operations of the company from the perspective of its owners, the shareholders. Its job is to review the strategic and operational decisions made by the company's managers and employees, with a view of determining whether they serve the interests of the shareholders. Because the board reflects the collective interests of the owners, it has a responsibility to provide direction to the enterprise's senior managers, particularly when it deems the enterprise's trajectory to be out of line with the owners' interests.

Councils can be vested with substantial decision-making power. This is particularly true of boards of directors, whose members have a legal responsibility to protect the interests of the people they serve. Among the most momentous decisions boards can make is to fire senior managers whose actions do not support the organization's well-being or disregard the board's directions. Boards should not become involved in the details of managing an enterprise's operations, but they do have the power to influence even small decisions by changing the management players who make the detailed decisions.

From a decision-making perspective, councils are vehicles of group decision making par excellence. While council members elect a chair to lead their deliberations, they typically operate according to one-person, one-vote rules, making them classic democracies. Being democracies, they are subject to the well-known panoply of strengths and weaknesses associated with democratic governance. When board members agree with each other on issues, their deliberations run smoothly. If a small minority disagrees with a board position, the majority may try to assuage them with concessions, and if that fails, the minority's concerns can be bypassed and decisions can still be forthcoming using majority rule principles. However, if there is a significant split in the outlook of board members on important issues, reaching decisions becomes problematic. Emotions may begin playing a significant role in the decision-making process, and political game playing may become significant. Things may get so bad that the council encounters decision gridlock, where no decisions are made.

Self-Directed Work Unit

Councils are decision-making bodies. However, they do not implement their decisions themselves; they direct others to do this. Self-directed work units, in contrast, both make decisions and implement them. They often operate in a production or project environment, charged with producing concrete deliverables. Their decision-making authority is derived from their work charter, and it may be severely restricted. For example, the members of the work unit may be empowered only to make day-to-day technical and administrative decisions. Any decisions beyond this limited range must be made by higher authorities. Or their decision-making authority may be comprehensive: the collective team may possess full hiring and firing authority; they may make all management decisions, from defining requirements, to scheduling tasks, to establishing and controlling budgets; they may be empowered to make key design decisions, and so on.

Self-directed work units depend heavily on group decision-making processes. Because their goals are usually well established—for example, to design, build, and market a new product—they entail far less decision-related conflict than groups such as councils with open-ended objectives. Ultimately their effectiveness is tied to their ability to achieve the targets they establish. Did we produce a deliverable by the October 15 contract deadline date? Did our product pass the customer's user acceptance test? Did the product meet the performance specifications that the customer established?

In some organizations, distinct business units have been established to nurture self-directed work units for the purpose of developing disruptive technologies. Perhaps the most famous example of this was the launching of the IBM personal computer team that worked in Florida, fourteen hundred miles away from head-quarters, and had substantial decision-making autonomy. The goal here is to buffer the work unit from the risk-averse propensities of the traditional corporate culture. These work units have the power to decide what they will do and how they will do it. One thing that keeps them effective is knowledge that if they do not produce things of value to their organizations, they will be disbanded. They have substantial motivation to produce results that work. This environment offers little room for ideological grandstanding and politics.

Community

When people think about group decision making, they most likely visualize a number of men and women together in a room around a conference table, batting ideas back and forth; or three or four people standing before a whiteboard, scrib-bling graphic images and jotting down key words; or in a virtual world, with people resolving issues during a teleconference call or through e-mail communi-cations. The point is that in thinking about the group, they picture specific players participating in the decision-making effort. They also see the group effort occur-ring in a defined organizational setting.

But things are changing. The social networking tools and perspectives that have emerged since the 1990s have created a new type of group-based decision-making process where images of the participants become blurry or even transparent. Clay Shirky captures the new process in the subtitle of his book, *Here Comes Everybody: The Power of Organizing Without Organization* (2008). The foundation for the successes of "disorganized" development, as reflected in prod-ucts such as Wikipedia, Firefox, and Flickr, was established in the mid-1980s with the breathtaking initiative of Richard Stallman to develop a process that taps into the volunteer contributions of independent software developers to create a free version of the Unix operating system. The actual development of the operating system, called Linux, was led by Linus Torvald using the free software principles Stallman established. Today Linux is a dominant operating system that continues to evolve through the efforts of volunteers working around the world through decentralized channels. Linux has been built by the people, for the people—and at no cost to the people.

The idea of people organizing their efforts independently to produce products outside an organizational setting extends to organizing events. Smart mobs illustrate this phenomenon. Smart mobs comprise people who at the last minute are apprised of an event occurring at a particular location and show up at the event concurrently, sometimes in large numbers. Some of the earliest manifestations of smart mobs occurred in Japan, where participants were notified that a celebrity would be at a specific spot at a specific time—perhaps emerging from a subway entrance. Crowds would descend on the locale quickly. In recent times, people have been notified of events through text messaging or Twitter messages. The practical power of smart mobs has been illustrated in political protests that were arranged quickly in repressive societies, foiling the authorities' efforts to quash them.

We have here a reliance on a community to make decisions in a decentralized fashion. Thomas Seeley relates how communities of honeybees provide a model of this in his fascinating book, *Honeybee Democracy* (2010). No central authority governs the decisions of individual bees, yet hives get built; foraging bees locate and retrieve nectar from flowers; the swarm makes a collective decision on where to relocate the hive; honey is produced from the nectar; and so on. Careful investigations show that bees are capable of learning and communicating, and they use these skills to aid in community decision making. This was initially revealed through Karl von Frisch's pioneering studies in the 1940s (von Frisch, 1967).

With human communities, members are tied together by common goals and a common interest in issues, not by membership in a discrete organization with a central command structure and power hierarchy.

MAKING DECISIONS IN GROUPS

A common exercise in team-building classes is to have students visualize five people in an elevator at a time when it gets stuck between floors. Once students indicate that they have the vision in their heads, the facilitator asks: "What does it take to transform this group of five people into a team?" The objective of the exercise is to get students to recognize the difference between a group of people and a team.

An important feature of teams is their need to organize their actions to achieve results. This entails working out a protocol to make decisions. In the elevator example, the five people must reach some measure of agreement on what steps to take to address their predicament.

In the case of a stuck elevator, the decision protocol is simple: after a brief discussion of alternative courses of action, the people in the elevator arrive at an informal consensus on what steps to take to deal with the situation. That's it. The options they face are limited: there is no need to undertake a formal decision-making effort or take a vote. They can push the alarm bell, under the presumption that the building is occupied and that the occupants will respond to the annoying alarm. If the elevator has an emergency telephone, they can use it to contact an operator—that is, if the telephone actually functions. If there is no built-in tele-phone, they can use their own cell phones to contact someone on the outside—provided that the cell phone signal can penetrate the steel casing of the elevator. They can even force the door partially open to see where the elevator is positioned in the elevator shaft. If they are aligned with a floor, they can force the outside door open and exit the elevator without further fuss. It works (I have done it three times).

The elevator case is as simple as it gets. But when the decision is nontrivial, often the steps a group should take to reach a decision are not clear. They have available many decision-making protocols to follow, ranging from the informal to the highly formal, with the most appropriate one depending on a variety of factors. For example, the size of the group is important: with large groups, formal protocols are required in order to handle scale and complexity, while with very small groups, affirmative nods of group members' heads might be adequate. Other factors contribute as well to defining an appropriate decision-making pro-tocol: the impact of the decision, its complexity, the political character of the problem, and the intransigence of group members, for example.

The point of defining a protocol is to facilitate the process of achieving con-sensus among group members as to what actions to take. This requires having an understanding of what constitutes consensus.

DEGREES OF CONSENSUS

The principal goal of group decision making is to achieve a measure of consensus among the decision-makers. Without consensus, there is no group decision. If in the absence of consensus, a decision is forced on the group by a third party (for example, the Big Boss), the decision that emerges is likely to be unsatisfactory to the people engaged in the decision-making effort, which does not bode well for the efficacy of the decision. As Chapter Three notes, the physical act of deciding to pursue option A over option B is only one step in achieving a workable decision. For a decision to be actionable, it must be implemented. If the decision-makers do not have a commitment to implement it, the chances are slim that it will yield the intended results.

When groups deliberate on an issue, two matters need to be addressed. First, a rule must be established that defines clearly what constitutes a consensus threshold. For example, if a group is using simple majority rule to decide things, then decisions require more than half the group members to support them. When this threshold is reached during deliberations, the group has effectively agreed on a decision, can now stop the discussion, and can move on to other matters. Second, a process must be established to identify what steps need to be taken to move toward consensus. Should the group vote? Should external facilitators be employed to move the group toward a common agreement? Should scoring sheets be used? In major deliberating bodies such as national parliaments, the process is highly formalized. In small groups dealing with small issues, it is usually informal.

DEFINING CONSENSUS

Achieving consensus means the group has reached a level of agreement on an issue that enables them to make an implementable decision. If you have been raised in a Western democracy, you may automatically assume this means that a simple majority of the "voters" agrees on a course of action, because a majority of 50 percent or more is the decision threshold that permeates Western thinking. It covers most formal group decision-making efforts, from electing public officials, to determining what restaurant to dine in, to making basic business decisions. In fact, simple majority rule is just one of many decision rules available to decision-makers. There are plenty of reasonable alternatives, and this section explores several of the frequently employed ones.

Nature of Consensus

Before looking at specific decision rules, it is helpful to develop a good understanding of the nature of consensus. At first blush, it appears to be an easy issue to deal with: when more than half the members of a group agree on a course of action, then sufficient consensus has been achieved and a decision is made. Through this process, you have assurance that the desires of most players have been satisfied. However, this outlook oversimplifies things. Quite often, sometime after a decision has been made using simple majority rule, people become disconcerted to see that it is not working out. Individuals who disagreed with the decision may actively work against its implementation. Even some of those who voted in its favor may grow lukewarm in their support for it. Others may complain that what is being implemented is not what they supported. And so on.

It is important to note that while more than 50 percent voted in favor of the decision, they did so with different rationales. If the players involved in the decision took into account the multiple perspectives of the group members, the decision outcome might have been different. To demonstrate this, consider one easily measured factor that varies substantially among decision-makers: the intensity of their feelings about a decision. Some group members may favor a decision passionately, while others may be equally opposed to it. Still others, perhaps most, may hold a position between these two extremes. A measure of intensity of support for a decision is easily assessed by surveying participants with one or two questions using a five-point scale, ranging from 1, which reflects strong opposition to a decision, to 5, which reflects strong support. The midpoint value of 3 reflects indifference.

Figures 7.2 through 7.5 show how the intensity of support for a decision suggests that it may hide more than it reveals. In Figure 7.2, an overwhelming majority of group members support a particular decision. Nine out of ten give it a rating of either 4 or 5. One individual, clearly a loner, opposes it strongly. In this case, support for the decision under normal circumstances is so strong that the group can go ahead with it without undue concern about the opposition of the holdout.

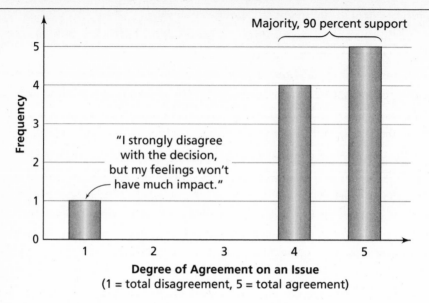

Figure 7.2 Strong Support, Weak Opposition for a Decision

Figure 7.3 presents a significantly different situation. As with the previous figure, a majority rates the decision with a score of either 4 or 5, but 40 percent are strongly opposed to it. What this means is that a significant minority of the decision-makers does not want to move forward with the decision, and they feel strongly about this. When only 10 percent oppose the decision, you have little problem in pursuing majority rule. But when you come closer to a fifty-fifty split in opinion, you need to give serious thought to the consequences of overriding the preferences of the minority, particularly in the case pictured here, where all the members of the minority express strong opposition to the decision. In a situation like this, if the decision is an important one, it makes sense for the winners to work closely with the losers to see if assurances or adjustments can be offered to allay their strongly felt concerns.

In Figure 7.4, we encounter yet another scenario. Although the majority supports a decision, a large minority expresses indifference toward it, giving it a score of 3. They do not support it, but neither do they oppose it. In my personal experience in working on boards and committees comprising people who do not subscribe to political agendas, this is a common situation. The indifferent players

Figure 7.3 Moderate Majority Support, Strong Minority Opposition for a Decision

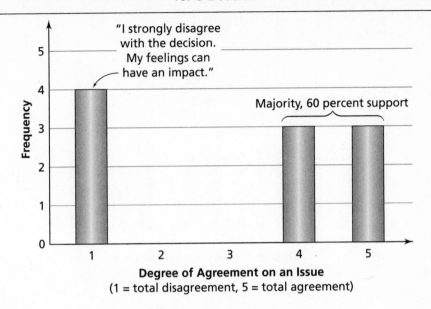

Figure 7.4 Moderate Support, Substantial Indifference: "I Can Live with the Decision"

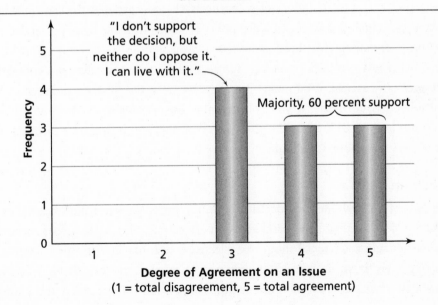

Figure 7.5 Absence of Consensus on a Decision

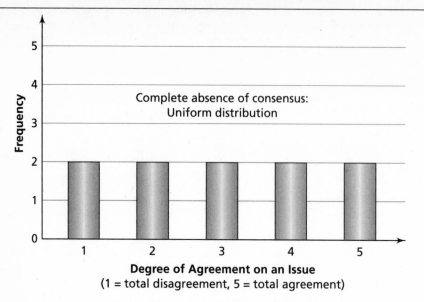

Degree of Agreement on an Issue
(1 = total disagreement, 5 = total agreement)

appreciate that reasonable arguments can be made in support of or opposed to most reasonable issues. The outlook is: "Although I don't actively support the decision, I can live with it." I think this reflects a healthy group of decision-makers whose principal goal is not to score political points to show their power but to get on with making decisions.

Finally, in Figure 7.5, we come across a group that experiences a complete absence of consensus on an issue. In a case like this, the smartest policy may be to table the issue. In the parlance of current group processes, this decision should be put into the parking lot. The group can come back to it later, or a different set of players can address the issue.

Decision Rules

By having a clearly defined decision rule, the group knows without ambiguity when a decision has been reached. No best rule applies to all circumstances. Whatever rule you choose should be selected in accordance with the context. In theory, there is no limit to the number of rules you can draw from. You may establish a rule that a decision can be made only when 100 percent of the council of elders support it, or when the court astrologer feels this is an auspicious moment to move forward with a decision, or when your benefit-cost analysis indicates that benefits will exceed costs by a 1.5-to-1.0 ratio.

Our concern here is restricted to rules that apply to group decision making. They should enable us to determine when a group achieves acceptable consensus. So we limit ourselves to looking at rules built around some kind of formal or informal vote taking. Following are six frequently employed rules employed in group decision making.

Simple Majority Decision Rule. Simple majority rule is the dominant approach to affirming consensus. Its underlying premise is that decisions should reflect what most people want. In taking into account the strength of feelings group decision-makers have when making decisions, Figures 7.2 through 7.5 show how a simple majority is not necessarily so simple. Depending on how large the majority is and how strongly the decision-makers feel about the issue, simple majority rule may reflect a true mandate (for example, when 90 percent support the decision) or may portend trouble (when there is a near fifty-fifty split, and the losers oppose the decision passionately).

Supermajority Decision Rule. According to the simple majority decision rule, if a decision you are promoting gains support from 51 percent of the voters, you are a winner and are officially authorized to implement the decision. If this is a routine decision that does not generate strong negative reactions, you are indeed a winner. However, if this is a decision of consequence and passions run high among the losers, basically half the voters may be unhappy with the outcome. This may bode poorly for implementation of the decision: it does not have big support to begin with and the losers may turn to sabotage.

To avoid this situation, you can impose a supermajority decision rule. Thus, you may require significant decisions to receive at least 60 percent of the vote (or 67 percent or 75 percent or whatever other figure you believe to be appropriate). Many organizations employ the simple majority decision rule for most decisions but set aside a subset of the most significant issues to be handled using a supermajority decision rule. A well-known example is found in the U.S. Congress. For a bill to become law, more than 50 percent of House and Senate members must vote in its favor. If the president vetoes it, both the Senate and House must muster a two-thirds supermajority to override the veto. Another well-known example of the application of the supermajority rule in the U.S. government is the requirement that an amendment to the Constitution be approved by at least two-thirds of the states.

The strength of employing a supermajority decision rule is assurance that decisions that are reached have reasonably strong backing and did not just squeak by. This gives the decisions moral strength. People whose views do not prevail need to acknowledge that their views reflect truly minority perspectives. Whenever possible, I employ supermajority decision rules in the committees I run. My feeling is that if a proposal cannot get support from a substantial portion of the decision-makers in the group, it may need to be reworked. Getting a decision approved is only part of the overall decision life cycle: it must be implemented effectively, and this may not happen if it has lukewarm support. With supermajority backing of a decision, the likelihood of achieving its desired results increases dramatically.

Weighted-Majority Decision Rule. There may be reason to believe that not all voters should have equal input into arriving at an outcome. For example, a technology review panel that examines proposals for new technology-based products may give the votes of the business members of the panel higher weight than the members with technical backgrounds, recognizing that even the most exciting new technologies are not worth pursuing if they do not sell in the market. With new technology, marketing trumps technology. In a case like this, the business votes may be multiplied by 1.25, while the technical votes are weighted with a value of 1.00. Let's say the review panel has five business members and five technical members. Let's say further that four technical members and one business member support the proposal, while four business members and one technical member oppose it. The weighted value of the pro votes is 5.25, whereas the weighted value of the con votes is 7.00. In this case, the panel members opposed to development of the new technology prevail, and the project is rejected.

The challenge is to come up with valid weights. These will be derived largely through experience-based intuition rather than science. In some cases, the views of senior managers might be given extra weight for a variety of reasons (perhaps they view the activities of the organization from all perspectives: business, technical, legal), whereas lower-level managers tend to have a narrower perspective of their department or division. In other cases, the views of technical managers may be given special consideration. In yet other cases the views of the business players will be emphasized.

100 Percent Consensus Decision Rule. When self-managed teams emerged in the 1990s and were empowered to make consequential decisions, many of them operated on the principle of achieving 100 percent consensus when making decisions, particularly smaller teams of three to ten players. They followed what I call the *three musketeers principle*: all for one and one for all—that is, everyone on the team needed to support a decision before it was implemented. While the cynical reader might believe that it is impossible to get two or more people to fully agree on anything, gaining 100 percent consensus among the members of small self-managed teams was easier than you would expect when the team members had a history of working together effectively over a long period of time. The explanation of why this is so is simple. Many of these teams had evolved into what Gerald Weinberg (1971) called "egoless teams"—men and women who worked so closely together for so long that they fully understood and respected each other's capabilities and viewpoints. In this environment, if a highly respected team member provided a strong argument favoring a particular decision, the other team members would likely ask a number of questions; when they were satisfied with the answers, they would support the decision fully. They did not demand a protracted debate-and-vote process.

The 100 percent consensus decision rule will not work in many situations. Cynics who believe that it is difficult to get people to fully agree on anything have a good point. However, in certain environments, full agreement of the players on courses of action that should be undertaken is common. One of the qualities of high-performing teams is members' trust in the judgment and capabilities of their colleagues. When trust exists, achieving 100 percent consensus is surprisingly easy.

Plurality Decision Rule. Up to this point, we have assumed that group decision making requires that at least half the players support a specific decision. This view is based on the premise that group decisions require consensus among the players, where the consensus threshold is defined as having most the players support a decision.

In fact, decisions are made in the absence of consensus in plenty of situations. The most obvious example is decisions based on plurality support. With plurality support, the winning decision is the one that has the greatest support among alternative options, even though it does not attain majority support. For example, in the United States, the Constitution holds that the presidential candidate who gains the greatest number of votes through electoral college voting becomes president. The Constitution does not require support from the majority of voters. It is instructive to recall that in the 1992 election, Bill Clinton became president with only 43 percent of the vote. (George H. W. Bush received 38 percent of the vote, and Ross Perot received 19 percent.) Clinton's biggest challenge in his first term was to gain the backing of a majority of the American people.

Decisions supported by a plurality of players face tough circumstances. Most the players have not expressed support for them, so their legitimacy is easily questioned. Israel is an example of a country whose politics are so fractionated that its ruling party, which historically has been unable to win majority backing by the electorate, owes its leadership position to support from smaller parties with which it has shaky alliances. This makes for roller-coaster politics.

I-Can-Live-with-It Decision Rule. Organizations that depend on governance through collegiality—including universities, nonprofits, volunteer organizations, and knowledge-based businesses—depend heavily on the I-can-live-with-it decision rule. This decision rule was discussed earlier in connection with Figure 7.4. With this rule, players who do not favor a decision may agree not to actively oppose it based on the principle that "I can live with it." In my experience working with universities, R&D enterprises, and professional societies, I have encountered this as the dominant decision rule employed with small- to medium-impact decisions that were not emotionally charged. If some players express concern about the decision during discussions of its merits, the decision's supporters strive to ease the concern. They may possibly reformulate it to satisfy the doubters. At a certain point, it becomes clear that almost everyone involved with the decision either supports it or can live with it.

This approach is a variant of what management scientists call Pareto optimality: a decision is supportable if it benefits at least one player without diminishing the benefits received by any other player. With ICLWI, the decision to support a given initiative can be made if it has a core of supporters and nonsupporters can live with it.

REACHING A DECISION

Even if decision rules have been carefully defined, there is nothing automatic about how they will be applied in order to arrive at decisions. The ultimate outcome of a decision-making process can be materially affected by the approach that group members take to reach a decision. It makes a difference whether people approach decision making by working face-to-face or virtually, whether they pursue formal voting procedures or vote by nodding their heads, and whether they are permitted unlimited debate or given three minutes to make a point.

Setting

Decision-makers must be sensitive to the impact of setting on the process of decision making. King Arthur recognized this when dealing with his contentious knights. In order to overcome their concerns with status and hierarchy, he had them sit at a round table, where the status implications of seating positions disappeared.

Perhaps the most significant issue of setting today is whether decisions are carried out face-to-face or virtually. The dynamics of group processes are quite different in these two settings. The immediacy of contact with fellow decision-makers in a face-to-face environment has its advantages and disadvantages, just as the remoteness of contact in a virtual environment has its pluses and minuses. For example, in face-to-face settings, participants can read others' body language, tone of voice, and facial expressions when discussing issues. This is a plus. On the minus side, the need to schedule different players at a single site at a particular time can delay decisions and can mean that some important players are excluded from the meeting. In virtual settings, the ability to work asynchronously offers participants time to reflect on subtle issues without feeling pressure to commit themselves to an immediate decision. This is a plus. The inability to account for body language and other nonverbal cues is a minus.

Clearly accounting for setting is important.

Steps Toward Making a Decision in Groups

There are many alternative paths that can be trekked to arrive at a decision. Regardless of the details of the approach that is employed, reaching group consensus on decisions entails going through three basic steps.

First, the issue to be decided is presented to the decision-makers, whether a small committee of two or three people or a dozen august directors on a corporate board of directors or the full faculty of an engineering school. Although the specifics vary from case to case, the typical presentation is captured in the following words: "We have a problem that needs to be resolved. Here are the basics." The initial presentation gets group members up to speed on the facts, alerts the decision-makers to the context of the decision, and therefore gets the ball rolling.

Second, once the discussion is underway, the group identifies different decision options and debates their pros and cons. In surfacing options, a common practice is to encourage brainstorming to let people generate ideas freely. The group can be broken down into subgroups that go off to tackle pieces of the problem before assembling in a plenary session to aggregate their suggestions. After the options have been sketched out, attention focuses on discussing their merits. During this step, proponents and opponents of the options present their arguments. Questions raised by the undecided decision-makers are addressed. New paths may be opened and old ones abandoned. Groups that want to maintain a semblance of order during the debate employ well-defined procedures governing the discussion, such as *Robert's Rules of Order* (Robert, 2011). Those who want to maintain an element of spontaneity (and possibly chaos) may promote free-form debate.

Third, the decision-makers vote on the decision, either supporting it, rejecting it, or putting it on hold. There are various ways this third step can be implemented. For example, once discussion has stopped, the group can take a vote. This can be an open vote, using a show of hands, or it can be a secret ballot, with participants submitting their votes on slips of paper. Another example is with groups using meeting-facilitating software, where participants enter their votes by pressing an appropriate button at their place or on their computer; the software immediately tabulates the distribution of votes and displays the results on monitors. This approach to counting votes can be employed in a face-to-face or virtual setting. Finally, during the course of discussion, after the sense of the group becomes clear, the group leader may simply say: "I think we have an agreement on what the decision is. Is there any further discussion? If not, let's move on."

In practice, reaching a decision on matters of consequence entails pursuing a mixed bag of approaches. This is readily illustrated with a personal example. I recently served on an eight-person committee of a large professional society. Our job was to formulate the criteria a selection committee should use to assess the qualifications of future board candidates when recruiting them for board positions. The committee had seven experienced volunteers and one sitting board member, who served as our committee chairwoman. Over three months, we conducted most of our business virtually, making ample use of teleconferences, discussion boards, and e-mail. During this time, the committee held two face-to-face meetings, which required most of the committee members to travel to the meeting site in Washington, D.C., from out of town.

At the outset of this process, we were given one day to conduct a workshop with sitting board members to get their thoughts on the selection criteria for recruiting future board members. Inasmuch as these board members would make the final decision on what the criteria should be, it was important to capture their perspectives early in the effort. During the workshop, the board members broke into groups, each one tackling different parts of the problem. By the time the workshop ended, they were able to provide guidance to our committee on what we should focus on. At the end of the three-month decision-making process, the final decision on the selection criteria for future board members was made at one of the board's quarterly meetings. After our committee chairwoman presented our recommendations, the board members raised questions, requested minor modifications to the selection criteria, and then voted unanimously to incorporate the criteria into the formal rules of the board. This eclectic approach reflects the practical reality of how decisions of consequence are often made.

THE WISDOM AND FOOLISHNESS OF CROWDS

I conclude this chapter on group decision making by addressing a question that I have heard debated since my days as an undergraduate: Do groups outperform individuals in making decisions? This question is politically charged because group decision making lies at the heart of democracy, while decisions based on the insights of individuals conjure images of elitism, at best, and bald autocracy, at worst. Today's *vox populi* appears to lean in favor of group solutions to problems, so managers who express a preference for solo decision making may find themselves branded as autocrats.

Individuals Versus Groups

The question of whether groups outperform individuals in making decisions extends back to the ancient Greeks. In *The Republic*, Plato argues that society is best off if governed by a super-wise philosopher king whose wisdom is based on his deep grasp of reality (as reflected in Plato's *forms*). What is interesting is that at the time Plato wrote, democracy had been practiced in Athens for at least two generations. It flourished during the reign of Pericles, who died just one year before Plato was born. Plato was aware of the practice of democracy—government by the group—and witnessed it in action, yet he promoted rule by a single, highly qualified individual, his philosopher king.

Proponents of each side can muster good arguments to buttress their positions. Those who believe individuals generally outperform groups adduce the history of great ideas and achievements, which are generally associated with individuals, not groups. Consider, for example, the achievements of the following people:

In governance	Queen Elizabeth I, Ataturk, Gandhi, Lincoln, Churchill
In religion	Siddhartha, Lao Tzu, Jesus, Muhammad
In business	Akio Morita of Sony, Jack Welch of GE, Steve Jobs of Apple
In art	Rembrandt, Monet, Picasso, Pollack
In literature	Charlotte Brontë, Leo Tolstoy, Günter Grass, Toni Morrison
In science	Galileo, Newton, James Clerk Maxwell, Albert Einstein, Stephen Hawking

Proponents of the superiority of the individual find it hard to visualize teams of people matching the achievements of the individuals in this list.

On the other side, proponents of group performance appeal to common sense and simple logic. They argue that the knowledge and insights of individuals cannot match the collective and more substantial wisdom of larger numbers of people. Furthermore, they continue, the interactions of people functioning in groups create a crucible where ideas are scrutinized, deconstructed, reconstructed, and strengthened through a Darwinian process of natural selection. Finally, they argue that the scale and complexity of the challenges we face today require solutions that go beyond the limited capabilities of even the cleverest, most creative individuals.

Who's got it right? Neither side (or both!). The framing of the question being debated understates the complexity of the issue by casting it in either-or terms. The confounding problem here is that the line distinguishing the individual and the group is often blurred. Consider the superior achievements of outstanding individuals. Their individualism may be deceiving, because all individuals depend on inputs from outside, from an extended group. In the history of great individuals, few were hermits cut off from the world. Although they may not have worked as members of a team, all the players on the list above functioned in a community of players with whom they interacted directly or indirectly. Their achievements reflected their times and the conditions under which they operated. For example, Jesus did not function in a vacuum. He lived in troubling times in a region that had bristled against foreign occupation since the Maccabean revolt against the Seleucids in the second century B.C.E. Messianic movements flourished as the Jews looked for their God to send them a leader who would liberate them from foreign oppressors. Jesus delivered his message in this context. He emphasized the need for Jews to connect to God personally during oppressive times; their liberation would be spiritual rather than political.

For his part, Monet's brilliant work was rooted in his close ties to the impressionist movement in France during the second half of the nineteenth century. To be understood, Monet's achievement must be examined in the context of impressionism and his communion with Renoir, Sisley, and the other impressionists.

Einstein's discoveries on the photoelectric effect, Brownian motion, and relativity (all reported in 1905, when he was twenty-six years old) were linked to his addressing questions raised by the greater community of physicists at the turn of the century. Furthermore, as a theoretical physicist, he depended on experimental physicists to confirm his theories. Thus it was not until Arthur Eddington, a

British astrophysicist, confirmed his predictions about the ability of mass to bend light after the total eclipse of 1919 that his general relativity theory was taken seriously. Einstein may have worked alone, but his discoveries were tied to a dependence on an extended group of colleagues in the scientific community (Isaacson, 2007).

In the arena of business, Akio Morita's industry-transforming innovations at Sony required give-and-take interactions with his engineers. In his autobiography, *Made in Japan* (1986), Morita describes the origins of the Sony Walkman. As an aficionado of classical music, it occurred to him that the massive headphones in use at the time were unnecessary to achieve high-fidelity sound. He reckoned that you could produce high-fidelity sound with featherweight earphones that fully covered the ear canal. Morita assembled his top engineers and whimsically speculated: "I wonder if we can produce a super-light tape recorder that can generate high-fidelity sound?" The engineers took it from there.

Much of what is viewed as individual decision-making behavior corresponds to the consultative leader designation described at the outset of this chapter. Consultative leaders do not operate alone: they gather input from an array of sources before making decisions. Certainly, with consultative leaders, the final decisions are made by individual decision-makers. However, their decisions are informed by the knowledge and insights of a network of other players: colleagues, employees, writers of scientific publications, opinion leaders, opponents, and more. John Donne had it right when he wrote: "No man is an island entire of itself; every man is a piece of the continent, a part of the main."

In software development, the exemplar of the consultative leader is Harlan Mills's *chief programmer*, popularized in Frederick Brooks's classic book on software development, *The Mythical Man-Month* (Mills, 1988; Brooks, 1995). Mills argues that a superior approach to developing complex systems is to employ what he calls the chief programmer team model (Brooks calls it the surgical team model). With the chief programmer team approach, key software is written by one individual—the chief programmer. He is a superprogrammer who can write ten times the lines of code with ten times the quality of average programmers. His sole job is to write software. He can solicit whatever support he needs to get his job done. For example, after developing a module, he hands it to software testers, who test it for him. At the end of each day, a program librarian documents what he has done, so that the all-important documentation chores are accounted for. If the chief programmer needs insights into a programming language, he can call in a language expert to provide him the guidance he requires. The goal is to free the chief programmer to do what he does best: write software. As a super-programmer, this individual writes superior code. Because the code comes from the mind of one developer, traditional problems of inconsistency that arise when patching together the contributions of different programmers will disappear, leading to a dramatic reduction in bugs that need fixing.

The Wisdom of Crowds Perspective

In 2004, James Surowiecki published a high-impact book on decision making titled *The Wisdom of Crowds*. Its subtitle captures its message: *Why the Many Are Smarter Than the Few and How Collective Wisdom Shapes Business, Economies, Societies and Nations*. When the paperback version of the book was issued the following year (2005), the subtitle was dropped—possibly to save space or possibly because it is misleading.

The origin of the book's title is interesting. In 1841, a Scottish writer, Charles Mackay, wrote a book with the intriguing title, *Extraordinary Popular Delusions and the Madness of Crowds* (Mackay, 1995). In his Preface to the 1852 edition, Mackay captures the essence of his work in the following words: "Men, it has been well said, think in herds; it will be seen that they go mad in herds, while they only recover their senses slowly, and one by one." He shows the folly of herd thinking in fifteen fascinating chapters that cover topics from tulipmania in Holland in the 1600s, to speculation in Mississippi land, to witch hunting.

While acknowledging the merits of Mackay's arguments about the downside of the herd instinct, Surowiecki strove to highlight the positive side of decision making by crowds. Hence he adopted the title *The Wisdom of Crowds*.

The book is best known for a story Surowiecki tells in the Introduction: an account of a visit by eighty-five-year-old Francis Galton to a county fair in England. Galton is famous in statistics for his seminal work on correlation and regression. (His fame is also tied to his being a cousin of Charles Darwin.) At the fair, Galton came across a weight-judging competition. Members of the crowd were invited to submit their estimates of the weight of an ox on slips of paper. Whoever provided the best guess would win a prize. Galton surmised that the average crowd member had no special expertise on livestock, so the guesses were provided by well-informed nonexperts. Eight hundred people submitted guesses, 787 of which were usable. Galton obtained access to the slips with the guesses and performed a statistical analysis on them. He was surprised to discover that the crowd's collective guess missed the true weight of the ox by only 1 pound: a weighing of the butchered ox found it to weigh 1,198 pounds; the crowd's guess was 1,197 pounds.

This story sets the tone for the entire book. Its message, as interpreted by Surowiecki, is that the judgments of inexpert crowds are often superior to those of experts. Throughout the book, Surowiecki supports his contention with anecdotal evidence from a variety of real-world experiences. One is a story of how in 1960 the U.S. Navy located a lost submarine, the *Scorpion*. The individual in charge of finding the submarine assembled a team of people with a wide range of knowledge and had them develop scenarios of what they believed transpired with the *Scorpion* and where it might be located, motivating them with bottles of Chivas Regal as prizes for good guesses. As a result of this effort, the team generated different pieces of information on what might have happened to the *Scorpion* and where it might lie. The leader of the search effort brought together the disparate data and subjected them to a Bayesian analysis, a special type of statistical analysis, to locate the missing craft. The collective judgment of the participants emerging from this process led to a location that was just 220 yards away from where the submarine was ultimately located.

Surowiecki provides other stories about the superiority of group judgments. He cites experiments carried out by professors in the classroom that show groups of students outperforming individuals in judging the weights of objects, the temperature of a room, and the number of beans in a jar. He maintains that Google's superior search engine performance is tied to its tapping into the wisdom of large numbers of searchers. He holds that decision markets such as the Iowa Electronic Market and Hollywood Stock Exchange provide superior estimates of hard-to-predict events in a variety of areas, such as who will win an election or win the Academy Awards. All these amazing accounts are crammed into the first chapter of the book.

The Wisdom of Crowds is a good read once you get beyond the largely unsupportable crowds-beat-experts hype found in the Introduction and Chapter One.

Regarding the story of Galton's adventure at the country fair, I believe it proves nothing. Assuming Galton's tabulation of data was correct, the fact that the crowd's collective guess of the ox's weight was off by only one pound is likely a matter of luck. In science, results like this would not be regarded as more than a curiosity until they had been replicated many times under controlled conditions. Surowiecki's references to professors replicating Galton's experience, where crowds of students accurately guess the number of beans in a jar, got me thinking: "I'm a professor. I teach large numbers of students. I can test Surowiecki's hypothesis with my students."

And so I undertook efforts to replicate Galton's experiment with my students. Here is an account of my recent experiments. In December 2011, I taught graduate classes first in Shanghai, then during the following week to another class in Beijing. In a Shanghai class, I related the Galton story to my students, then told them: "Pretend I am an ox. How much do you think I weigh fully dressed in kilograms?" I paraded myself before them in the front of the classroom. The following week, I repeated the experiment, this time with a class of graduate students in Beijing. The results of the weight-estimating experiments in the two cities are shown immediately below:

Shanghai Class 1: Body Weight Estimates

N = 26 students

Actual weight (fully dressed, with jacket) = 97.0 kilograms

Estimated weight = 91.4 kilograms

S.D. = 6.45 kilograms

Beijing Class 1: Body Weight Estimates

N = 21 students

Actual weight (dressed, without jacket) = 94.0 kilograms

Estimated weight = 88.6 kilograms

S.D. = 7.4 kilograms

In Shanghai, the students underestimated my weight by 5.6 kilograms, which translates to an error of 5.7 percent. In Beijing, the students underestimated my weight by 5.4 kilograms, which translates to an error of 5.7 percent. I thanked the students for their underestimates and reveled in feeling svelte for a couple of weeks.

With these two experiments, I attempted to replicate Galton's weight-estimating experiment. While the students' estimates were a respectable 94 percent of the actual value in both experiments, this is hardly confirmation of Galton's results, which were dead-on in the county fair experiment. There were no miracle results in Shanghai or Beijing. To my thinking, the results were not surprising. I would expect good guesses when a group of adults estimates a man's weight, because those guessing are familiar with the weights a normal male can reach. One simple strategy they could follow would be to begin with knowledge of their own weight and then make adjustments to accommodate the corresponding size of the individual whose weight is being guessed.

What about estimating the weight of other, inanimate objects? I recently conducted a quick-and-dirty experiment at my school, asking staff who package and ship books to students to guess the weight of a number of objects hidden in a cloth bag. Because each day they computed the weights of books in order to ship them, they were expert in assessing the weights of smaller objects. Then I asked student counselors, clerical staff, and professors to guess the weight of the same objects. The professionals in the shipping room consistently outperformed the amateurs. That makes sense to me: the professionals weigh books every day as part of their job and should be good at guessing weights. My little experiment suggests they were better at this task than amateurs. Is there anything surprising about this result?

Surowiecki points out that crowd estimates are best when dealing with large crowds. Clearly I did not conduct my experiments using large crowds, and perhaps that affected my results. But I do not think so. I see no underlying reason that working with a large group would yield miracle results when estimating the weight of people and smaller objects.

Surowiecki's account of students' making accurate estimates of beans in a jar led me to carry out a counting experiment. While in China, I had plenty of access in local convenience stores to bags of peanuts with shells (the Chinese love peanuts in shells). In Shanghai and later in Beijing, I bought three bags of peanuts with shells and arranged the loose peanuts in piles on a table. Following are the results for the Shanghai and Beijing experiments:

Shanghai Class 2, Peanut Counts

$N = 36$ students

Actual count = 499.0 peanuts in shells

Estimated count = 405.5 peanuts in shells

S.D. = 172.6 peanuts in shells

Beijing Class 2, Peanut Counts

$N = 27$ students

Actual count = 451.0 peanuts in shells

Estimated count = 367.4 peanuts in shells

S.D. = 158.3 peanuts in shells

Performance on the peanut-counting experiments was substantially weaker than on the weight-estimating experiments: in Shanghai, students underestimated the actual number of peanuts by 23.1 percent; in Beijing, by 18.5 percent. And in both cases, the standard deviations were large, indicating that student guesses were all over the map.

At the end of each peanut-counting experiment, students were rewarded for their participation in the experiment with handfuls of peanuts, which they consumed as the class continued. They were happy students.

I am not surprised that the guesses for peanut counts were worse than for a man's weight. All the students possess a measure of expertise in dealing with body weight, but none had prior experience attempting to count piles of small objects: peanuts, beans, or something else. I suspect that other experiments like this would show that experts consistently outperform amateurs when dealing with simple, well-defined problems. As to the accuracy of Wall Street experts in predicting stock market trends and other outcomes tied to complex social phenomena, that's another story and warrants further investigation.

Distributed Collaboration

Surowiecki's points supporting the wisdom of crowds are based in large measure on recent experiences in distributed collaboration tied to developments on the

Internet. The Internet has made possible large-scale collaboration among people scattered across the globe. The Internet itself is a product of large-scale collaboration, emerging from U.S. Defense Department efforts in the 1960s to promote collaboration among scientists and engineers through a large distributed network: the well-known ARPANET initiative. Ultimately the growth of the Internet with its attendant advances in technology enabled highly creative people to use its reach to create distributed decision-making communities through mechanisms such as crowd sourcing and open sourcing. Wikipedia and Linux are two of the best-known results of these initiatives.

Historically, decision scientists have given distributed collaboration little thought. In going through my personal library of decision-making books, I have not found any that devotes attention to decision making rooted in distributed collaboration. Presumably that will soon change. Suddenly distributed collaboration is big news. Popular works like Surowiecki's *The Wisdom of Crowds* and Shirky's *Here Comes Everyone* (2008) have played a significant role in drawing attention to the impact of distributed collaboration on decision making. Their suggestions that in many cases crowd-based decisions offer superior results to traditional expert-based decision making are being taken seriously.

As we hear drumbeats promoting the discovery of distributed collaboration, we need to remind ourselves that it is not a new creation of the Internet. History offers a number of impressive examples of successful distributed collaborative efforts that predate the Internet by centuries.

The writing of the King James Bible provides one well-known example. People who believe that creative literary works cannot be developed through committees need to read up on the translation of the King James Bible in the early seventeenth century (Nicolson, 2005). The effort, carried out from 1604 through final publication of the finished work in 1611, entailed the collaboration of forty-seven Hebrew and Greek language scholars who worked together in six committees. It was potentially a risky undertaking: some seventy years earlier, William Tyndale had been strangled, impaled, and burned at the stake for translating the Bible into English. The outcome of the committee effort of the Bible translators was the creation of one of the greatest literary products of the English language.

More recently, the compilation of the *Oxford English Dictionary* (*OED*) was made possible through the work of thousands of volunteers contributing millions of quotations that illustrate the actual use of words in the English language. This effort began in the mid-nineteenth century. Volunteers pored through English language writings to identify examples of how words are used in practice. They submitted these examples to the *OED* editors on slips of paper, and the editors incorporated them into the ever-growing dictionary. The fascinating story of the development of the *OED* is masterfully related in Simon Winchester's book, *The Professor and the Mad Man* (1998). The *OED* is generally acknowledged to be the greatest authority on word definitions and usage in English. It currently contains some 600,000 entries. It was Wikipediaesque in a world before Wikipedia.

The global scientific enterprise is another example of a pre-Internet distributed collaborative undertaking. From the outset of modern science in the fifteenth century, its advancement has depended on the distributed collaborative efforts of members of the scientific community scattered across many countries. Discoveries are communicated through scientific journal articles, monographs, correspondence, and colloquia. The community collectively determines what scientific questions are important and deserve the attention of scientists. It collectively sits in judgment of new findings, separating those that are accepted from those that are not. Without the distributed guidance and scrutiny of the scientific community, there would be no science as we know it.

The most impressive example of human-distributed collaborative decision making is the marketplace, whose functioning dwarfs the achievements of Wikipedia and Linux by light-years. The first documentation and explication of this phenomenon appeared in Adam Smith's *Wealth of Nations*, published in 1776 (Smith, 1990). Smith showed how independent buyers and sellers, operating in the marketplace and pursuing their own self-interest, set the price and quantity of goods and services produced by society. These findings formed the foundation of modern economic thinking.

Most people who have thought about distributed collaboration attribute its successes to two simple points. First, through distributed collaboration, you have an opportunity to bring more people to the problem-solving effort than you do when working with one very smart individual or a small team of qualified experts. By working with larger numbers of people, you can draw on a broader and deeper store of knowledge and insights. Second, a large group of people coming from a diverse population will contain a greater diversity of viewpoints than an individual or small team. Insights are strengthened when they are challenged from multiple perspectives. These two points have commonsense appeal, but they do not explain much. They do not tell us, for example, how assembling a large number of independent and diverse computer aficionados produces a masterpiece like Linux.

The mere fact of having large numbers of people reflecting different perspectives provides no assurance that crowds will decide wisely. Political elections involve large, diverse crowds of voters using the ballot box to decide who should lead them. Is there anyone who believes that crowds consistently make wise choices on election day? Mackay believed strongly that crowds typically get things wrong and supplies plenty of convincing evidence to buttress his views. That is why he talked about the madness of crowds. Plato's confidence in the superiority of the philosopher king was based on the special insights he possessed that distinguished him from the crowd.

Still, I am intrigued by Surowiecki's claims, although many are unsupported. Some are thought provoking and may have merit. His points make those of us who work in the realm of decision science squirm a little. We have not given much thought to decisions reached through distributed collaboration. The problem I have with his uncritical and enthusiastic support of crowd wisdom is that the examples he showcases do not offer compelling explanations of why groups, and crowds in particular, outperform individuals and experts. It reminds me of the well-known cartoon of a scientist standing in front of a blackboard filled with impenetrable equations; where the final results should be displayed, the following words are written: "And then a miracle happens."

I am aware of only two cases of distributed decision making that have unassailable explanations that account for the good results they produce: Adam Smith's invisible hand and honeybee democracy. I will not cover how the free market yields optimal results through the power of distributed collaboration, because it is well known. But we encounter a different story when dealing with honeybees. Not many people realize that these near brainless insects have developed a remarkable approach to making smart, democratic decisions that ensures the well-being of the entire community. Let's look at honeybee democracy for unassailable evidence of the wisdom of crowds in at least one instance.

HONEYBEE DECISION MAKING

A community of honeybees is often likened to a single organism comprising many independent pieces functioning collaboratively. A typical hive of honeybees numbers in the tens of thousands of bees. Its inhabitants comprise one queen, thousands of workers, and a handful of drones.

While her title as queen suggests an all-powerful monarch ruling over a hive of obedient subjects, the reality is that the queen bee is more a slave to the hive than its leader. Her job is to become fertilized by drones and then to lay roughly two thousand eggs a day. She is not involved in the governance of the beehive. She typically lives three to four years and can be mother to 1 million offspring.

The worker bees provide the brains and brawn of the beehive. They are sisters, and the queen is their mother. They build and maintain the hive, forage nectar, produce honey, care for the queen and bee larvae, defend the hive, and locate a new hive site when the existing one becomes crowded. They have a short life of several weeks in summer to a few months in winter.

Drones are the only males in the hive. Their numbers are small, ranging typically in the hundreds. They have one job: to fertilize the queen bee when she flies her nuptial flight. Once they have achieved this goal, they die. Any drones that remain in the hive when winter arrives are driven out by the worker bees.

When conditions in the colony become too crowded, it is time for the colony to split in two. This often happens in spring. When a move is imminent, the worker bees create a dozen larger queen bee cells in the hive. The queen deposits eggs in a number of them, and the worker bees then nurture the larvae with a special nutrient called royal jelly. The larvae evolve into pupae and emerge from their cells as developed queen bees. The entire process from egg-laying to emerging virgin queen takes only sixteen days.

Before the new queens emerge, a subset of worker bees called scouts muster more than half of the colony, including the queen, out of the hive and have them congregate on a nearby tree branch as a swarm. Then a remarkable feat of democratic decision making begins: the community of honeybees will decide collectively where to move. The scouts play the lead role in finding a new home. A hundred or so fan out to explore sites surrounding the swarm. Some travel distances of 5 kilometers (about three miles) or more. They are looking for knot holes in trees or cracks in rock walls. The volume of living space they seek is roughly 20 liters (about twenty-two quarts), a good size to accommodate a new honeybee colony. When a scout finds a possible candidate site, she flies back to the swarm and carries out a waggle dance. Energetic, prolonged waggle dances indicate a good find. The attitude of the dance reveals the direction of the site (for example, it can be found 20 degrees to the left of the sun). The number of waggles indicates distance (for example, six waggles might indicate a distance of 300 meters from the swarm site, roughly 330 yards).

If several surrounding scouts find the message of the dancing bee to hold promise of a good site, they fly to the site to explore it themselves. If they agree it is a good one, they return to the swarm and repeat the energetic waggle dance, thereby recruiting more scouts to explore the site. If they deliver a convincing presentation, more scouts fly to the site to investigate it. If they disagree with the original scout, they either perform a lackluster waggle dance or forgo the dance entirely.

What happens with a process like this is that good sites attract visits from ever-growing numbers of scouts, while weak or mediocre sites attract few if any visitors. Through this process, good sites are distinguished from less desirable ones. At a certain point, when twenty to thirty visiting scouts congregate at the target site concurrently, a decision quorum is reached (Seeley, 2010). This triggers the selection of this site as the new home for the colony. The scouts return to the swarm and initiate a process called piping: all the honeybees in the colony vibrate their wings in order to warm up for a flight to the new site. The loud hum associated with piping also alerts the colony that a decision on a new home has been reached and deliberations on other sites should cease. After an hour or two of piping, the scouts lead the queen bee to the new site with the entire swarm accompanying them. The democratic process of selecting a new site takes anywhere from several hours to one or two days. It is important for the bees to decide on the new site quickly, because they have only enough food stored in their bodies to sustain them for a short period of time.

Meanwhile, at the original hive, a new queen bee reigns. As her queen bee sisters emerge from their cells one by one, she systematically stings them to death so that the hive has only one queen. During a nuptial flight, she is fertilized by a dozen or so drones. Then she returns to the hive and begins laying eggs. Through the laying of new eggs, the original hive population quickly returns to an optimal size.

This democratic decision-making system has served honeybees well for 30 million years. It enables insects with no notable individual intelligence to function effectively with a collective intelligence. Decades of studies by apiologists confirm that the home-finding process described here leads to the optimal selection of the best site for a new hive. Honeybee democracy works! In the honeybee world, Surowiecki's contention holds true: the crowd is wiser than the individual.

It is mind-boggling to witness such an elegant process of high-order thinking among low-order thinkers arising naturally in nature. A review of how the honeybees decide on the site for their new home reveals that their peculiar consensus-building process makes sense—except for one puzzling point: the use of a quorum decision rule to trigger the final decision. The quorum decision rule is a crucial component of the decision process. Without it, honeybees would not be able to bring the decision-making process to closure. So what is the rationale underlying the quorum decision rule?

As noted, a quorum is achieved when twenty to thirty scouts congregate concurrently at a prospective new home. This number of scouts reflects only a portion of the visitors to the site. Others came earlier, then returned to the swarm, where, through their waggle dance, they recruited more visitors. The original scouts visit the site only one, two, or three times, then remain at the swarm. So by the time a quorum of twenty to thirty visitors collects at the site at the same time, this corresponds to visits by many more scouts. Apiologists speculate that after 30 million years of home-hunting experiences, nature has foreordained a quorum of twenty to thirty visiting scouts as the ideal number. It is not an arbitrary value but captures what has worked over the eons. We must recall that the scouts face great urgency in locating a new site for the swarm. They do not have the luxury of spending several days for their search, because members of the swarm will not replenish their nutritional needs until the new site is occupied. Using a quorum-based decision rule, they can come to a decision quickly.

The case of honeybees offers solid evidence of a situation where the crowd operates more wisely than the individual. The functioning of free markets offers additional evidence. Had Charles Mackay had an opportunity to witness honeybee democracy in action, I am sure he would have agreed that under some circumstances, though not many, we can have crowds eschew their propensity for madness and act with sublime wisdom.

8 The Biology of Decision Making

Decisions are made by people. They may be made collectively through elaborate social mechanisms, such as national legislatures, economic markets, and international organizations. They may be made by teams of coworkers, family members, corporate boards, and other collective bodies operating cooperatively, or contrariwise, they may be the outcome of conflict. They may be made by individuals operating alone with no input from others. But ultimately the origin of all decisions, whether collective or individual, traces back to what's going on inside people's heads.

This chapter and the next peek into people's heads to see how they arrive at decisions. I have titled this chapter "The Biology of Decision Making." It focuses on the brain and the neurological processes that underlie decision making in individuals. If you are going to appreciate the role of the brain in decision making, you need to have a sense of how it works, and that is what this chapter addresses. The next chapter, "Toward an Empirically Rooted Understanding of Decision Making," looks at current scientific investigations into decision-making behavior based on neurological and behavioral studies. While philosophers have speculated on the mind and its functioning since the time of Plato twenty-five hundred years ago, only recently have scientific advances in examining the functioning of the brain enabled us to begin systematically studying the behavioral consequences of neurological activity.

The traditional approach to decision making paid little attention to the role of the brain in formulating decisions. The brain is treated as a black box. In this chapter, we peek into the black box to see how it works.

At this time, neuroscientists are at the earliest stages of discovery, and very little is certain. And although scientists and engineers have developed extraordinarily sophisticated technology to look into the brain, we're not quite sure what we see. Popularizers of brain research broadcast all sorts of discoveries that make big news on television and popular Web sites, but the findings are mostly speculation and seldom firm. Frequently, in fact, they are shown to be off-target, but their invalidation seldom makes the news.

BRAIN BASICS

Scientists are obtaining insights into the brain's structure and function at a great rate. But the brain is so complex that even big increases in understanding leave us with meager insights as to how it works. If complete understanding of the brain is visualized as a 1 kilometer journey, we have perhaps traveled a few centimeters. It is hard to say, because at this stage of understanding, we are still traveling through terra incognita. We have little idea of what it takes to fully comprehend the workings of the brain. We don't know the length of the course. Whatever the distance traveled may be, it is meager because the challenge of decoding the brain is formidable.

The typical brain, as I have already noted, contains 100 billion neurons, and each of these is connected to an average of 10,000 other neurons. When the brain processes information, the information is transmitted through neural pathways. Because there are 100 billion neurons to work with, each linked to 10,000 other neurons, there are trillions of potential pathways a datum can travel. Even if you were able to track the path taken by a specific datum, this would not be very enlightening, because human perceptions are formed from countless data flows, each following a unique path. The fact that this light organ can contain and handle so many information channels (100 billion neurons! Trillions of channels!) is astonishing. However, the real mystery is how it can make sense of the overwhelming volume of data it handles each second and bring together disparate data flows into actionable perceptions. Through the conversion of photons to electrochemical pulses traveling through neurons, it enables a human to identify a cow as a cow rather than as a toaster.

This section lays out basic information on what scientists think they know about the structure and function of the brain. The insights they have garnered are rough approximations of the truth. Fifty years from now, neuroscientists will reflect on many of today's findings and speculations with patronizing smiles, as parents do when listening to their children's first explanations of how the world functions.

For all their imperfections, our newly acquired insights on the functioning of the brain have opened our eyes to possibilities that were unimaginable a few years ago. For example, until recently, it was believed that the brain ceased development in childhood: that is, anatomically, the brain you have at the age of thirty is more or less the same one you had when you were an adolescent. Now we know this is not true and that the brain continues to develop through early adulthood. Even in advanced years, the plasticity of the brain enables it to rewire neuronal channels in the event it is damaged.

In order to conserve energy, the brain is constantly taking shortcuts to perceiving things by working from templates drawn from experience. What you think you have perceived is often an artifact of the brain's extrapolations from prior experience and does not capture objective reality.

The more we learn about the brain, the more we marvel at how it works. In this chapter, we look at some key features of the brain that ultimately affect how people make decisions. The chapter provides just a sampling of what we think we know. In the next chapter, I examine the behavioral consequences associated with the way the brain functions.

THE LAZY BRAIN

It may seem ludicrous to call the brain lazy because we know that it is astonishingly busy, processing some 11.2 million bits of information per second (Dijksterhuis and Nordgren, 2006). Yet for all of its activity—actually, because of this activity—the brain is constantly looking for shortcuts to conserve energy. This search is important and has several significant, interrelated consequences. First, as noted earlier, the brain works with templates in order to save energy. As you experience phenomena, the brain is steadily trying to match your current experience with previous experiences that are captured in those templates so that it does not need to process the incoming stream of data de novo. Second, because it is trying to address new situations with template solutions, it creates an environment of resistance to change: it wants to stick to the templates. New scenarios demand the expenditure of more energy, so it seems better to stay with old solutions, if possible, in order to conserve energy. Third, the shortcuts prevent people from experiencing the "real world." Everything you experience undergoes intermediation by the brain, reflecting your experiences or projections of future scenarios.

Template Solutions

Neuroscientist Robert Burton (2008) calls the nexus of connected neurons in the brain the *hidden layer*, a term he borrows from the discipline of artificial intelligence. The hidden layer comprises the nexus of connected neurons in the neural network and the rules that govern the firing of neurons. These rules focus on functioning efficiently. And in order to operate efficiently, the brain relies heavily on prior learning. If a newly perceived stimulus has been encountered before, it sees no need to reinvent an energy-consuming strategy to deal with it. So when the hidden layer encounters a new stimulus, the operating rules focus on whether this stimulus has been experienced before.

For example, a loud bang might tie to the following prior experiences: the sound of a firecracker exploding on July 4, a gunshot heard at a firing range, a balloon popping at a party, or a book falling onto a desk. Meanwhile, other support information is being captured and processed by the brain, and the loud bang is assessed accordingly. If it is night and you are alone in a dangerous neighborhood, the bang might be associated with gunshots, and your brain (specifically, the amygdala) will put you on hyperalert status. If you are in a library, the loud bang might be associated with a book hitting a desk, something that the experienced brain might treat as so unnoteworthy that the bang might not even be raised to the level of consciousness and may be treated simply as background noise.

The brain's search for efficiency has major impacts on how decisions are made. The brain builds your perceptions on experience. When you encounter a related experience at a future time, the brain recalls the prior experience and uses it as the foundation of perception. Rather than handle each experience as a brand-new event, the brain saves energy by employing templates to anticipate appropriate actions and fill in the blanks. If the current reality differs from the template, the brain revises the template accordingly. It learns and consumes additional power in doing so.

Owing to its lazy nature, the brain often forms perceptions along predetermined lines. In doing so, it constrains the decision-maker's vision of what is transpiring. It's something like a tourist stuck with the limited options of a prix fixe menu in a restaurant that serves limitless entrees. When facing a prix fixe menu, tourists do not encounter a decision-making challenge: they get one glass of the house wine, their soup is preselected, they get to choose between beef and chicken, and their vegetables are preselected. Often their biggest decision-making dilemma is whether to order flan or gelato for dessert.

Resistance to Change

The brain's corner cutting means that the range of options facing decision-makers is circumscribed, defining a decision-choice comfort zone that they will be reluctant to abandon. It encourages resistance to change rather than breakthrough thinking. When decision-makers go through a decision-making process, either consciously or unconsciously, the brain works to frame problems in accordance with template-rooted perceptions. This is important, because how problems are framed defines how they will be approached and solved.

In fact, the template-driven framing of problems does not usually lead to bad decisions. The brain employs templates to transform raw stimuli into perceptions because it works. If it didn't work, evolutionary forces would have created a different kind of brain from what we have. This feature of the brain's functioning makes sense. Most of the stimuli the brain addresses are recurring. If it approached each stimulus as if it were a brand-new happening, the brain would quickly become bogged down in its attempts to separate the wheat from the chaff. Most problems people encounter fit recurring patterns that can be captured in templates. For example, when you are walking on a slippery surface—ice on a stairway, water on a marble floor—you unconsciously adjust your walking style to avoid slipping. You function in accordance with a "slippery surface" template.

It is important to note that the brain does not handle all the events it encounters with template shortcuts. When it encounters truly novel situations that do not fit prior experience, it processes the event as a new experience and adds it to its storehouse of templates for future use. It is only when trekking familiar ground that it reverts to using templates to conserve energy. Of course, most of the ground the brain treks is familiar, because we encounter very little in our daily experiences that is truly unique. As noted in Ecclesiastes 1:9, "What has been is what will be, and what has been done is what will be done; there is nothing new under the sun."

Reversion to templates is not salubrious in two obvious situations. First, serious problems can arise when the brain misreads a situation, handling it in a predetermined way as if it were a well-known recurring event although it really represents a new experience that requires novel action. For example, let's say that while in the library, the bang sound your brain attributes to a dropped book is in fact a gunshot! You may be in danger and need to respond appropriately.

Second, opportunities for innovation may be lost if the brain directs decision-makers to follow paths requiring standard solutions to familiar challenges. In a static social or business environment, this may be a good thing, because in a static world, often your job is to maintain things as they have always been maintained. However, in a dynamic environment of rapid change, decisions guided by the brain's conservatism can harm the interests of decision-makers and their constituents. In warfare, the army that fights using the same strategies and weapons of the last war is at a disadvantage when confronted by an army that embraces innovation. The same circumstance holds true in business: the company that builds its strategies on milking cash cows finds that eventually the milk runs dry and business goes to the players who leverage change to their advantage.

It is difficult to overcome the brain's tendency to stick with template responses to stimuli. Visualize a river cutting into soil and rock to create a riverbed. The longer a river proceeds along one course, the deeper it cuts into an established channel and the harder it is for the water to jump the channel and travel another course. The Grand Canyon is an extreme example. With canyon walls that in places stand more than one mile above the Colorado River, it is difficult to visualize how the river can overflow its banks and follow a new course. As it is with rivers following well-established channels, so it is with the brain adhering to template responses to stimuli.

Elusive Reality

Through the brain's efforts to function efficiently, human perception does not capture reality exactly; it approximates it. This fact strikes at the foundation of our faith in science, which holds that truth is ultimately discerned through observation, a perspective that is called empiricism. A key tenet of empiricism is that the only thing you can trust is what you observe directly. But neuroscience suggests that you cannot even trust that.

The elusive character of human perception can be convincingly demonstrated with an example from baseball (Burton, 2008). Consider a top-rated batter who is facing a top-rated pitcher in a baseball game. Let's say the pitcher can propel the ball forward at speeds of ninety miles an hour. This means that it takes less than half a second from the time the ball leaves his hand until it lands in the catcher's mitt if it is not hit (a very fast pitch can take only 0.36 seconds).

There is a delay between the time an action physically takes place and the action is perceived by the brain. Photons of the pitcher and his pitch pass through the eye's lens and hit the batter's retina. From the retina, the data travel along the optic nerve and are forwarded to the occipital lobe (via the thalamus), where they are converted into preimages; then these data are transmitted to the cerebral cortex, where they are interpreted and turned into a perception. When accounting for the delay between physical action and human perception on a very fast pitch, it turns out that the ball has already traveled nine feet toward the batter at the moment the batter first sees the ball leaving the pitcher's hand. If the batter is going to swing at the ball, this intent needs to be processed by the brain and sent to the appropriate muscles. More time passes.

Simple arithmetic suggests that the batter does not have enough time to track the ball's trajectory visually and react appropriately. Mark Changizi (2010) estimates that it takes about a tenth of a second to process the visual information. By the time a fast-thrown ball is truly perceived by the batter and the body's muscles have been ordered to respond appropriately, it would already be just short of the catcher's mitt. Weekend batters who have tried to hit baseballs pitched by machines that throw fastballs have experienced this reality. They find that the ball is already passing them as they begin their swing. So how do great hitters consistently connect with the ball and knock it into the stands?

The consensus among neuroscientists is that the batter's brain is able to read the visual cues coming from the pitcher's windup and ball release and anticipates the ball's trajectory. It processes the data so that the batter "sees" the oncoming ball sufficiently early to enable him to swing and hit it. Only he does not see the actual ball; rather, he sees the brain's image of the ball following an anticipated trajectory. For exceptionally gifted batters who have trained hard and have carefully studied the pitcher's prior performance, the ball's trajectory is computed more accurately than could be done by supercomputers using the most advanced formulas of motion provided by physicists. In this case, the batter's response to the pitch is more akin to a reflex than a decision.

Brain trickery is a common experience. Consider that when observer A and observer B view an object, they do not perceive exactly the same thing because of their own brain's intermediation. Vision and perception are not the same thing. The vision phase of the seeing process is fairly straightforward, akin to a camera capturing and storing an image: photons strike the retina, and the resulting data are sent to the occipital lobe via the thalamus through the optic nerve. In the perception phase, the cortex interprets the data forwarded to it from the occipital lobe. The data are interpreted as they travel down neural pathways. The brain determines which pathways a datum travels according to the experiences of the individual observer. Given the countless pathways tied to countless individual experiences, it is clear that the data for observer A will travel different paths from the data for observer B and that the perception of the object will be different in some degree for the two observers. No two people see the exact same thing. The point is that reality lies in the eyes of the beholder. More accurately, it resides in a beholder's cerebral cortex.

The ephemeral nature of reality is an old idea. Plato wrote that what humans perceive is a dim reflection of what is real (Plato, 2004). What is real is captured in what he called *forms*. The chair you see is an approximation of an ideal chair-form, and the cup you hold an approximation of an ideal cup-form. While this idea of ideal forms may sound silly and can be written off as the speculations of naive philosophers in a prescientific world, modern science offers us possibilities that are more fanciful than anything Plato could have cooked up. An intriguing current theory of vision is that what we see is not literal reality, but rather a probability distribution of past retinal images associated with a visual stimulus (Purves and Lotto, 2003). In other words, the visual perceptions we experience can be likened loosely to averages of retinal images we have experienced in our lives. What we see is *not* what we get.

Our growing understanding of how the brain works supports the view of philosophers who have long argued that humans cannot perceive objective reality firsthand. Scientists have struggled with this issue for centuries. In 1637, in his *Discourse on Method* (1965), René Descartes argued for complete skepticism when dealing with perceptions: "Seeing that our senses sometimes deceive us . . . and because some men err in reasoning . . . I was convinced that I was as open to error as any other. I supposed that all the objects that had ever entered into my mind when awake, had in them no more truth than the illusions of my dreams." Searching for the most fundamental truth that he could articulate with certainty, he uttered his famous dictum: "I think, therefore I am."

In recent times, Norwood Russell Hanson has played a leading role in articulating the view that perception is defined contextually. Hanson was educated as a physicist and held two Ph.D.s: the first from Oxford in 1955 and the second from Cambridge in 1956. During World War II, he was a marine fighter pilot in the Pacific, where he earned the Distinguished Flying Cross as a combat pilot. After completing his studies abroad and returning to the United States, he received a fellowship to serve at the Institute for Advanced Study in Princeton, Einstein's bailiwick from 1933 until his death in 1955. Later, he established the Department of the History and Logic of Science at the University of Indiana, then moved on to Yale University. He died in 1968 at the age of forty-three when the Grumman Hellcat he owned and piloted crashed in fog.

In the United States, Hanson turned his attention to the history and philosophy of science. He argued strongly that the facts do not speak for themselves, even in the sciences (Hanson, 1958). Rather, they are interpreted contextually. If a thirteenth-century scientist and a twentieth-century scientist observe a sunrise, he asked, do they see the same thing? He notes that it is tempting to say yes, because in both cases photons from the sun strike photoreceptors in the retinas of both scientists, which forward the sensation to the brain, where the data are converted into perceptions. But Hanson answered the question with a no, noting that the thirteenth-century scientist operated in a world where truth held that the earth stood at the center of the universe, while the views of the twentieth-century scientist were colored by Copernicus's assertion that the sun sat at the center of the solar system, Newton's laws of motion, and Einstein's views on relativity.

To Hanson, context affects perception. To him it was inconceivable that the thirteenth-century scientist would view a sunrise the same way as a modern scientist owing to the radically different context in which each operated.

In his 1958 work, *Patterns of Discovery*, Hanson anticipated the research of neurologists four decades later, when he stated: "Seeing is an experience. A retinal reaction is only a photochemical excitation . . . People, not their eyes, see. Cameras and eyeballs are blind."

VISUAL ILLUSIONS: WHAT YOU SEE ISN'T WHAT YOU GET

You don't need to be a neuroscientist to encounter evidence supporting some of the points raised in this discussion. You need only draw on your experiences with the visual illusions you have encountered throughout your life. Visual illusions (often called optical illusions) provide evidence that brains intermediate reality by cutting corners to conserve energy, working from templates, and filling in blank spaces.

People have been fascinated by visual illusions for a long time. Artists have employed them for their own purposes for millennia. One of the best-known stories about illusion in art comes to us from Greece's Golden Age (fifth century B.C.E.). Two artists challenge each other to see who can create the most realistic painting. Artist One (Zeuxis) paints berries that are so realistic that birds fly down and try to eat them. Artist One says, "Let's see you beat that." Artist Two (Parrhasius) responds, "Wait until you see my painting. Pull the curtain aside and see what lies behind it." Artist Two was declared the winner of the contest after Artist One unsuccessfully attempted to part the curtain. Artist Two's painting was the curtain!

Artists in the Byzantine Empire (the Greeks again) employed visual illusions on a grand scale in some of their large religious mosaics that decorated the interiors of their cathedrals. The ceilings and soaring walls of these cathedrals were often covered with religious scenes. Because the upper reaches of the cathedral were far from observers down in the sanctuary, artists consciously distorted the images they created to eliminate the shrinking effects of distance: heads of depicted people would be enlarged, while feet would be scaled down. The figures appeared balanced to those looking at the images from the sanctuary floor because the effects of distance had been adjusted visually.

Since the time of the Renaissance, artists have had fun with trompe l'oeil (which means "deceive the eye" in French). Its most common form entails painting objects in two dimensions that appear to be three-dimensional. When walking through old palaces in France and Italy, tourists should look carefully at the cornices that run under the ceilings in many grand rooms. They appear to be three-dimensional moldings, but there is a good chance that they have been painted onto the wall to establish a trompe l'oeil effect. Just for fun.

Trompe l'oeil; deceive the eye. Yes, it is possible to trick the eye, particularly when the images of three-dimensional objects are projected onto a two-dimensional retina. However, we recognize that in many cases it may be that the eye is not being deceived. Rather, it is the brain that is deceived. This happens when the brain takes data forwarded to it by the eye and misinterprets them, in which case the proper French expression would be *trompe le cerveau* (deceive the brain).

Almost everyone views visual illusions as being interesting diversions. One of the best-known visual illusion pieces, originating in the nineteenth century, is an image that when viewed one way looks like an old hag, while when viewed differently appears to be an elegant young lady (Figure 8.1). I remember encountering this image as a boy and trying to see how quickly I could flip from one perspective to the other, then back to the first, then to the second, and so on. To me it was magical to have a single image portray two opposing images.

Visual illusions are more than interesting diversions, because they offer insights into the functioning of the brain. When object A looks substantially smaller than object B but is shown by objective measurement to be larger, we must acknowledge that the brain has led us astray. When object X seems dimmer than object Y, yet objective measurement shows them to possess equal luminance, we have more evidence of the brain's capacity to be tricked as it employs shortcuts to do its job.

The following section looks at a handful of specific well-known visual illusions in order to illustrate the brain's capacity to be deceived. Scientists have different theories of why we experience these illusions. One thing that seems certain is that different types of visual illusions have different proximate causes. For example, some visual trickery may be tied to distortions created when three-dimensional objects are projected onto a two-dimensional retina. In this instance,

Figure 8.1 Old Hag or Young Lady?

we experience bona-fide trompe l'oeil: the eye itself is being tricked (although you would think that a truly smart brain should be able to work around such distortions). In other cases, the visual deception may be rooted in context: if you place a baby in a room where furniture, windows, toys, and other accoutrements have been scaled down by a factor of two or three, the baby will look like a giant. In yet other cases, when the brain possesses inadequate data to see a complete image or when it is plain lazy and relies on templates, the visual illusions may entail the brain's using best guesses to fill in the blanks.

Some of the most intriguing arguments along this last line are offered by the neuroscientist Mark Changizi (2010), who believes that the brain is steadily cranking out visual guesses of what will happen in our environment one-tenth of a second from now in order to compensate for delays of one-tenth of a second in processing visual data. To Changizi, a broad range of visual illusions can be explained by this phenomenon. In the next section, I provide an interesting example that Changizi uses to support this view.

Of course, some visual miscues are simply tied to the way the brain is hard-wired to handle visual information. We know, for example, that when visual data are sent from the occipital lobe to the cerebral cortex, the data travel along different pathways that handle different types of information: information on the location of the objects being observed travels on an upper pathway along the top of the brain through the parietal lobe, while information on the basic content of the images travels along a lower pathway through the temporal lobes above the ears. We also know that visual data are coded in different ways (for example, data on human faces are given special treatment; data involving images of moving objects are processed differently from data for stationary objects). As flexible as the brain is, it is certain that as with any process based on well-defined procedures, there are exceptional circumstances that the procedures are ill equipped to handle properly.

EXAMPLES OF VISUAL ILLUSIONS

It seems as if there is no end to the number of ways the brain can trick us into seeing what is not there. The Internet is rich in providing illustrations of a wide variety of visual illusions. Some are rooted in misperceptions of color, others to variations in light intensity (called luminance), others result from strange animation, and still others are tied to misconstrued context. If visual illusions were not so abundant, magicians would be out of business. Visual illusions are easy to access on the Internet: simply type the words *optical illusion* or visual illusion into a search engine, and you will encounter many well-executed sites. The great danger of these visual illusions is that viewing them can become addictive.

In this section, we look at a small number of well-known visual illusions that provide a glimpse into how the brain functions when dealing with stimuli from the outside world. The implications for understanding decision making are substantial. Philosophers can argue as to whether there is an objective reality that defines the world. However, an examination of the visual illusions that humans routinely encounter makes us recognize that on a practical level, the mechanics of perception place comprehension of objective reality beyond the capability of humans. We can move no further forward than our brains allow us.

Filling in the Blanks with Established Images

There is agreement among a large number of neuroscientists and ophthalmologists that a brain accumulates a storehouse of images that it draws on when creating percepts that serve as their "owner's" visualization of reality. There is less agreement on what the storehouse contains. On the one hand, it could be a limited inventory of a thousand basic shapes hardwired in our brains, such as triangles, squares, rhomboids, and so on. I recall reading once that if you live in New York City and want to keep pigeons off your balcony, you should paint squiggly lines on the floor of the balcony, because the visual systems of pigeons store snake images for defense purposes, and pigeons and other birds will stay away from your balcony to avoid being eaten by what they see to be hungry snakes.

Purves and Lotto (2003) suggest that everything you see reflects a statistical distribution of visual images you have accumulated over your life. In their opinion, all the images you see as you go about your business are some kind of statistical average of what you have seen before.

Whether you subscribe to the small storehouse model of perception, or the all-images-are-statistical-artifacts model, it is hard to deny that the brain uses stored images in some manner to form percepts.

Figure 8.2 offers evidence of the brain's capacity to employ template images to fill in the blanks. In Figure 8.2a, we see six items arranged haphazardly on the page. When looking at them in this state, we encounter no discernable pattern. However, when we rearrange the six items, as in Figure 8.2b, we clearly see a white square superimposed over another square, and both superimposed over two black circles. Careful consideration of the image shows that no squares have been drawn. However, the brain sees squares. The white box is constituted from empty space. The boxes seem totally palpable, but that is because the brain has made them so. This visual illusion supports that contention that the brain draws upon a storehouse of images.

Filling in the Blanks for Events That Have Not Yet Happened

Earlier, we examined what happens when a batter faces an oncoming baseball that is traveling ninety miles an hour. Knowledge of the reaction time needed to process visual information and translate this into muscular action suggests that

Figure 8.2 Seeing What Is Not There: (a) Six Objects with No Pattern
(b) Six Objects with an Illusion of Squares

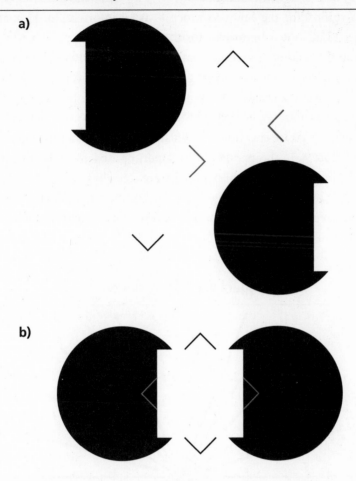

the batter does not have enough time to connect with the ball except by chance. What appears to be occurring is that the brain anticipates the ball's trajectory, and this is what the high-performing batter sees—not the true flight of the ball but the brain's image of the ball following a predicted trajectory. In this case, the brain is filling in the blanks not to conserve energy, but in order to provide information that will enable its "owner" to respond effectively to challenges arising in the environment.

Mark Changizi and his colleagues maintain that the brain does this steadily during our waking hours (Changizi, 2010). They calculate a neural lag of one-tenth of a second for the brain to process visual information. Humans are in constant motion, so it is important for the brain to anticipate what might transpire during the one-tenth second of missing time. Thus, as you walk down the street, what you see is the brain's best guess of what will eventuate one-tenth of a second from now. In a sense, you are always living in the future.

According to Changizi, evidence of this anticipatory vision is found in some of the visual illusions we encounter. To illustrate this, consider the Hering illusion shown in Figure 8.3. The parallel lines superimposed over the radiating lines appear to be bowed outward although they are straight lines. Changizi's hypothesis is that the radiating lines suggest forward motion to the brain. Let's say the parallel lines represent the sides of a doorway you are entering while walking forward. As you pass through the door, the sides of the door at eye level appear

Figure 8.3 Hering Illusion

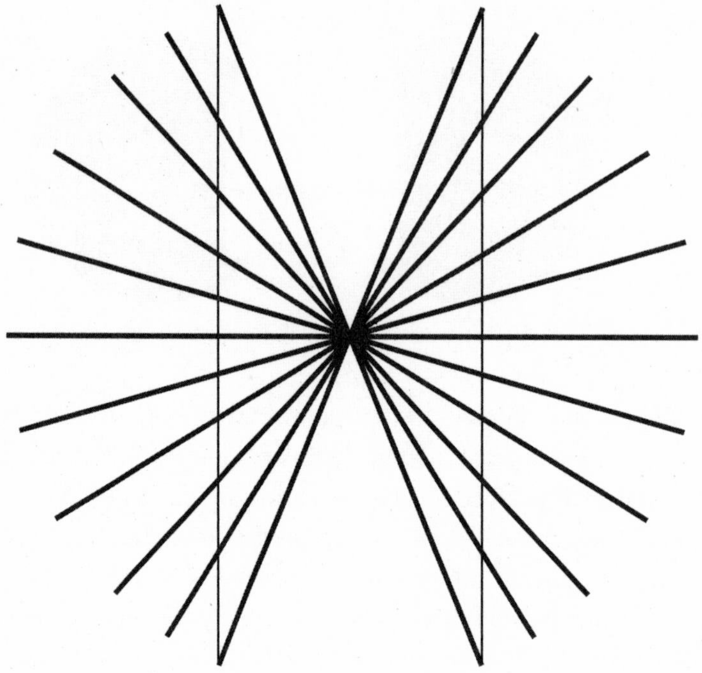

to bow out while the sides toward the upper and lower reaches of the door curve in. It's simply a matter of perspective. The Hering illusion suggests that the brain is anticipating what you will see one-tenth of a second from now as you pass through the parallel lines. If Changizi's speculation is correct, this supplies evidence of the brain's steady employment of anticipatory vision.

When Things Aren't Quite Aligned

In Figure 8.4, the horizontal lines running across the rows of black and white squares on the top portion of the image appear mildly curved, while the lines on the bottom portion of the image appear straight. Actually all the lines are straight. In fact, each row of black and white boxes is identical to every other row. (I can guarantee this because I drew this image with graphics software.)

Note that the top seven rows of black and white boxes are slightly out of line with each other, while the bottom four rows are aligned perfectly in a checkerboard pattern. In processing the image, the brain has no problem dealing with the consistent order of the perfectly aligned black and white boxes in the bottom rows. Consequently, it detects that the lines running across each row are straight. However, the brain has difficulty handling the out-of-line rows on the top portion

Figure 8.4 Illusion of Curved Lines Caused by Pattern Disruption

of the image. If you move a row of boxes to the right or left, the straight line will appear to bend upward or downward. This illusion suggests that the brain has difficulty handling scenarios that do not match its predetermined sense of order. In this case, it has a tough time seeing well-ordered straight lines when handling the misaligned squares.

Compensating for Environmental Conditions: Example 1

Figure 8.5 offers an especially impressive visual illusion, one that illustrates trompe le cerveau at its most powerful. When you look at Figure 8.5a, it seems clear that the luminance of the three stars differs, with the star in the upper-left

Figure 8.5 Luminance Affected by Background Shading: (a) Illusion of Differing Luminance of Stars (b) Equal Luminance of Stars

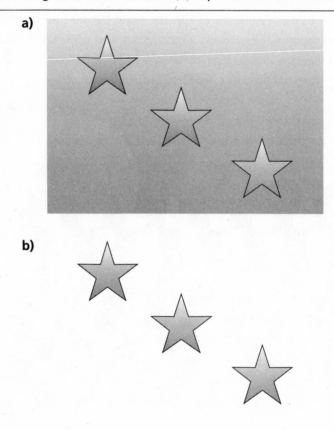

corner having the darkest hue and the star in the bottom-right corner having the lightest. In fact, the three pictured stars are identical. There are no differences in hues. This is seen when the gradient background is removed (Figure 8.5b).

What is happening here is that the brain is compensating for ambient lighting, perhaps to strengthen the contrast between the observed object and its background or perhaps to make it easier to perceive the object's details. When the background hue is light, the brain creates a darkened image of the star in the foreground, strengthening the contrast between the star and the background. When the background hue is dark, the brain creates an image of the star that appears lighter than it really is. It is roughly analogous to the way camera light meters open or close the diameter of the lens diaphragm that brings light into the camera. When an object is underlit, the diaphragm opens; when it is overlit, the diaphragm closes. It is understandable why evolution would have contributed to this phenomenon: when walking through a dark jungle, it is helpful to highlight a tiger lurking in the brambles, or to darken the tiger's form in a snowy field to raise awareness of its presence.

Compensating for Environmental Conditions: Example 2

Figure 8.6a is one that causes many people to reach for their rulers to confirm that line segments AB and BC are indeed the same length. Segment AB looks longer because the parallelogram it is embedded in is larger than the parallelogram containing segment BC. What we encounter here is the same effect as with the illusion referred to earlier, where a baby sitting in a room with scaled-down furniture will look like a giant. When segment ABC is viewed outside the confines of the two parallelograms (Figure 8.6b), it is immediately evident that segments AB and BC are the same length.

Seeing Things as Three-Dimensional Objects

Figure 8.7 illustrates a variant of the Shepard tabletop illusion, one of my favorites. It shows two benches. The left one clearly appears squatter than the one on the right, with a broader bench top. In fact, the size and shape of the two bench tops are identical. Skeptical readers can trace the dimensions of the right bench top onto a clear transparent acetate sheet, then place the traced drawing over the left

Figure 8.6 Effects of Context: (a) Illusion of Varying Line Lengths (b) Equal Line Lengths

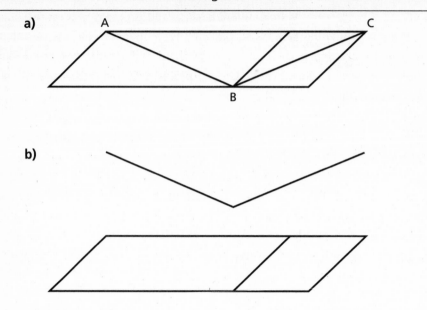

Figure 8.7 Park Bench Variant of Shepard's Tabletop Illusion

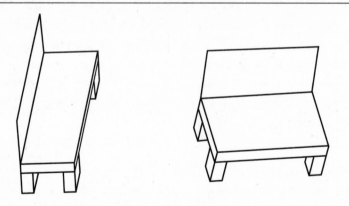

Source: Adapted from Roger N. Shepard, *Mind Sights: Original Visual Illusions, Ambiguities, and Other Anomalies, With a Commentary on the Play of Mind in Perception and Art*, New York: W. H. Freeman & Co., 1990, p. 43.

bench top. The two will match perfectly. Even though I know what is happening here, I find that the fully rational portion of my brain is trumped by raw perception (and deception) processed in another part of the brain.

The illusion is tied to the portrayal of the two benches as three-dimensional objects. The eye-brain visual system sees them in three-dimensional space, and it interprets the right bench as extending back in space, while the left bench stands in the foreground.

BRAIN DECEPTION BEYOND VISUAL ILLUSIONS

I have focused on visual illusions because they palpably reinforce an important theme of this chapter, which is that there is nothing straightforward about how the brain creates perceptions. In its efforts to handle enormously complex tasks, it employs a rich variety of coping strategies to deal with seemingly limitless permutations of stimuli. Its neuronal components contribute to making decisions that range from lifesaving executive decisions ("Jump left out of the oncoming car's path!"), to the humblest background decisions needed to maintain the neuronal machinery. One consequence of the brain's processing contortions is that they yield constant deception. The deceptions are not a willful effort to lead people astray. Rather, they are a natural consequence of the brain's approach to conserving energy and handling complexity.

By themselves, visual illusions do not provide absolute evidence of how the brain works. However, they give some credence to a number of hypotheses we explore in this chapter:

- The brain cuts corners to conserve energy, which entails employing templates whenever possible.

- When it encounters gaps of information, the brain fills in the blanks with its best guesses.

- Owing to its proclivity to favor templates, the brain operates conservatively by resisting nontemplate solutions.

- Everything we experience is intermediated by the brain: we do not perceive reality directly.

When addressing visual illusions, we are concentrating on tricks of the eye and brain (trompe l'oeil and trompe le cerveau, respectively), harmless diversions that are instructive at the same time. But sometimes the brain creates a patently false reality that goes beyond innocent visual tricks, as with hallucinations and delusions. The false reality can be triggered chemically or psychologically or can be tied to brain damage. Of particular interest to this book's primary concern—decision making—is how the brain can convince us we are absolutely correct in our assessments of things even when it can be demonstrated that we are not. Consider how many battles were lost, ill-fated products launched, and marriages ruined because key decision-makers were totally convinced of the correctness of their incorrect insights.

In his best-selling book, *The Man Who Mistook His Wife for a Hat* (1998), the neurologist Oliver Sacks uses cases from his clinical practice to describe twenty-four instances where neurological disorders contribute to hallucinatory and delusional behavior. He launches his book with the story of an accomplished professor of music, Dr. P., who has developed visual agnosia, also known as face blindness. Dr. P. cannot recognize people from their faces. On occasion, he confuses inanimate objects with faces and faces with inanimate objects. For example, as he prepares to leave Dr. Sack's office toward the end of one visit, he mistakes his wife's head for his hat and, grabbing it, tries to lift it to his head. On another occasion, he mistakes a fire hydrant for a little child. Visual agnosia can be triggered by a head injury, brain lesions, strokes, tumors, or an illness that affects the brain. Dr. P.'s ailment falls under the umbrella of delusional misidentification syndrome.

Burton (2008) points out that an interesting feature of brain-rooted delusions is that the people who suffer from them are fully convinced of the correctness of their outlook, even when confronted with clear evidence to the contrary. He discusses the case of Ms. B., a patient recovering from viral encephalitis (an inflammation of the brain), who suffers from Cotard syndrome. She believes that she is dead. True, she is ambulatory, can hold a conversation, and can eat a meal, but she nonetheless believes that she is dead. When her doctor has her listen to her heartbeat through a stethoscope, she admits that her heart is indeed beating, but still her feeling of being dead is so strong that it outweighs any evidence demonstrating she is alive. After Ms. B. fully recovers from her bout with viral encephalitis, the symptoms of Cotard syndrome disappear.

To Burton, the most interesting feature of Ms. B.'s story is the fact that she has a strong feeling of certainty about being dead despite contrary evidence. In his book, *On Being Certain*, he fully explores the feeling of certainty that people possess. He notes that schizophrenics have feelings of certainty about the often bizarre subjective realities they experience. The voices they hear and the images they see are completely real to them. Similarly, he notes that the hallucinations experienced by people who take psychotropic drugs are real to them. Hallucinations can even be induced when brain surgeons touch different areas of the exposed brain with a probe.

Burton argues that the brain can deceive people into feeling absolutely certain about things that are not true or real. The examples I have provided are tied to clear-cut hallucinations or delusions. But deceptions are also common in the realm of the normal. Burton holds that the feeling of certainty that normal people have about ordinary events is identical to the feeling possessed by people who are delusional. Examples from ordinary life include things like being certain that Aunt Sylvie wore a yellow flower to cousin Myron's wedding (photos reveal that it was a red flower) or being certain that in your favorite movie, the hero's sister slaps the hero's best friend (a replay of the DVD shows that she slaps the florist). The frailty of feeling certain about something has been exposed in numerous studies that demonstrate that witness testimony in legal cases can be highly unreliable and that false memories of bad childhood experiences can ruin the fabric of families.

The feeling of uncertainty is not a mere curiosity; like visual illusions, it provides insights into the functioning of the brain. Burton (2008) believes that the feeling of certainty is a special function of the brain that operates outside the realm of consciousness. He writes: "Despite how certainty feels, it is neither a conscious choice nor even a thought process. Certainty and similar states of 'knowing what we know' arise out of involuntary brain mechanisms that, like love or anger, function independently of reason" (p. xiii).

It is in fact inured to appeals of reason and logic, which leads Burton to speculate that it has neurophysiological roots independent of conscious deliberations. He writes: "When such a sense of conviction overrides obvious logical inconsistencies or scientific evidence, what is happening? Is it possible that there is an underlying neurophysiological basis for the specific sensation of *feeling right* or of *being right* that is so powerful that ordinary rational thought *feels* either wrong or irrelevant?" (p. 20).

If this speculation is correct, it has major implications for decision making. It tells us that although we may feel certain that we have a full understanding of the facts that will lead to a decision, we cannot count on this feeling of certainty to guarantee that we have got things right. It also tells us that although we may be absolutely certain that the decision we are making is the right one, this sense of certainty may be misleading. When people insist they are right when it can be demonstrated they are wrong, they are not being arbitrarily pig-headed; their outlook is being controlled by a feeling of certainty that lies outside the cognitive realm and is tied to neurophysiological factors.

THE MATURING BRAIN

Much of the brain's functioning has implications for decision making. The functioning of the olfactory nerve will certainly affect a professional chef's culinary choices when selecting fresh cilantro. The malfunctioning of the auditory nerve may cause an executive to mishear important components of a briefing, leading to a misunderstanding of important facts. Reduced levels of dopamine may influence an individual's attitude toward life and lead her to question the worthiness of a simple decision. Each of these examples illustrates how brain function can affect decision making. If a writer were to write about all the aspects of the brain's effects on decision making, it would be easy to put together a large book on the subject. My goal here is not to explore the whole realm of the brain's impact on decision making, but to focus on the big picture: to acquire a general sense of how the basic functioning of the brain influences the making of conscious decisions. Consequently, I am restricting my coverage of brain basics to one final topic.

This last brain basics topic examines how the brain develops and matures. Recently, neuroscientists have made discoveries that are changing our views about how the brain physically becomes a brain. Many of the new insights have substantially updated our understanding of the anatomy of the brain, focusing particularly on the development of gray matter and white matter in the cerebral cortex (respectively, the thinking and perceiving parts of the brain). The traditional view has been that the brain grows rapidly in our earliest years and that sometime during adolescence, growth stops. Thanks to advances in functional magnetic resonance imaging (fMRI) technology, which provides colorful maps of the brain that have bright red, blue, yellow, and green colors, indicating brain activity, scientists have discovered that from the time of conception through the mid- to late twenties, the nervous system and its brain undergo dramatic transformations.

By the age of two, the brain reaches 80 percent of its adult weight. Three years later, at age five, it reaches 90 percent of its adult weight, and at age six, 95 percent of its adult weight (Lenroot and Giedd, 2006). The brain grows quickly. In the early stages, there is an astonishing proliferation of neuronal branches—the so-called gray matter. This process is called arboration (referring to the growth of branches on trees). Then somewhere around the age of eleven or twelve, a grand pruning endeavor commences, and a significant portion of gray matter is dramatically cut away. When this trimming of gray matter was discovered, scientists were understandably surprised, since it appeared to suggest a process of dumbing down in humans. Further reflection, accompanied by further studies, led to a different conclusion.

What appears to be happening parallels the pruning activities of gardeners. In order to strengthen the plants under their charge, gardeners cut away branches that interfere with plants' future development. These branches add no value; in fact, they detract from the plant's strength. So it appears to be with the pruning of gray matter. The rapid growth of neurons yields a bramble of neuronal branches. By early adolescence, evolution has declared it is time to clear the mess. Neuroscientists generally believe that the neuronal branches that have not been used are discarded, while those that have been used are kept—the so-called use-it-or-lose-it theory. Recent research suggests that the pruning occurs selectively in different areas of the brain at different times, with initial pruning occurring in the parietal region at around the age of ten and final pruning beginning in the late teens in the temporal regions.

If the use-it-or-lose-it theory is correct, it gives rise to interesting questions. If young Bobby is very active in sports but does little to strengthen his reasoning skills (for example, by reading books, studying nature, and building things), will the neuronal pruning hardwire superior motor skills in his brain and leave him at a disadvantage in the arena of reasoning? Or if little Natuski spends a large part of her day playing the violin from the time she is three years old and eschews other physical activity, will the neuronal pruning hardwire violin-playing skills in her brain and leave her with average sports capabilities?

Many neuroscientists and psychologists believe this is what happens with neuronal pruning, pointing out that nearly all of history's great musicians and athletes were heavily engaged in building their special skills when they were young, during the crucial prepruning years. Similarly, men and women who became great scientists tended to spend their prepruning years with a disproportionate interest in exploring the world around them and solving puzzles. By the time the pruning process begins, the brains of life's superperformers have experienced substantial activity in certain areas of effort—sports, dance, science, chess—and from this time forward, their strengths are pronounced in these areas.

Another exciting finding has been the discovery that even as gray matter is pruned and its mass reduced, white matter experiences a steady growth through the mid- to late twenties. White matter (technically myelin) is the fatty sheath that envelops neurons. It can increase the information-processing capabilities of neurons by a factor of one hundred. The growth of myelin suggests that the brain is functioning more efficiently. The continued growth of myelin into the twenties correlates with the maturation of personalities and the growth of cognitive capabilities. Long before scientists knew anything about myelin, psychoanalysts such as Freud and Jung noted that psychoanalysis should not be carried out on young subjects because the human personality does not fully gel until the midtwenties. Their clinically rooted insights anticipated recent discoveries of the brain's evolving anatomy.

What appears to be happening is that from conception through adolescence, the human brain develops its core functions in the same manner as with other mammals. For humans and other mammals, brain development begins from the bottom up and from the back forward. Through this development process, the brain establishes its basic functions. Then in early adolescence, the human brain moves on to acquire higher cognitive functions. It gradually transcends its core features and begins the process of transforming itself into a mature organ capable of employing good judgment and solid reasoning capabilities to make decisions. For a typical person, the process is completed sometime in the mid- to late twenties. At this point, the adolescent has evolved into a mature adult.

Much has been written in the popular science literature about this phenomenon, suggesting that it explains how humans progress from thoughtless and selfish adolescents into mature adults. Some writers, including a number of well-known neuroscientists, talk about the distinction between the teenage and adult brain. The propensity of teenagers to behave impulsively and sometimes destructively is correlated with underdevelopment of the prefrontal cortex (among other things), which is associated with self-control and reasoning. Add to this the fact that through the pruning process, the brain is rewiring itself to play to its "owner's" strengths, and that with the growth of white matter, it is functioning with increasing efficiency, you find that the mature brain looks quite different from the teenage brain.

Among the best-known studies distinguishing adolescent and adult brain processes are those conducted by Harvard's Deborah Yurgelun-Todd. In one study, she carried out fMRI brain scans on sixteen normal adolescents whose ages ranged from eleven to seventeen years old (Yurgelun-Todd, 2002). She showed her subjects photographs of fear-filled faces. Interestingly, the younger adolescents did not detect fear when they looked at the photographs, but instead indicated that the subjects in the photographs were experiencing sadness or anger. In contrast, all of the adults in another of her studies detected fear. With adolescents, fMRI images showed high levels of activity in the amygdyla when the young subjects viewed the photos, whereas with adults, activity levels were high in the frontal lobes (the reasoning lobes). Older teens experienced more brain activity in the frontal lobes than younger adolescents, suggesting a shift in brain processing from the amygdyla to the frontal lobe as a correlate of maturity. Yurgelun-Todd's work is often offered as evidence of a distinction between the so-called teen brain and adult brain.

I suspect that many readers who are parents of children in their teens and early twenties will nod their heads in agreement when reading these words. Even the most intelligent, thoughtful, and responsible children in this age range occasionally engage in bizarre, sometimes self-destructive behaviors that have their parents wondering: "What were they thinking?" These are young people who post photos of their drinking binges at parties on public social network sites, experiment with prescription and illicit drugs, and pack into cars to take joy rides down winding country lanes. A major trait of these behaviors is the absence of awareness of the consequences arising from their actions. Disregard for consequences is attributed to the underdeveloped prefrontal cortex region of the brain—the portion associated with judgment, planning, and rational decisions.

Not everyone buys into an anatomical explanation of teenage turmoil. The psychologist Robert Epstein (2007), for example, challenges the idea that teenage brain anatomy is programmed to yield irresponsible behavior. He argues that teenage conflict is largely a cultural by-product of modern industrial society and cites the cross-cultural works of Alice Schlegel and Herbert Barry and Beatrice and John Whiting that suggest that in non-Western, preindustrialized cultures, there are few signs of adolescent turmoil. What distinguishes adolescents in industrialized cultures from those in preindustrialized cultures is that in the former, teenagers socialize almost exclusively with other teenagers, whereas in preindustrialized cultures, they socialize with adults. In industrialized societies, young people are often isolated from exposure to adult norms. This results in their infantilization, which in turn yields the turmoil of immaturity.

Epstein is also critical of efforts to draw behavioral conclusions from fMRI images, arguing that even if patterns of localized brain activity appear to correspond to the specific behaviors of teenagers, they are correlational, not causal. The fact that the amygdala lights up red in a brain scan when a teenager sees a photo of a frightened face suggests that the image may trigger activity in that part of the brain. Or perhaps not. Good science requires that an experiment be carried out multiple times with large samples of subjects who have been selected randomly in order to avoid selection bias. Even if the amygdalas of five hundred randomly selected teenagers light up red when teenaged subjects are exposed to the photograph of a frightened face, this observation by itself does not explain anything. At best, it suggests a correlation between seeing the photo and experiencing some kind of activity in the amygdala. Interpretation beyond this is speculation given our current state of knowledge.

Whether you accept or reject the view that there is an adolescent brain, the important thing is to recognize that judgment skills evolve with physical changes in the brain's structure and that the brain as a thinking, reasoning, judging, rational organ emerges from a lengthy process of internal wiring and rewiring from the time of its initial development in the womb through the late twenties.

Two insights about decision making that we gain from a cursory understanding of how the brain develops anatomically stand out. The first is obvious: our understanding of the evolving brain anatomy of humans suggests that the maturity they achieve by their late twenties has neurological underpinnings. Most people believe that individuals become mature through the accretion of experience: immature individuals have a paucity of experience and mature individuals have an abundance. This perspective holds that at birth, the cognitive brain is a blank slate. Experience fills it in. The greater the level of experience gained, the greater the wisdom individuals attain.

People have long recognized that the capacity of most individuals to make good judgments is tied to maturity. That is why in preindustrialized societies, the community delegates the most important decisions to the elders. In a similar vein, contemporary business and government organizations do not usually confer significant decision-making responsibility on employees before they have reached the age of thirty.

To the extent men and women are deemed fit to assume significant decision-making responsibilities in their late twenties or early thirties, their fitness is attributed to their accumulation of a critical mass of experience by this age. Certainly, experience counts. However, while experience can help people become wiser and contributes to their maturity, the final anatomical development of the brain provides the platform that enables them to make adult judgments, understand the consequences of their actions, and exercise a measure of discipline. By the late twenties, neuronal wiring is stabilized and white matter stops growing. The finishing touches on the development of those parts of the brain that support judgment, decision making, and discipline are finally complete. At this point, a normal, healthy individual has become a fully developed, mature adult capable of making mature decisions.

Thus, the development of sound decision-making skills is tied to two factors. One is the final formulation of a fully developed brain, particularly in the frontal cortex region, which plays an important role in enabling people to exercise good judgment and assess alternatives. The other is the accumulation of pertinent experience, which provides people with the specific skills and knowledge they need in order to make effective decisions within a given context.

The second insight that bears on decision making is more subtle. It arises from recognition that most of the high-impact academic studies of decision making use undergraduates as their subjects. Daniel Kahneman's famous behavioral economics studies that won him the Nobel Prize were carried out chiefly using undergraduate students at Hebrew University, Stanford, and Princeton. Wilson's often-cited studies on decision making employed undergraduates at the University of Virginia. Daniel Ariely's studies on rational decision making that are reported in his best-selling book, *Predictably Irrational*, employed undergraduate subjects at MIT. And so it goes with a large portion of decision-making research carried out by university professors. Because of their reliance on undergraduate subjects, a problem with these studies is that they lack external validity, an important methodological concept that examines the degree to which subjects in a study truly reflect the population they are purported to represent. The big validity question is: To what extent do findings based on studies of teenagers matriculating at elite universities accurately reflect the decision-making behaviors of the adult decision-making population at large?

As we just saw, an anatomical look at the brain suggests that the brain is not fully developed until the mid- to late twenties. The parts of the brain that play a role in judgment and decision making are among the last to develop. Consequently, the findings of some of the most authoritative empirical studies that are routinely cited to explain human decision-making behaviors are based on subjects whose judgmental and decision-making capabilities are not yet fully developed. It is not clear that these findings have a bearing on the decision-making behavior of adults who are twenty-five years old and older. Beyond this, the fact that these subjects study at elite universities suggests that they possess IQs, discipline, and drive that look very different from what you would find in the population at large.

What has happened is that these professors have been seduced by easy access to research subjects: a captive audience of undergraduate students. They resort to using what are called *samples of convenience*, that is, employing whoever happens to be available to participate in the behavioral experiments they have cooked up. What they should do—a fundamental practice of good empirical research—is make an effort to select a representative sample of the decision-making community, comprising mature people ranging in age from thirty to sixty-five. This generally entails employing some form of random sampling. If their study focuses on young decision-makers, they can employ well-established sampling techniques to do so, just as they can elect to overrepresent older decision-makers. In such a case, they need to identify their samples: "Our study focuses on the decision-making practices of men and women whose ages range from thirty to forty-five" (or whatever age range they used). One thing is clear: a worthwhile study that seeks to understand the decision-making practices of real decision-makers in an enterprise setting would not focus on individuals in the eighteen-to-twenty-two-year-old age range.

I return to some of the methodological failings of many empirical studies of decision making in the next chapter.

CONCLUSION

An examination of brain basics yields several important conclusions that bear on decision making. First and most significant, we see that the brain intermediates everything that people experience. The process of intermediation goes beyond mere filtering of incoming data. In its pursuit of energy conservation, the brain supplies template perceptions based on prior experience as well as inborn hardwired templates. In cases where it faces a paucity of information, it fills information gaps with its best guesses through a process called *predictive coding*. Beyond this, experience with visual illusions indicates that the brain can be readily fooled.

What all this suggests is that the external reality humans encounter is chimerical. This is not a new idea. Philosophers have argued for millennia that humans are incapable of experiencing reality directly through their senses. What is new is that recently gained scientific knowledge confirms the speculations of philosophers. The evidence demonstrates that for a variety of reasons, the brain's intermediation in the perceptual process ensures that the reality people perceive is colored by the way their brains process information.

The impact of this phenomenon on decision making can be substantial. Common sense dictates that to make good decisions, you need to get your facts straight. But knowledge of how the brain works shows that this is problematic, because whatever facts decision-makers surface are a product of their brain's intermediation. The perceived facts are not objective facts. This is true even in the hard sciences. In referring to the subjectivity of the facts scientists deal with in their research, Thomas Kuhn (1996) called on Norwood Russell Hanson's (1958) concept of *theory ladenness*. He noted that scientists working with carefully controlled experiments are not looking at wholly objective facts, because their perceptions of the data are colored by their life experiences.

For the commonplace decisions people make each day, the implications of this reality are largely inconsequential. But for significant decisions, the implications can be substantial. Consider how the strong economic performance of the United States during the 1990s and early 2000s (following the deregulation initiatives that began with Ronald Reagan in the 1980s) confirmed the Federal Reserve chairman's free market ideological orientation, convincing him that government regulation of business activity was unnecessary because free markets are self-correcting. This perception of reality led chairman Alan Greenspan to pursue easy money policies and promote increased deregulation. After the near collapse of the world economy in 2008–2009, triggered in part by the absence of effective regulation in the financial arena, Greenspan publicly acknowledged that his lifelong commitment to deregulation and unfettered free markets was rooted in shaky premises.

A second important conclusion emerging from an examination of brain basics is that humans are programmed to resist change. Almost everyone recognizes that the introduction of new ideas or products or routines often generates resistance. The resistance may be rooted in one or more factors, including concern that with change, benefits that are currently enjoyed will be lost (a big concern of labor unions), that change erodes cherished traditions (a big concern of religious fundamentalists), or that the perceived benefits of change do not outweigh the effort of implementing it (an argument of those who abide by the maxim: "If it ain't broke don't fix it").

Knowledge of brain basics leads us to conclude that resistance to change is more fundamental than these explanations suggest. From a biological perspective, the brain's primary objective in resisting change is to conserve energy. Sticking to template solutions consumes less energy than dealing with stimuli in new ways. As the neuroscientist Gregory Berns highlights in *Iconoclast* (2010), truly innovative and creative people are able to overcome the brain's inherent conservatism—a conservatism that can be traced to individual neurons "deciding" on whether to fire based on the anticipated energy that would be expended if they fired. This is what makes creative people special and enables them to do things that others cannot. Because of this brain-rooted conservatism, most people are unable to think innovatively. The important insight here is that conservative decision making is not simply a manifestation of people's risk aversion; it is a characteristic of the brain's laziness.

The brain's inherent tendency to resist change has obvious impacts for decision making. Under most circumstances, decision-makers are most comfortable sticking with what has worked in the past. It takes a special mind-set to see new opportunities and pursue them. This gives Berns's iconoclasts an advantage over other people. Berns suggests that for decision-makers to be more boldly innovative, they need to be conscious of the brain's tendency to resist change. They can overcome this tendency by exposing themselves constantly to new ideas and experiences, in their personal lives as well as in their work lives.

A third conclusion emerging from a review of brain basics is that the brain can produce a sense of certainty that something is true when it is not. This is evident among people who suffer delusions—for example, paranoid schizophrenics. Although the world they perceive may be viewed as unreal by the community at large, it is real to them. Even normal people experience unsupportable feelings of certainty. They occasionally encounter situations where they are absolutely sure that they are correct about something, recalling supporting evidence in detail. When external facts show them to be wrong, they are surprised to learn that they were so wrong when they *knew* they were right. The neuroscientist Robert Burton holds that this feeling of certainty is not an anomalous quirk, but is rooted in a neurophysiological process outside of conscious thought.

A final conclusion stemming from a study of brain basics is that decision-making maturity is linked to a person's stage of brain development. The brain's anatomical structure does not assume its final form until people reach their mid- to late twenties. It is at this point that it achieves full decision-making maturity, because the finishing touches of brain development are directed at refining higher-level brain functions, such as understanding the consequences of actions and exercising good judgment.

While experience is important in acquiring decision-making maturity, by itself it does not fully define such maturity. Ultimately decision-making maturity arises after the pieces of the brain are put together properly in an anatomical sense. The fully developed brain provides a platform that enables people to strengthen their decision-making maturity through life experiences. Even here, there are variations among people in how the brain is wired (particularly in the important frontal cortex region), so there is no assurance that a mature adult has a brain that is wired to exercise good judgment when making decisions.

Two decision-making implications stand out here. First, as a general rule, when dealing with problems of consequence and complexity, it may be smart to select key decision-makers who are thirty years old or older. Of course, there are exceptions to the rule. History provides examples of individuals who demonstrated great decision-making capabilities at a young age: Alexander the Great and Bill Gates are two cases. But even here, we need to recall that young Alexander and young Bill were smart enough to solicit guidance from smart elders (Alexander's principal teacher was Aristotle).

Second, we should continually remind ourselves that while experience is a great teacher, by itself it does not yield wise decisions. Experience must be wed to a brain that is fully developed and wired to understand the consequences of action.

9 Toward an Empirically Rooted Understanding of Decision Making

Traditional approaches to the theory and practice of decision making have largely been normative. By *traditional*, I am referring to what is taught in standard decision-making courses and written in most decision-making books and articles. By *normative*, I refer to the fact that the traditional approaches are prescriptive, pointing out optimal ways to make decisions through the use of mathematical and statistical formulations or by following a series of well-defined, logical problem-solving steps. They place great emphasis on being rational, with many books offering tips for avoiding irrationality. The greatest beneficiaries of traditional approaches have been engineers, operations managers, and economists—people who make things, run things, and are charged with identifying optimal solutions to well-defined problems.

In an attempt to go beyond prescription, there has been a move afoot to get a better grip on the theory and practice of decision making through empirical studies. This chapter takes a critical view of what an empirical approach can reveal about how decisions are made and their consequences. Empirical research in the behavioral arena entails the systematic collection of data on how people function as they make choices in their lives. To the extent possible, an empirical outlook enables us to replace speculation on human behavior with fact.

Empirical investigations can be carried out in a number of ways. What makes them empirical is their employment of observation in a systematic, objective manner. In the case of decision making, this entails looking at the conditions leading to the making of decisions, the actual decision-making process, and the consequences of the decisions (or nondecisions) that are implemented. In some circles, the term *empirical* is often associated with the conduct of experiments. I employ the term in a broader sense here: my concern is with using factual observations to help us understand decision making.

Empirical research can assume many forms:

- *Experimental*—designing and executing scenarios under controlled conditions to see how experimental subjects make choices in response to different stimuli

- *Anthropological/unobtrusive*—observing how people behave in their natural environment without direct intervention by the observer

- *Survey-based*—systematically collecting information from the subjects being studied through questionnaires or interviews

- *Historical*—collecting, collating, and interpreting data on how decisions have been made in specific instances

- *Case study*—a variant of historical and anthropological approaches, where a detailed examination is made of something—individuals, work units, enterprises, industries, processes, products, or something else

- *Exploratory*—an investigation that does not employ rigorous scientific methods but is designed to get a rough understanding of a phenomenon

- *Basic research*—an attempt to acquire knowledge for the sake of knowledge, with no practical application in mind

In this chapter, I look at several examples of the use of empirical research to investigate decision making. My goal is to employ these examples to provide a taste of what empirical approaches entail. I do not offer a comprehensive exposition, but focus mostly on work in psychology and the neurosciences. Psychologists alone have cranked out hundreds of papers since Tversky and Kahneman published their seminal article in 1974. Other social science disciplines conduct empirical studies as well. For example, political scientists routinely carry out surveys to determine citizen attitudes on policy issues and examine voting patterns of politicians in legislatures. The discipline of market research is built on empirical investigations of consumer buying preferences. And of course, most research in economics is empirically rooted and has been since the time of the classical economists.

IN THE BEGINNING: TOWARD AN EMPIRICAL VIEW

The birth of the social sciences was a protracted one, starting with the insights offered by the classical economists (Adam Smith, David Ricardo, and Thomas Malthus) and stretching through the nineteenth century. In the late eighteenth century and early part of the nineteenth century, these men recognized and documented the behavioral underpinnings of economic activity. Their contributions were based on empirical data—the first time human behavior and its consequences were studied systematically—so these first economists deserve credit for getting the social science ball rolling.

While the classical economists and their immediate successors engaged in a form of proto-social science, social science as we practice it today really began with the work of the French sociologist Emile Durkheim, who stands among the earliest scholars to approach the study of human behavior in a scientific way. He aspired to do in the social arena what physicists, biologists, and chemists did in the physical. Two contributions establish his credentials as a modern social scientist. In his 1895 book, *The Rules of Sociological Method*, he provided a road map that showed how scholars interested in studying human behavior should carry out their efforts (Durkheim, 1982). In *Suicide*, an empirical study of differences in the suicide behavior of Protestants and Catholics, he provided a model of solid, empirically rooted social science research that others would emulate (Durkheim, 1951). Durkheim emphasized the need for social scientists to employ facts, buttress their findings with statistical analysis, and adopt the norms of good scientific practice, which includes objectivity.

Identifying the behavioral origins of decision-making theory and practice is trickier than for standard social science disciplines, because great thinkers have reflected on the human role in decision making for thousands of years, expressing views that predate social science perspectives by millennia. Plato's *Republic*, for example, defined the traits and responsibilities of the philosopher king, and Aristotle's *Politics* examined all aspects of governance. Lest anyone forget, Aristotle was Alexander the Great's teacher, and if the lives of students reflect the wisdom of their teachers, it appears that Aristotle knew a thing or two about decision making.

An important work that deserves the attention of students of empirically based decision making is Cyert and March's *A Behavioral Theory of the Firm* (1963).

Cyert and March were colleagues of Herbert Simon at Carnegie Mellon University. As with Amos Tversky and Daniel Kahneman a decade later, they were bothered by the abstract formulations of conventional economic theory and sought to develop an economic theory of how enterprises really function. Conventional economics treated business enterprises as black boxes. Cyert and March wanted to get into the black boxes to see what they contained.

They articulated four goals in writing their book, goals that set their work apart from the teachings of conventional economic theory and practice. First, they would examine a small number of economic decisions firms made to see how they were carried out in practice. Not only would they review price and output decisions, but they would investigate internal allocation and market strategy decisions as well.

Second, they would carefully study the business processes firms employed, with a view to identifying how these processes led to decisions. One category of firm they examined in detail was retailers.

Third, the models they developed would be tested with empirical data from real-world businesses to make them rooted in the real world to as great an extent as possible.

Finally, based on their examination of the functioning of real-world enterprises, they would create a general behavioral theory of the firm that would offer a dramatic contrast to the prevailing abstract theory of the firm promoted by conventional economics.

In 2007, the journal *Organizational Science* showcased a retrospective examination of the impact of *A Behavioral Theory of the Firm* four decades after it was published (Argote, 2007). The conclusion was that the impact has been substantial.

EVIDENCE OF UNCONSCIOUS DELIBERATION IN DECISION MAKING: THREE EMPIRICAL APPROACHES

One of the most interesting and important issues facing decision-makers is the role of unconscious deliberation in decision making. Each of us wrestles with this issue each day. Consider the following examples:

- After visiting the Cadillac showroom on a whim on a Sunday and test-driving a fully loaded new model car, which you adore, you find that the salesperson is pressuring you to commit to a purchase. If you wish to behave wisely, you should smile, thank the salesperson, then say: "I need to sleep on the decision. I'll get back to you later in the week."

- You and your colleagues have interviewed five applicants for a student counselor job. None of the candidates thus far is acceptable. After the sixth candidate has spoken two or three sentences of introductory comments, you think: "This is the one! I can feel this candidate is the person we are looking for." If you wish to behave wisely, you should let this candidate proceed with the interview process, then interview the remaining candidates. You should hold off selecting a new student counselor until the next day.

- Your presentation to the executive committee requesting their support for a new project is going well until the chief information officer derails the presentation by declaring that your project ignores the latest communication protocols adopted in industry. You know that he is wrong in his assessment but remain quiet. After the meeting, you return to your office and bang out a three-page piece highlighting the CIO's errors of fact. It's okay to write such a letter, because it lets you vent your anger and frustration. But if you wish to behave wisely, you should not send out your missive until you have a chance to reread and reconsider it the next day.

Each of these stories exemplifies the workings of unconscious deliberation in decision making. In each case, you trust your unconscious brain to put things into the proper perspective. Quite often, after sleeping on a decision and revisiting it the next day, you wonder what you were thinking when you were so intent to commit to a particular course of action.

The question we look at here is: What are the relative merits of conscious versus unconscious deliberation when making decisions? This question lends itself to empirical investigation. We can address it with real-world data to determine the relative merits of conscious versus unconscious deliberation in decision making. In this section we look at three levels of empirical investigation. The first is the weakest from a methodological standpoint. It is the "blink" argument

Malcolm Gladwell raised in his best-selling book, *Blink* (2005). Gladwell holds that spur-of-the-moment decisions often provide better results than carefully deliberated decisions. The approach he takes is anecdotal: he "proves" his case with interesting stories that corroborate it.

The second approach is methodologically stronger in its use of controlled experiments to test the hypothesis that unconscious deliberation can yield superior decisions to those made through conscious deliberation. The study we look at, conducted by Timothy Wilson at the University of Virginia, is well known and highly cited in the decision-making literature, but a close look at how it was carried out shows it to suffer serious methodological shortcomings. These obvious shortcomings have not been highlighted in the experimental psychology or decision-making literature, but they are real and require us to question the study's conclusions.

The third approach looks at the relative merits of conscious and unconscious deliberation in decision making by carrying out experiments that employ classical good-practice methodology. It is illustrated by the research of Ap Dijksterhuis and his colleagues in the Netherlands. Their experiments build on the work of Timothy Wilson but avoid some of its methodological shortcomings. They explain their results in the context of a clearly posited theory. Still, even this good-practice research has its methodological shortcomings, which I examine briefly.

The Blink Phenomenon: Anecdotal Speculation

In this section, I use a simple phenomenon, intuitive blink insights, to illustrate how empirical speculation on decision making is often carried out: through the use of intriguing yet unsupported narrative stories.

From time to time thoughtful books appear in the popular literature that trigger spirited debates among scholars and laypeople. Examples include John Kenneth Galbraith's *The Affluent Society* (1969), Francis Fukuyama's *The End of History and the Last Man* (1992), and Stephen Hawking's *A Brief History of Time* (1988). Malcolm Gladwell has proven to be a superstar in this arena, knocking three homers into the stands in quick succession with the publication of *The Tipping Point* (2002), *Blink* (2005), and *Outliers* (2008).

Gladwell's *Blink* is the book that interests us here. Its central thesis is captured in its subtitle: *The Power of Thinking Without Thinking*. The book is filled with stories of instances where conscious thinking and attempts at due diligence fail to deliver good results while snap judgments succeed. The success of the snap judgments is attributed to the mysterious workings of the unconscious brain, where an individual suddenly experiences a total certainty of truth that cannot be explained rationally.

The book's Introduction recounts a story of how California's J. Paul Getty Museum was investigating whether it should spend $10 million to purchase a sixth-century B.C.E. Greek *kouros* statue that depicted a young man standing. After devoting fourteen months to examining the authenticity of the *kouros*, which included geological tests of the dolomite marble material, the museum director decided the statue was authentic and purchased it. However, the moment Thomas Hoving (former director of New York's Metropolitan Museum of Art) saw it, he knew there was something wrong with it: it was too "fresh." Other experts had similar cautionary feelings that were hard to pin down. Ultimately a police-like investigation determined that the statue was a fake. Gladwell's point was that the flash of insight Hoving and others experienced provided better guidance on the provenance of the *kouros* than careful scientific study.

Gladwell concludes his book with a story about Abbie Conant, a professional classical trombone player who happens to be female and auditioned for a trombone-playing position with the Munich Philharmonic Orchestra. It was a screened audition, meaning that the judges could not see who played the pieces they heard. Thirty-three trombone players were invited to participate in the audition. When Conant played her piece as the sixteenth performer, the Philharmonic's music director exclaimed, "That's who we want," and sent the seventeen remaining performers home. The twist in this story is that when the music director discovered that the trombone player was a woman, he wanted to back out of the deal because he did not feel the trombone was a woman's instrument. Ultimately, after years of legal and administrative hassles, Conant prevailed and became principal trombonist in the orchestra.

In his *New York Times* best-seller, *How We Decide* (2009), Jonah Lehrer recounts a similar tale. His story is about Herb Stein, director of daytime television soap operas. Stein's days are filled with blink moments, because when he is directing a daytime program that operates under nonnegotiable deadlines, he cannot reshoot bad scenes. He needs to get it right the first time. He does not have the time to be analytical about camera angles and such and therefore depends heavily on his instincts. This extends to his hiring of actors. Lehrer tells of one occasion when Stein spent hours auditioning dozens of actors by having them recite a set of lines. The results were discouraging. Then after hearing one actor say just a few words, he knew this was the man he was looking for. "I couldn't say why, but for me, he completely stood out. What they say is true: you just get a feeling."

In his *Thinking, Fast and Slow* (2011), Daniel Kahneman relates a story reported by the psychologist Gary Klein to illustrate expert intuition at work. In Klein's story (1998), the lieutenant leading a team of firefighters fighting a kitchen fire in a home develops a feeling that something is terribly wrong. He orders his men out of the house, and moments later, the kitchen floor collapses. By getting his men out of the house in a nick of time, the lieutenant averts a catastrophe.

These are intriguing stories. But after carefully reading these and other accounts of the blink phenomenon, it is not clear what the authors are saying. Are they advising that when you have a strong intuitive feeling about something, you should follow your intuition? Are they asserting that in contests pitting due diligence against powerful yet inexpressible feelings, you should go with the strong feelings? What are they suggesting beyond the obvious point that sometimes grandma's premonitions hit the mark?

The authors point out that in each of the examples covered here, the individuals experiencing the blink moment are experts in their fields. Thomas Hoving, the music director, Herb Stein, and the firefighting lieutenant are highly experienced and respected professionals. But what does this mean? Are the authors suggesting that their intuitions are unfailing?

From the scientific perspective, if you want to aver that Hoving's blink experience is real, you need to review a broad range of intuitive decisions Thomas Hoving made in his several decades in the art world. Was he always right? Did his intuition ever lead him astray?

Gladwell tells us that the director of music of the Munich Philharmonic was so sure that the unseen trombone player was the perfect match for his needs that he sent seventeen auditioners home without listening to their performances. Could it be that one of the seventeen would have surpassed the capabilities of the candidate who was chosen? Did the music director ever reflect on the irony that in following his intuition, he selected the individual who was the worst match when assessed against his personal values?

Lehrer tells us that Herb Stein proudly boasts that he knows whether an auditioning actor is right for his daytime TV programs after three to five seconds. Does this mean he doesn't choose clunkers? If objective observers were to examine Stein's choices over the past ten years, would they agree that he hits the target more often than not?

As to the firefighting lieutenant Kahneman references, given the enormous danger he faces each time he enters a burning building, isn't it normal for him to have occasional premonitions of disaster? Isn't it likely that some of these premonitions will come true and others don't? Are his premonitions any more accurate than grandma's?

There is no science in these narrative accounts. There is no use of empirical evidence beyond the telling of a story. It is clear what the blink boosters are trying to say: that there are times when the unconscious processing of the brain can handle phenomena people experience better than the conscious processing. I agree that there is possible merit in this supposition. As Chapter Eight points out, in order to conserve energy, the brain incorporates experience into template perceptions that help people cope with the challenges they face in their lives, from crossing a busy street to deciding whether to take an umbrella to work. It has ready responses to challenges that work unconsciously. But where is the connection between the employment of these templates and making unconscious judgments that are smarter than conscious judgments? This is a testable proposition. So where are the tests? What evidence can the blink boosters provide beyond anecdotes?

Before leaving this treatment of the blink phenomenon, I want to make a final point that addresses an important feature of the blink experience: the feeling of absolute certainty about the correctness of the insight experienced by the individual. In each of the stories narrated here, the individual experiencing a blink insight *absolutely knows* what is right or wrong. This should make you nervous if you recall Robert Burton's work on feelings of certainty (2008) addressed in Chapter Eight. As Burton points out, feelings of certainty usually offer unreliable reflections of reality. For example, the unreliability of eyewitness testimony is well documented. Based on abundant medical evidence, he speculates that these feelings have neurophysiological roots independent of conscious deliberation. When people feel absolutely certain about something, they are inured to appeals of reason and logic. Paranoid schizophrenics know they are right when they recount what others view as delusions. People suffering from Cotard syndrome know they are dead even as they listen to their heart beat through a stethoscope. Men and women under the influence of hallucinogenic drugs know that the fantastic images they perceive are real.

It isn't necessary to revert to these dramatic examples to make the point. All of us have suffered embarrassing situations where we have sworn to the truth of something we experienced when evidence is provided that shows us to be wrong—perhaps a photograph, or written words, or a glance at the calendar, or the statement of someone we respect shows us with finality that we are mistaken in our certainty. So it may be with the blink phenomenon.

In the next two sections, I look at the use of social experiments to examine the efficacy of conscious versus unconscious judgments.

Unconscious Deliberation in Decision Making: Use of Experiments 1

In the early 1990s, the cognitive psychologist Timothy Wilson carried out experiments supporting the view that the conscious deliberation of decisions can yield suboptimal results. His studies led newspapers and popular magazine to proclaim that the best decisions are those that you sleep on. These findings resonated with large numbers of people who favor intuition over analysis.

In one famous experiment that is heavily referenced in the decision-making literature, he had undergraduate students carry out a blind taste test on five samples of strawberry jam (Wilson and Schooler, 1991). Half the students were asked to write down their opinions of the merits of the different jams they tasted. This constituted the group of decision-makers deliberating through conscious thought. The other half were asked to rank the different jams without conscious reflection. The rankings of the second group of students (the unconscious deciders) were significantly closer to independent assessments of the quality of jams by external experts, leading Wilson and his colleagues to conclude that the effort to deliberate consciously on a decision can yield suboptimal results.

In 1993, Wilson and his coauthors published findings of a more sophisticated experiment: "Introspecting About Reasons Can Reduce Post-Choice Satisfaction"

(Wilson and others, 1993). The goal of the study was to determine whether people can overanalyze their choices in making decisions, leading ultimately to unsatisfactory decisions. This is an interesting question with practical as well as theoretical implications.

The subjects in the study were forty-three female undergraduates at the University of Virginia. The researchers conducting the experiment created a bogus research project that purportedly examined the kinds of aesthetic effects in pictures that people find pleasing. Thus the research subjects did not know the real objective of the study. The women were randomly assigned to two groups: twenty-one to a control group and twenty-two to a treatment group. One by one, individuals in both groups were brought into a room where five posters were displayed. Two posters pictured serious paintings, one by Monet and the other by van Gogh. Three pictured humorous depictions of cute animals.

Participants from the treatment group were asked to look at the five pictures, then write a half-page description for each poster of what they liked and disliked about it. After this, they filled out a scoring sheet that had them rank the appeal of each picture on a nine-point scale. These participants constituted conscious deliberators.

Participants from the control group were asked to look at the five pictures, then write a short piece on a number of extraneous topics: why they chose the major they did, why they decided to attend the University of Virginia, and their career prospects. Then they were asked to fill out a scoring sheet that had them rank the appeal of each picture on a nine-point scale. These participants constituted unconscious deliberators because they were not given the opportunity to reflect consciously on the posters they viewed.

At the end of the poster assessment exercise, each participant was told that she could select one of the five posters as a gift of thanks for her participation in the study. Each participant selected one poster.

An analysis of the data confirmed the researchers' hypothesis that the conscious deliberation on the merits of each poster by the subjects influenced their view of what they liked. While twenty of the twenty-one control group participants best liked one of the two fine art posters, eight of the twenty-two treatment subjects expressed preference for one of the humorous posters.

The experiment did not end here. Several weeks after the subjects participated in the experiment, they were contacted and asked to indicate how happy they were with their choice of the posters they took away. For example, did they keep the posters? Did they hang them in their rooms? While all of the control group participants indicated satisfaction with their choices, a number of those who selected the humorous posters indicated dissatisfaction.

The study concluded that by consciously reflecting on the choices you face, you can generate outcomes that may not serve your interests. This is an interesting study that addresses a question that most decision-makers would deem important, showcases a clever way to answer the research question, and yields results that appear to confirm the hypothesis articulated by the researchers. But the study is seriously flawed because its participants were a sample of convenience of young women just a few years beyond adolescence and enrolled in one of America's most prestigious universities. Is it a surprise that young women who had not yet achieved full emotional maturity could talk themselves into favoring humorous and cute posters? As Chapter Eight noted, the brain does not develop executive processing capabilities fully until people reach their mid- to late twenties. If the participants were in their teens or early twenties (the paper does not stipulate the age of the research subjects), another five to eight years would need to pass before the executive processing capabilities of their brains would be fully developed, that is, before they became mature decision-makers.

Would a study of mature women produce the same results? For the validity of the findings to be strengthened, the study should have been repeated using women who were unambiguously mature—women, say, in their midthirties who were experienced in making consequential decisions. Personally I have trouble believing that mature women would make the same choices as postadolescent women and opt to select humorous, cute posters over works by either Monet or van Gogh. But I may be wrong. A simple extension of the experiment to cover mature women would help to resolve the issue. Better yet, to avoid potential problems of gender bias, the experiment should be conducted on a representative sample of both males and females.

The obvious biasedness of the sample subjects taints the research results. Owing to their youth, their sex, incomplete brain development, and lack of life experience, they do not represent a broader population of people who make consequential decisions at work and in their personal lives. Another source of biasedness is that they come from one of America's top-ranked undergraduate programs. Consequently, it is likely that their intellectual capability, cultural perspectives, and need to achieve are substantially different from their peers. A third potential source of biasedness is based on my suspicion that the subjects, presumably humanities and social science students, reflect only one portion of the intellectual spectrum. Unfortunately, the paper does not provide information on this point, even though it could affect the results. Specifically, to what extent did the participants reflect a broad range of academic preferences? It appears likely that some, perhaps many, were psychology majors. Were there any economics majors? Any engineering majors? Any physics majors? Why is this important? Because it is plausible that individuals with analytical proclivities would handle the poster-ranking decision differently from those with little analytical orientation.

We have here a cleverly designed study that addresses an interesting research question. However, its employment of readily available undergraduate students at a prestigious university taints the subject pool. In the real world, decisions of consequence at companies and in government are made by mature adults whose brains are fully developed and who have accumulated a full portfolio of real-world experiences. This research effort rates low on external validity. While it may accurately reflect the decision-making behaviors of undergraduate women at prestigious schools, its bearing on the broader population of mature decision-makers is questionable.

Unconscious Deliberation in Decision Making: Use of Experiments 2

In this section, we look at another example of experiments carried out with a view to study decision making empirically. However, in this example, we encounter research that pays greater heed to employing good methodological practice.

As with the University of Virginia researchers, Dutch professor Ap Dijksterhuis and his colleagues, who were influenced by Wilson's work, use experiments to investigate the making of small decisions. Their experiments focus on the relative efficacy of conscious versus unconscious deliberation in making decisions and the degree of satisfaction with decisions that have been made through conscious versus unconscious deliberative processes (Dijksterhuis, 2004; Dijksterhuis, Bos, Nordgren, and van Baaren, 2006). Their findings suggest that in dealing with simple decisions, a measure of conscious deliberation is helpful. It yields better decisions and greater long-term satisfaction with the decisions. Their findings also support the hypothesis that with more complex problems, it is better to take a break and let unconscious deliberations guide you. Their studies suggest that with more complex problems, experimental subjects operating at an unconscious deliberative level develop better solutions and express greater satisfaction with their decisions than subjects who apply conscious thought to the decision process.

In one of their early studies, the researchers presented sixty-three undergraduate students with information on four apartments situated in Amsterdam. Each apartment was described by twelve attributes, including location, size, cost, and friendliness of the landlord. The subjects were randomly assigned to three groups. Members of the first group were asked to rate each of the four apartments on a scale of 1 to 10 immediately after reviewing the data on the apartment attributes. Members of the second group were given three minutes to think carefully about the four apartments. After three minutes, they were asked to rate each of the apartments. Members of the third group were given a distracting assignment for three minutes, which did not enable them to think consciously about the attributes of the four apartments they had just reviewed. After three minutes, they were asked to rate each of the apartments.

In putting together information on the attributes of the four apartments, the experimenters consciously varied the attractiveness of the apartments. Apartment 2 was the most attractive, with eight positive and four negative attributes. Apartment 4 was the worst, with four positive attributes and eight negative attributes. Apartments 1 and 3 fit in between.

The results of the experiment showed that the subjects who were distracted for three minutes and unable to reflect consciously on the attributes of the four apartments were most able to distinguish the best from the worst apartment. Their average score for the best apartment was significantly greater than for the worst apartment. While subjects in the two other groups generally rated the best apartment higher than the worst, the difference in the scores was not significantly different from zero. (Dijksterhuis's team carries out statistical tests on estimated statistics, even though the sample being examined was not selected randomly.)

Dijksterhuis and his colleagues believe that these results suggest that the third group's thought processes employed powerful unconscious information processing capabilities to work on the problem, even as the subjects were unaware of what was transpiring. It enabled them to identify the best solution. To appreciate the processing capability of conscious versus unconscious deliberation, consider that the conscious effort of reading text entails information processing requirements of forty-five bits per second. However, even as you read the words on this page using your brain's 45 bps information processing capabilities, your unconscious brain is operating at *11.2 million bps*! The information processing capabilities of the conscious brain are puny when compared to the capabilities of the unconscious brain (Dijksterhuis, 2004).

It is hard for us to digest the possibility that our unconscious brain grossly outperforms our conscious brain. This is understandable, since we are stuck with using the conscious brain as the vehicle for comprehending our world. It is the mechanism that enables us to make sense of things. But our conscious brain gives us only a keyhole view of the world because of its limited information processing capabilities. From the perspective of an individual looking through a keyhole, reality is defined by the constrained range of what can be seen. Whatever exists outside the field of view is not perceived and therefore is discounted.

Another experiment examines whether conscious versus unconscious deliberation is affected by the complexity of the problem being investigated. Dijksterhuis carried out a number of experiments that explored this question, all of which generated similar results. I will summarize one experiment (Dijksterhuis, Bos, Nordgren, and van Baaren, 2006). Subjects were randomly divided into two groups, and all were provided information on four cars. They were told that they would be asked to select what they viewed to be the best car of the four. The experimenters wrote up one car to be the most desirable, another to be the least desirable, and the remaining two to be moderately desirable. One group of subjects was given descriptions of the four cars that listed only four attributes. The members of this group were faced with a simple decision. The members of the other group were given descriptions of the four cars that listed twelve attributes for each car. These subjects faced a more complex decision. Within each group, the subjects were further divided into two categories: one was given four minutes to think about the cars and their attributes, and the other was distracted for four minutes by working on anagrams. After four minutes, both sets of subjects were asked to select the best car. The results showed that with the simple decision condition (four attributes), subjects who consciously thought about the cars did better at selecting the best car than those who were restricted from thinking about them consciously. However, with the complex decision condition (twelve attributes), subjects who did not think consciously about the cars did better at selecting the best car than those who thought about them consciously. The conclusion is that when dealing with simple problems, conscious deliberation yields superior results. When dealing with more complex decisions, unconscious deliberation generates superior results.

The researchers' explanation of the findings is that with the increased complexity of decisions, the underperforming conscious brain lacks the capacity to make decisions effectively. However, it does a good job of deciding things when dealing with well-structured, simple problems, because such problems lie within its information processing capabilities. In contrast, the high information processing capacity of the unconscious brain enables the brain to handle more complex decisions unconsciously. The obvious difficulty here is that because problems are being resolved at an unconscious level, they remain below a threshold that makes them actionable. Regardless of whether conscious or unconscious deliberation yields better solutions, decision making ultimately requires conscious awareness that leads to conscious action. That is, the decision-makers must say: "Here is our decision. Now implement it."

Dijksterhuis and his colleagues have developed what they call unconscious thought theory (UTT), which explores their perspectives on the functioning of conscious versus unconscious decision deliberations (Dijksterhuis and Nordrgren, 2006). UTT has its challengers. The leading challengers are Ben Newell and T. Rakow, whose own research on unconscious deliberation brings into question the principal premises of UTT. In one study, Newell, Wong, Cheung, and Rakow (2009) describe the results of their attempts to replicate the findings that underlie UTT. In their experiments, they found that if subjects who deliberate consciously are given more time to review the facts associated with the choices facing them, they are able to make better decisions than if they are given only three or four minutes of deliberation time, as occurs in the Dijksterhuis experiments. They also found that the performance of unconscious deliberators was unstable: their performance on the experiments was sensitive to such things as the order in which attributes of objects were presented to them.

For readers interested in the details of how empirical experiments on decision making can be carried out, it is worthwhile reading the study by Newell, Wong, Cheung, and Rakow because it provides substantial detail on the methods and materials employed in the experiments, including specific descriptions of the attributes of cars being ranked. You can use their material to launch your own experiments of conscious versus unconscious deliberation!

In another paper, Newell and Rakow (2011) carried out a Bayesian analysis of the results of sixteen experimental studies on conscious versus unconscious deliberations and found that only one demonstrates a significant difference between the two modes of deliberation.

This type of dispute among scholars is common in science and reflects a healthy airing of opposing points of view. It sets in motion a Darwinian process of selecting the perspectives that demonstrate they are strongest. But no one remains king of the hill for long: even the best theories ultimately are toppled as new knowledge and insights expose the weak points of prevailing theories.

In what sense is the Dijksterhuis approach to empirical research superior to the Wilson approach? In my view, the Dijksterhuis team exercised greater methodological care in conducting their research than the University of Virginia team did, and this strengthens the credibility of their findings. For one thing, they are cognizant of the methodological limitations of any given experiment, so they have carried out many experiments, varying troublesome features in order to test if the outcomes are caused by unanticipated, extraneous factors. As with the Virginia team, the Dijksterhuis team depends heavily on experiments conducted on undergraduates, which I see as a weakness, but it overcomes some of my concern by testing the core hypotheses in multiple ways. They even extend their research to the field, investigating the decision-making process of shoppers purchasing simple products versus more complex products. Regardless of the approach they adopt, the results support their basic UTT hypotheses. The situation here is similar to what we encounter in a criminal trial, where the prosecutor's team hopes to get a conviction of an alleged criminal by presenting a preponderance of evidence rather than a smoking gun to support their case.

For another thing, the fact that they are being second-guessed by the Newell-Rakow team strengthens the credibility of their work. It is good that these two groups are eying each other closely: it keeps the research effort honest.

THE CONTRIBUTION OF EMPIRICAL RESEARCH: WHERE DO WE STAND?

We have just reviewed three empirical approaches to examining the research question: What is the role of unconscious deliberation in decision making? It is time to ask: In the final analysis, how much value do we derive from these approaches? Do empirical investigations of decision making in these three cases provide any advantages to decision-makers?

The first approach barely qualifies as empirical. It employs anecdotal accounts that buttress a particular point of view. Gladwell's arguments favoring the employment of snap judgments to guide decisions is typical of this approach (Gladwell, 2005). I have placed it under the empirical umbrella because it is based on observed facts. However, the facts are not handled scientifically. The problem is not that the facts are wrong. I do not doubt that after examining the newly purchased *kouros* at the J. Paul Getty Museum Thomas Hoving had an intuitive feeling about its authenticity. I also believe that the geologist who examined the chemistry of the *kouros*'s dolomite marble undertook a good-faith effort to determine its provenance. In relating his anecdotes, Gladwell does not make up the facts. But he is selective in the facts he chooses to use to tell his story.

This is the principal problem with anecdotal accounts: the adduced facts are chosen selectively to support a particular perspective. *Blink* would not be an interesting book if it were filled with stories of how people's gut feelings lead nowhere. Who would read a book that focused on the following storyline?

> When he woke up Tuesday morning, Andrew had an overwhelming premonition that he would be caught up in a terrorist attack while traveling to work on the subway. He knew it would occur. He called his office and said he was taking sick leave. He spent the day at home. Tuesday passed peacefully. The biggest news event was that Congress voted to raise postage rates on first-class letters by five cents.

The vast majority of premonitions and intuitive insights do not play out. In his perceptive and highly readable book, *Innumeracy* (2001), Temple University mathematician John Allen Paulos supplies many examples of how innumeracy can lead to misunderstandings of how the world works. In an examination of the occurrence of improbable events and coincidences, he points out that statistically, in a country the size of the United States, the odds are that even the most improbable events will surface. One example he employs has a direct bearing on our discussion: Paulos estimates that if one out of ten thousand dreams matches some real event in life (a conservative assumption), 3.6 percent of the people who dream every night will have a predictive dream in a year. This may look like a small value, but when you multiply it by a count of the U.S. population (more than 300 million people), you see that millions of dreams come true each year in America, purely on the basis of coincidence. As it is for dreams, so it is with intuitive speculation.

Do anecdotal accounts have value? Absolutely. They employ factual observation to demonstrate that a particular point of view is plausible. Consider the following hypothetical dialogue between Graham and Sabrina:

Graham: In my opinion, the prospect of the unconscious brain solving problems more effectively than the conscious brain is utter nonsense. That's not how it works.

Sabrina: Not so fast, Graham. Think about how Thomas Hoving's intuitive sense about the authenticity of a Greek *kouros* was dead-on. Or how soap opera directors survive in the tough world of daytime TV by making snap judgments on casting, camera angles, and things of this sort.

Sabrina is not saying that the unconscious brain hypothesis is correct: she is simply referencing anecdotes to inform Graham that there are times when snap judgments seem to work.

Another strength of anecdotal accounts is that they make the speculation real and interesting. One thing is for sure: Gladwell's success with *Blink* stimulated more interest in the value of snap judgments than a hundred academic papers written about the unconscious deliberation of the brain.

But the final verdict is that anecdotal accounts do not prove anything. However, they have value in that they enable us to identify and address interesting problems that we might otherwise ignore.

The second of the empirical approaches we reviewed examines decision making in a systematic way but lacks valid results because it employs methodological shortcuts. This approach is illustrated in Timothy Wilson's highly referenced study of how "thinking too much" can yield suboptimal decisions (Wilson and others, 1993). In defense of Wilson, his group is not alone in taking methodological shortcuts. In researching this book, I reviewed close to one hundred peer-reviewed articles written by experimental psychologists and discovered that employment of samples of convenience among them is the rule and not the exception. Nearly all the experiments I encountered were carried out by academics using undergraduate students as their research guinea pigs. In some of the best-known studies, the students attend highly prestigious schools. To what extent do these students—particularly those from schools like Stanford, Princeton, and the University of Virginia—reflect the traits of the population at large?

The disregard for representative sampling that I encountered in many published studies surprised me. This isn't how I was trained to do research. Early in my professional life, I executed some fifteen surveys for U.S. federal agencies over six years. Perhaps a third of the work effort in conducting these surveys entailed identifying an appropriate sample frame, randomly selecting subjects from the sample frame, distributing questionnaires to the subjects, then following up on nonrespondents until we hit an 85 percent response rate. Sometimes circumstances made it difficult to employ representative samples. In these cases, we had to be creative, because we realized that without a representative sample, our conclusions were not defensible. On one project, my group worked with the U.S. Navy to reduce shipboard racial tensions among sailors. An important part of the project was to determine the sailors' attitudes on a number of critical issues. But how to put together a representative sample of sailors? Our solution was to visit the ship mess hall at appropriate times during the day and to have every tenth sailor entering the mess hall fill out an attitudinal questionnaire. It took a lot of work to implement this sampling strategy properly, but at the end, we were confident we had a representative sample.

Here is a description of the sampling methodology employed by Tversky and Kahneman in one of their most famous studies, which is reported in their article, "The Framing of Decisions and the Psychology of Choice": "[In this article] we present selected illustrations of preference reversals, with data obtained from students at Stanford University and at the University of British Columbia who answered brief questionnaires in a classroom setting" (Tversky and Kahneman, 1981). In other words, the authors handed out problems in their classroom, gave students time to work on them, collected the results, analyzed them, and then wrote an article that was ultimately published in a prestigious journal. Where is the regard for external validity here?

Cavalier sampling isn't restricted to the use of undergraduate students. One study I encountered based its findings of public perceptions of risk on a study sample of thirty college students, forty members of the League of Women Voters, and twenty-five business and professional members of a local community club in Eugene, Oregon (Slovic, Fischhoff, and Lichtenstein, 1981). What kind of valid generalizations regarding perceptions of risk could possibly emerge from the use of this obviously nonrepresentative sample of survey respondents? The authors of this paper have used undergraduate students in other studies on perceptions of risk. This is disturbing. In what sense do inexperienced twenty-year-old undergraduates who are just emerging from the lifelong protection of their parents reflect the risk perceptions of the citizens of a diverse, multigenerational society?

As a general rule, samples of convenience are suitable for exploratory studies. For example, if you want to test the reliability of a questionnaire you have developed and want to see whether it confirms the relationships you have hypothesized, samples of convenience provide a handy and cheap mechanism to get a handle on your approach. But they have a serious drawback: because no steps have been taken to ensure that they represent the population being addressed, the researchers cannot meaningfully generalize from the results of their experiments to the characteristics of the broader population. This is a basic lesson from Statistics 101.

The third of the empirical approaches we reviewed, Dijksterhuis's experiments, is reasonably attentive to following good methodological practice. While it has its share of deficiencies (for example, the experiments are chiefly carried out on undergraduates and the interpretation of some results are dependent on questionable statistical tests), its use of multiple studies to examine unconscious deliberation from different perspectives strengthens our confidence in the validity of the findings.

Taken together, we have learned from these three levels of empirical studies that there appears to be evidence that when making decisions, the unconscious brain is at work. The blink anecdotes provide examples of how unconscious, template-rooted thinking might function, but they prove nothing. There is no evidence that blink insights offer better results than Grandma's premonitions. The experiments carried out by academic researchers provide some evidence that an unconscious brain works on problems in parallel with the conscious brain, although the two brains do not operate in concert. They also offer a dollop of confirmation that the high-powered processing capability of the unconscious brain can handle complex problems even as the conscious brain struggles to accommodate complexity with its limited processing capacity. They support the view that when we sleep on problems, we are letting our unconscious brain earn its keep.

EMPIRICAL RESEARCH ON DECISION MAKING IN THE NEUROSCIENCES

Human consciousness and the ability to reason have puzzled people since the earliest times. Historically, the workings of the mind fell under the purview of philosophy and religion. In the West, Plato and Aristotle wrote about the mind and soul more than two thousand years ago. Over the centuries, philosophers and theologians debated where the mind and soul reside. René Descartes saw the mind as being distinct from the body in what is called the dualistic mind-body perspective. Monism viewed the mind and body as inextricably interrelated.

Philosophical speculation gave way to empirical initiatives as scholars and practitioners in the medical arena began to study the structure and function of the brain and early psychologists struggled to understand and explain human behavior. In the twentieth century, empirically rooted neuroscience emerged and blossomed. Advances in understanding were closely tied to advances in observational technology. Ever stronger microscopes, brain imaging technologies, and the improved capacity to measure electrical and chemical activity in the brain enabled neuroscientists to garner the information they needed to begin understanding the workings of the brain. But the brain is so complex that even great advances in knowledge just scratch the surface of total comprehension. We know much more today than fifty years ago, but we acknowledge that we have just begun the journey.

Brain Basics Review

Neuroscience research that touches on decision making can be divided into two categories: general research on the structure and function of the brain and neuropsychological research, where neuropsychology addresses the cognitive, emotional, and behavioral functioning of the brain. We covered general neurological research in Chapter Eight, which looked at brain basics. In this section, I summarize key points addressed in that chapter. Developments in neuropsychology are treated in the next section.

Following are brain basics findings that have an impact on decision making:

- *Finding*: The brain cuts corners to conserve energy, which entails employing templates whenever possible. *Consequence*: On the positive side, template-based thinking enables us to make small, inconsequential decisions quickly, without excessive deliberation. Without template-based thinking, we would spend a large portion of our days weighing the pros against the cons of action for trivial issues. However, the templates work against thinking outside of the box. This is a theme fully explored in Gregory Berns's book, *Iconoclast* (2010). We need to recognize that in our own thinking, as well as the thinking of others, there is a tendency to resist change. This leads to overly conservative decision making.

- *Finding*: When it encounters gaps of information, the brain fills in the blanks with its best guesses. *Consequence*: This phenomenon, sometimes referred to as *predictive coding*, is valuable for top-rated athletes who operate in an environment of quick change and often have less than one second to make a decision. They do not have time to assess all the facts, so the brain takes the limited information they possess and fills in the blanks. All of us experience predictive coding continually, but we are unaware of it. Ophthalmologists tell us that the images we see are not perfect representations of external reality but are the consequence of predictive coding that the brain carries out as it translates signals from the occipital node to meaningful images. The downside of this phenomenon is that it provides us with guesses, not hard facts. If the guesses are wrong, the decisions based on them will likely be wrong as well.

- *Finding*: The physiological development of a human brain does not finish until about the age of twenty-six; mature decision-making capabilities are one of the last functions to develop fully. *Consequence*: The last stage in the development of brain functioning entails the growth of myelin sheathing around the neurons—so-called white matter. The myelin leads to substantial improvements in the efficiency with which neurons function. In the last stages of brain development, which occur in the mid- to late twenties, the brain's executive processing capabilities finally mature. This suggests there is a biological basis for providing major decision-making responsibilities to people after they have reached their midtwenties.

- *Finding*: Everything we experience is intermediated by the brain: we do not perceive reality directly. *Consequence*: Because each brain possesses trillions of neural pathways, we are assured that two people, even twins, who examine the same object or facts will perceive them differently. In some cases, the brain can be readily tricked by illusions, so that what it perceives is completely off-target. This suggests that our perceptions, which feed into our decision-making process, may not reflect the real world or possibly the perceptions of others. We must always be sensitive to the fact that our perceptions of reality may be wrong.

Experimental Findings in Neuropsychology

Neuropsychology focuses on the cognitive, emotional, and behavioral ramifications of the brain's structure and function. If someone has hallucinations, what is their source? If a young woman suffers from meningitis, then develops Cotard syndrome (a feeling that she is dead), what triggered this event? In *The Man Who Mistook His Wife for a Hat*, the opening story is about a patient suffering from face blindness, meaning he wasn't able to recognize the faces of people he knew well (Sacks, 1998). Why did this malady arise? These are the kinds of situations neuropsychology addresses.

My treatment of neuropsychology is restricted to a brief discussion that concentrates on the functioning of the brain's ventromedial prefrontal cortex (VMF). This area, located at the front of the brain, is believed to play a significant role in decision making, which is why I single it out. There isn't a single decision-making locale on the brain. Neuroscientists agree that decision making is distributed throughout the brain. Decision making arises from activity in a large-scale system that includes the amygdala, the somatosensory/insular cortices, and the peripheral nervous system.

Earlier in this chapter is a three-stage review of empirical research that examined conscious versus unconscious deliberations of the brain. I repeat that methodology here, but this time I engage in a three-stage review of research carried out on the VMF. I start with a look at a famous medical case, a clinical review of a young man name Phineas Gage who suffered serious damage to the front of his brain owing to an accident. Gage's behavior after suffering brain damage provided clues that suggested the prefrontal cortex plays a significant role in enabling people to make decisions. I then move on to experiments carried out by contemporary neuroscientists who investigate the role of the VMF in decision making by comparing the behaviors of normal people with those of people suffering damage to the VMF. Finally, I look at the use of advanced brain scanning technologies to examine the functioning of the VMF. Thus in a few pages, I cover a gamut of empirical research approaches taken in the neuropsychological arena.

Clinical Study: The Case of Phineas Gage

This is the story of Phineas Gage, a twenty-five-year-old foreman of a work crew blasting a roadbed for the Rutland and Burlington Railroad. A horrific accident occurred on September 13, 1848, outside the town of Cavendish, Vermont. In the greater scheme of things, it was a small tragedy that took place in a small corner of the United States. But it is recorded in the history books because, in the words of Gage's biographer, Malcolm MacMillan (2008), it was "the first reported case in which brain damage caused alterations to personality."

On September 13, Gage was preparing to blast rock to establish a rail bed. The standard blasting process required drilling a hole into rock, adding a quantity of black powder, inserting a fuse, adding a quantity of sand, then tamping the sand with a weighty, meter-long tamping rod. It is speculated that Gage or an assistant neglected to cover the black powder with sand. When Gage began the tamping process, the black powder exploded, driving the tamping rod clear through his head. The force was so powerful that the tamping rod landed eighty feet behind him. The tamping rod itself weighed thirteen pounds and had a diameter of one and a quarter inches. Gage was knocked down by the blow but did not lose consciousness. After the accident, he was able to carry on a conversation with coworkers and sat upright in a cart during the three-quarter-mile trip to town. The damage was substantial: the attending physicians witnessed brain matter spill from the open wound.

At the time of this incident, medical doctors were amazed that an individual could survive so much damage to the brain and continue to function effectively. Gage's claim to fame was having survived a horrendous experience. His important role in advancing brain research would be triggered by the 1868 publication of a medical paper by his physician, John Martyn Harlow. In a short piece appearing in the *Bulletin of the Massachusetts Medical Society* (published eight years after Gage's death), Harlow indicated that the accident caused a dramatic change in Gage's personality. Whereas prior to the accident, Gage was a reliable individual respected by his work crew, after it he became foul-mouthed and petulant and displayed deficiencies in planning. Harlow reported that Gage's personality had changed so much that his old friends said "he was 'no longer Gage'" (Damasio, 1994). Inasmuch as the damage to Gage's brain occurred in the prefrontal cortex and appeared to correlate with retrogressed maturity and diminished planning capacity, it encouraged speculation among neurologists that the prefrontal cortex region of the brain governed personality and planning capabilities in humans (Damasio and others, 1994).

In 1994, the neuroscientist Antonio Damasio parlayed Gage's story into a best-selling book, *Descartes' Error*. In the book, he uses Gage's history, as described by his physician, Dr. Harlow, to develop the argument that the damage to the young man's ventromedial prefrontal cortex led to diminished social capacity, as reflected in a reduction of emotional feeling and the loss of effective judgment. Damasio uses the Gage story to lay out his somatic marker hypothesis, which holds that decision making has a strong emotional component.

Damasio's speculations created a bit of controversy. An Australian academic, Malcolm MacMillan, spent several years digging into Gage's life. The result of his effort was the publication of Gage's biography, focusing primarily on the meager evidence that exists on his life before and after the accident (MacMillan, 2000). MacMillan's conclusion is that the neuroscientists who use Gage to demonstrate the clinical consequences of damage to VMF are making much ado about nothing. Notwithstanding Dr. Harlow's brief description of Gage's postaccident symptoms, published eight years after Gage's death, there is little evidence to show that Gage was dramatically transformed by the accident. He lived a productive life for nearly twelve years after the accident, before dying in 1860. MacMillan's comments raise the possibility that Damasio is reading more into Gage's story than can be sustained by the evidence. On the other hand, *Descartes' Error* includes clinical accounts of other people who suffered damage to the VMF, including a personal patient named Elliott. Irrespective of the accuracy of the Gage account, Damasio maintains that other clinical cases support his somatic marker hypothesis.

The situation we face here is similar to what we encountered in our earlier discussion about the use of anecdotes to support a specific point of view. Instead of anecdotes, we are dealing with clinical case studies that reveal an interesting story but lack scientific muscle. The account of Phineas Gage and others suffering VMF brain lesions presents interesting speculation that warrants further investigation. But by itself, it has not proven anything.

Experimental Studies of the Link Between the VMF and Decision Making 1

Antonio Damasio and his colleagues at the University of Iowa School of Medicine carried out a series of experiments in the 1990s and 2000s as they continued to seek evidence for the validity of the somatic marker hypothesis. Their approach was to test the decision-making capabilities of people with VMF damage by contrasting their performance in contrived exercises with the performance of "normal" people. They developed the Iowa gambling task, a neuropsychological test that assesses a participant's capacity to make decisions that lead to his or her ultimate benefit. The test employs four decks of cards, labeled decks A to D. The goal is to draw cards in such a way as to maximize gains and minimize losses. By drawing cards from decks A and B, participants can realize substantial gains, while cards from decks C and D generate smaller gains. The decks are set up so that participants are penalized from time to time. The penalties associated with decks A and B are greater than those associated with decks C and D. In fact, the game has been rigged so that the winning strategy is to select cards only from decks C and D. The participants know nothing about how the game plays out. They simply begin drawing cards and learn quickly that the payout of decks A and B is greater than that of decks C and D. It's only when they begin drawing penalty cards that they begin to think about developing a card-drawing strategy because if they stick with the high-payout, high-penalty decks, A and B, they will ultimately lose more than they gain.

The Iowa team's high-impact study published in *Science* magazine in 1997 came up with two conclusions (Bechara, Damasio, Tranel, and Damasio, 1997). First, the results of the tests suggested that by the eightieth draw of cards, normal people learn that the winning strategy is to pick cards from decks C and D. The patients with VMF damage do not learn this lesson.

A second conclusion is tied to taking skin conductance response (SCR) measurements of all participants as they make their choices. SCR measurement is akin to a lie detector test. When people experience stress, the autonomic nervous system causes them to perspire, and this can be measured with SCR devices. The uncontrolled perspiration is viewed as a type of emotional response. The researchers found that as they played the game and developed a sense of the patterns of wins and losses, normal people would perspire lightly prior to drawing cards from unfavorable decks. The perspiration would be detected by the SCR device attached to them. Thus they experienced anticipatory emotional responses before drawing from decks A and B. Patients with VMF damage did not register anticipatory SCR reactions. The authors view these results as support for the somatic marker hypothesis, demonstrating that decision making has an emotional component.

One problem with this early study is that the number of subjects in the study is minuscule: only ten normal subjects and six suffering VMF lesions. In 2004, Bechara reported an expansion of the study that used more subjects. The results of the second study were essentially the same as with the earlier one. In 2004, other neuroscientists disputed the conclusions of the early study based on methodological grounds (Maia and McClelland, 2004). That's the way science works.

Experimental Studies of the Link Between the VMF and Decision Making 2

In the discussion of experimental research on conscious versus unconscious deliberation in decision making, we saw that the second-generation experiments were methodologically superior to the first-generation studies. We encounter the same situation here. The Iowa team's studies stimulated several significant follow-up studies by other scientists, who carried out experiments that were tightly controlled. I focus on one whose methodological standards are exemplary.

In a 2007 issue of the journal *Cerebral Cortex*, Lesley Fellows and Martha Farah describe a study they carried out on the role of the VMF in decision making. It occurred to the authors that while prior studies focused on the VMF, it could be that other areas of the frontal cortex contributed to decision-making capabilities as well, so they set up an experiment on three sets of players: individuals with VMF damage, individuals with frontal cortex damage that spared the VMF, and a control group.

The care the scientists took in selecting subjects is admirable and contrasts dramatically with the sampling strategies that experimental psychologists often employ. The authors spell out the details of how they selected subjects:

- The brain-damaged subjects were selected from the databases of neurological patients at the University of Pennsylvania and McGill University.

- A criterion for selection of brain-damaged subjects was that the damage was of more than six months duration.

- In establishing baselines for the subjects, they employed the most recent brain scans.

- The process of selecting subjects focused on three categories of people: those with VMF damage, those with frontal cortex brain damage where the VMF was spared damage, and a control group.

- The VMF lesions were caused by aneurysms or ischemic stroke.

- The non-VMF lesions were caused by aneurysm, ischemic stroke, or surgery.

- Controls were carefully matched with the brain-damaged subjects: their IQs, education levels, verbal skills, and age were indistinguishable from the traits of corresponding brain-damaged subjects.

- Controls were carefully screened to eliminate subjects who had ever experienced brain-related or psychiatric problems.

The goal of the experiment was to see whether the decision-making performance of VMF subjects differed from the performance of brain-damaged subjects without VMF damage. The experiment assessed the degree to which the subjects made consistent decisions. The experimenters put photographs of eight types of food, six different people, and six brightly colored watches on cards. With each of these three categories, they had subjects look at pairs of items and identify which of the two they preferred. For example, they would show the subjects photos of a pizza slice and a chocolate bar, and ask: "Which do you prefer?" Then they might show them a photo of a slice of cake and a carrot stick and ask: "Which do you prefer?" After all possible pairwise comparison had been made, the experimenters were able to determine the degree of consistency in the making of choices. An example of inconsistency would be where subject X prefers pizza to chocolate and chocolate to carrots, but prefers carrots to pizza. The pairwise comparison of cards of people's faces and brightly colored watches was carried out separately.

The findings showed that in making judgments, subjects with VMF damage were significantly less consistent than either non-VMF brain-damaged subjects or the control group. There was no significant difference in the performance of the non-VMF brain-damaged subjects and control group subjects. These results led the authors to conclude that the VMF is indeed the locality of the frontal cortex that is associated with decision making. They also noted that when making their choices, the VMF subjects appeared to choose one card over the other haphazardly. There was no pause for deliberation. This is a trait other studies found in VMF subjects.

The Fellows and Farah study did not examine the emotional state of VMF subjects. However, a study by Mah, Arnold, and Grafman (2005) investigated whether VMF-damaged subjects had significantly greater emotional deficits than other frontal cortex brain-damaged subjects who had their VMF intact. In their study, the authors showed photographs of human faces and asked the subjects to interpret the emotional expression of the faces. Only the VMF-damaged subjects had difficulty interpreting the emotional expressions of the faces in the photograph. The control group subjects and the other brain-damaged subjects were able to interpret the expressions readily. The authors' conclusion is that their findings support the view that there is an emotional component in the functioning of the VMF.

One further paper has a bearing on this discussion (Phan, Wager, Taylor, and Liberzon, 2004). The researchers reviewed fifty-five experiments that attempted to examine human emotion and concluded that the brain's emotional response to stimuli can indeed be captured in fMRI images. Although the study does not examine the link between emotion and decision making, it notes that the amygdala (the flight-or-fight portion of the brain) lights up when subjects encounter certain stimuli. In view of the fact that the fear response of the amygdala affects decision making in some circumstances, this suggests that fMRI-based studies might be helpful in testing the hypothesis that decision making has a strong emotional component to it.

THE CONTRIBUTION OF NEUROPSYCHOLOGY RESEARCH: WHERE DO WE STAND?

Each of the three stages of empirical studies on the role of the ventromedial prefrontal cortex has contributed to our knowledge of the VMF's role in decision making. It began with the offhand, clinically based speculation of Phineas Gage's physician in 1868. Based on his observations, Dr. Harlow surmised that the damage Gage experienced in the front portion of his brain had a discernible impact on his personality. More than a century later, Antonio Damasio, a neurologist, followed up on this speculation and hypothesized that damage to the ventromedial prefrontal cortex caused Gage's changed behavior. He drew on his own clinical experience with a patient named Elliott to elaborate on Gage's experience. Elliott was known to have damage to his VMF that resulted from a surgical procedure. Changes in his personality that appeared to be tied to the VMF damage were well documented: prior to the damage, Elliott was a responsible business executive who possessed good planning skills and was emotionally normal. After the damage, he grew unreliable, was unable to plan even the simplest things, and was emotionally detached.

This clinically based speculation led to serious studies of the role of the VMF in decision making. What made the research interesting wasn't just its attempt to identify a location in the brain that supports decision making, but Damasio's contention that decision making has a strong emotional component to it. Damasio and his team at the University of Iowa led the effort to carry out experiments to test his somatic marker hypothesis. The initial research was methodologically crude. The results appeared to support the hypothesis, and this triggered additional, tightly controlled research by other scientists. The additional research suggests that the VMF does indeed play a significant role in decision making. It also shows that VMF damage appears to diminish emotional capabilities, but it is not clear that this indicates that emotion plays a role in decision making. No doubt research in this area will continue to grow, and through these efforts, greater knowledge will accrue on the brain's role in decision making.

The findings I discuss here are not immediately useful to decision-makers. At this point, the principal value of neuropsychology experiments is to provide a solid understanding of how the brain supports the decision-making process. We are not able to take the findings that are emerging and use them to make better decisions. This is not surprising, since serious neuropsychological examinations of the brain's role in decision making began just two decades ago, and the knowledge being generated is of the most fundamental kind. What we experience here is typical of basic research: at the outset, it clarifies issues that have no immediate application. However, after time, it becomes an important cornerstone in contributing to practical knowledge.

THE NEED FOR RESEARCH ON DECISIONS OF CONSEQUENCE

In 2003, soon after winning the Nobel Prize in economics, Daniel Kahneman wrote a reflective piece, "A Psychological Perspective on Economics" (2003). In it, he points out that after twenty-five years of research contributions by behavioral economists, the economics community resists incorporating the psychological perspective into the discipline's mainstream canon. His explanation is that the existing economics paradigm serves economists well, and they do not see how they will benefit by adopting the insights of psychologists.

I think Kahneman has it only partially right. An additional factor is that economists find the results of psychological research to be marginally relevant to their discipline. As a general rule, psychologists concentrate on the behavior of individuals while economists work with aggregates of people. The experiments that behavioral economists carry out often aim to demonstrate that the assumption of rational decision making does not hold up in the study of individual behavior. For example, in making decisions, individuals tend to be inconsistent ("I like A better than B, B better than C, and C better than A"), unduly influenced by how problems have been framed, and overly reliant on inappropriate heuristics. For their part, experimental psychologists such as Timothy Wilson, Ap Dijksterhuis, and their colleagues carry out experiments on individuals to assess the workings of the unconscious brain. So it is with other psychologists who study the effects of priming on decision making, perceptions of risk, and an assortment of allied topics.

The insights these experiments offer pertain to small, inconsequential problems. Tversky and Kahneman tell us what happens when people multiply $8 \times 7 \times 6 \times 5 \times 4 \times 3 \times 2 \times 1$ versus $1 \times 2 \times 3 \times 4 \times 5 \times 6 \times 7 \times 8$. Wilson and his colleagues inform us that people who don't introspect about strawberry jam do a better job of choosing good strawberry jam than those who do. Dijksterhuis and his colleagues inform us that when you purchase simple products such as toothpaste, your decisions are best when made consciously, but when you purchase complex products such as bedroom furnishings, you may make better decisions by relying on unconscious deliberation. I believe these examples are not the exception, but the rule. To test my belief, I went through a compendium of the best-of-the-best psychology-oriented papers on decision making (Lichtenstein and Slovic, 2006) and found few that would resonate with anyone functioning outside the realm of experimental psychology. Furthermore, the great majority of papers reporting experimental results were based on the use of undergraduates from elite universities. And nearly all employed statistical tests of significance on their findings, even though the samples were not representative.

In going through the behavioral economics and other experimental psychology literature, you seldom encounter studies that examine decisions of consequence that affect aggregates of people: employees in companies, boards of directors, citizens of municipalities, and leaders of whole nations. Economics, political science, and sociology are concerned with human behavior in the aggregate. The decisions of greatest interest to their adherents are decisions of consequence, which are not addressed by most experimental psychologists. To be fair, I need to point out that some of the studies on the irrational choices individuals make are of interest to marketers concerned with buyer behavior, and other studies of public perceptions of risk have a bearing on public policy.

Economists are spoiled by the work of Adam Smith. Their discipline was founded by a man who established a link between the choices and actions of individual men and women and people functioning in the aggregate. If you think back to Adam Smith, his great contribution to social thinking was his realization that individual people operating in their own self-interest function as if guided by an invisible hand to set the price and quantity of goods produced and sold in the marketplace. The market, he determined, was the ultimate arbiter of individual decisions.

Consider also the decision-making behavior of bees. As Chapter Seven shows, what enables bee communities to survive is the collective decision-making behavior of the hive, not the efforts of individual bees. We may be experiencing the emergence of the same type of phenomenon in humans as developments in open sourcing demonstrate the efficacy of leaderless, distributed decision making.

Certainly psychologists are capable of studying aggregate human behavior. The experimental efforts of the pioneers of social psychology bridged the gap between individual behavior and the aggregate behavior of individuals. Their studies had clear implications for decision making. In well-known experiments on the autokinetic effect carried out in the 1930s, Muzafer Sherif (1935) convincingly demonstrated that when collaborating in groups, group members naturally strive to accommodate the range of viewpoints held by the members. Through experiments, he showed that when functioning alone, individuals may hold a particular point of view, but when engaged in group decision making, they adjust this point of view to accommodate the viewpoints held by group members. In his most famous experiments, the robber's cave experiments, he demonstrated how conflicting groups can overcome their mutual animosities when challenged to achieve superordinate goals (Sherif and others, 1988).

Sherif's contemporary, social psychologist Solomon Asch, also carried out high-impact experiments of practical value to decision-makers. His best-known experiments demonstrated that in a desire to conform to a group norm, many individuals are willing to supply obviously incorrect answers to problems (Asch, 1955). In the 1960s, Asch's student, Stanley Milgram, continued with this line of research in the famous experiment that showed that real experimental subjects were willing to administer nasty shocks to "subjects" of a bogus experiment when ordered to do so by an authority figure (Milgram, 1963). The implications of these findings on conformity are obvious in the context of decision making: when decisions are made in groups or larger communities, they may be more heavily influenced by the desire of individuals to conform to group norms (however distorted) than to follow objective reasoning.

It would be nice to see more empirical studies addressing decision making for consequential decisions. Knowledge of how decision making works would be strengthened if researchers continue to conduct empirical studies on how decisions are carried out. However, I would argue that for the research to possess value for the theory and practice of decision making, it should deal with more important questions than those the behavioral economists and other experimental psychologists have been addressing. In line with the orientation of this book, attention should focus on mindful decisions of consequence.

10 Seven Lessons

This last chapter takes a look at the major lessons that distinguish what this book argues from what is proffered by the conventional wisdom on decision making. It is useful at this point to recall its subtitle: *Decision Making That Accounts for Irrationality, People, and Constraints*. I do not see irrationality, people, and constraints as impediments to good decision making. Instead, I see them as lying at the heart of the decision-making process when dealing with decisions of consequence, and that is my message.

What I write here is quite different from what you encounter in other decision-making books. During the two years that I immersed myself in the decision-making literature to prepare this book, I was surprised to discover big holes in mainstream writings. My surprise was largely rooted in the fact that the missing points were significant omissions that entail commonsense insights. Here are three examples of important decision-making principles that are not covered by canon.

The first is that *decisions are made by people on behalf of people and with impacts on people*. In the process of decision making, primary attention should focus on people issues—what I call *social space* in this book. That's common sense. Who are the players? What are their interests? How capable are they? How do we handle their differing points of view? Strangely, these obvious points aren't covered in standard treatments of decision making.

The second example is that *the world is filled with scalawags*. Small business owners certainly know this. If they want to stay in business, they must spot the lies, half-truths, illegal propositions, and wishful thinking they have been bombarded with from the day they opened their doors for business. Nobody needs to tell them that in making a decision, they should reflect on its moral dimension. What small business owners encounter in the moral arena of business practice is pertinent to all decision-makers, who should routinely ask: Is the information provided to me by the players I deal with truthful? To what extent are the actions of the people I rely on guided by their self-interest? Again, we are dealing with common sense here. And again, you won't find these matters discussed in standard decision-making fare.

The third example is that *we cannot know more than what our brain allows us to know*. There is an absolute limit on the depth and breadth of our knowledge and understanding. When acting as diligent decision-makers who are intent on collecting the facts for fact-based decisions, we must acknowledge that our perception of the facts is intermediated by the brain. If we know something about how the brain functions, we recognize that the facts we work with are imperfect reflections of reality and can lead us to off-target decisions. We encounter common sense once again. Until recently, little attention has focused on what I call the biology of decision making. The good news is that the biology of decision making has begun to receive attention in segments of the decision-making community, and its role in decision-making processes and actions will become increasingly evident.

The gap we encounter when we look at what's happening with real-world decision making and compare it to the decision-making canon reminds us of the old adage that there is nothing more uncommon than common sense. Let's now take a final look at significant, often ignored commonsense lessons that have been surfaced in this book. Mimicking Stephen Covey (2004), I present them as seven lessons for highly effective decision-makers.

SEVEN LESSONS FOR HIGHLY EFFECTIVE DECISION-MAKERS

Following are seven lessons emerging from this book that decision-makers should master.

Lesson 1. Decisions of Consequence Occur in a Social Environment That Strongly Affects Decision Outcomes. These Decisions Should Always Accommodate Social Space

The concern here is mindful decisions of consequence, not decisions on purchasing flat panel televisions, or determining what university to apply to, or whom to vote for in the next election. These are personal decisions whose scale and impact are small. They may be important to the decision-maker, who may find it difficult to make a decision, but in the greater scheme of things, the decision-making effort is trivial. This book also doesn't look at well-defined decision problems that have unambiguous optimal solutions—for example, deciding how to configure equipment on the factory floor to optimize throughput. These can be highly consequential decisions, but resolving them can be done mechanically through the employment of effective operations research procedures. With these decisions, if you know how to set up the problem properly, you effectively push a button and get an answer.

Decisions of consequence have an effect on, and are affected by, multiple sets of players. The scale and impacts of the decisions are nontrivial. Examples include President Kennedy's decisions on how to respond to Khrushchev during the Cuban missile crisis, a city manager's decision on whether to promote the floating of municipal bonds to upgrade a community's sewage treatment capabilities, a marketing manager's decision on whether to launch a new advertising campaign, or a bid review committee's decision on whether a company should bid on a proposal to deliver technical training courses to a government agency.

A characteristic of decisions of consequence is that they are carried out in social space. As discussed in Chapter Three, social space incorporates an array of players whose desires and actions are crucial in defining the outcomes of a decision-making process. The social space associated with a decision has five sets of players:

- *Stakeholders*, who stand to benefit or suffer as a consequence of the decision. They may attempt to influence a particular decision outcome actively.

- *Decision-makers*, who deliberate and make the decision, taking into account inputs from stakeholders, the community, and external forces.

- *Decision-implementers*, who are charged with implementing the decision and are usually different people from the decision-makers.

- *The community*, that is, people who are largely bystanders who may be affected by the decision and whose support or opposition to it can make the difference between success and failure.

- *Outside forces* that are important to a decision, including such things as general economic conditions, the passage of new regulations, and acts of God (force majeure).

It is important that the decision-makers take into account the perspectives of each set of players in the social space when making decisions of consequence. They must recognize, for example, that after their careful deliberations, their decisions may not be executed properly if the decision-implementers do not implement them effectively. As another example, they need to recognize that a decision may go astray if stakeholders who disagree with the decision bypass the process by actively pressuring the decision-implementers to follow their orders.

Effective decision making must go beyond the narrow concerns of optimizing objective functions, striving to achieve rationality, working from weighted check-lists, setting up Bayesian models, and implementing a panoply of other tools and techniques showcased in decision-making books and courses. I don't advocate discarding these important tools and perspectives. I use them frequently myself. But they are secondary concerns. As I have tried to demonstrate in this book, they have little value if decision-makers do not account for the much bigger issue of individuals, groups, and communities, and all they entail, in the decision process. Carefully considered decisions will fail if they do not accommodate the realities of the decision social space.

Lesson 2. Decisions of Consequence Entail Dealing with Aggregates of People Who Have Contending Interests. Frequently the Decision-Makers' Primary Job Is to Work Through These Contending Interests

A corollary of lesson 1 is that in addressing a decision's social space, we find ourselves dealing with aggregates of people. I'm not just talking about juggling the five sets of players I mention above. The number of people affecting a decision or being affected by it can be substantially larger. Each of the five sets of players in social space has its multiple actors, and these actors often hold contending points of view. This reality is often lost when we frame decision-making problems. Frequently the default perspective we adopt is what Graham Allison calls *the rational-actor* model, which I discussed in Chapter Three. That is, we treat a group of people as if they hold a single outlook on issues. For example, we say "the position of senior management is . . ." or "What the customer wants is . . ." or "What the Chinese want is . . ." as if senior management, the customer, or the Chinese have a single, consistent perspective on issues.

Clearly this position does not reflect how the world really works. Senior managers make decisions that they mandate their organization to implement, but these decisions may not have the full support of all the senior players. In the real world, different executives argue different points in getting to the final decisions. The discussions might grow contentious. In fact, a substantial minority might heartily disagree with the decisions that are being promulgated within the organization and might work behind the scenes to sabotage them. (This scenario is covered in Chapter Seven.) The same can be said about "the customer." The customer is a fiction, occasionally the artifact of a focus group exercise or market research survey. If we say, "Our primary goal is to satisfy the customer," as if the customer is a homogeneous entity, we may be in for some unpleasant surprises. Regarding "the Chinese," at the time of this writing, there are 1.3 billion Chinese citizens who could very well reflect 1.3 billion separate points of view on issues. It is not clear whom we are talking about when we make reference to the perspective of "the Chinese."

Because decisions of consequence entail working with aggregates of people, decision-makers need to be able to sort through their contending needs and wants, then fashion a workable decision that reflects an appreciation of the different perspectives. Pushing forward with a decision that goes against the sensibilities of key players or does not account for the imperfections of the implementation process will most likely lead to unhappy outcomes that do not satisfy the decision-makers' desires. Chapter Seven provides insights into how aggregates of people can be accommodated when making decisions. It points out the variety of approaches to dealing with the perspectives of multiple players, ranging from pure autocracy ("Do what I say"), to collaborative consulting ("Tell me what you think"), to democratic councils ("We'll vote on the options"), to leaderless, distributed decision making ("Let's look at honeybees").

Those who teach, study, and practice decision making need to acknowledge these significant realities. They must acquire a mind-set that holds: "First, let me be sure to have mastery of a decision's social space, with its multiple actors who hold contending points of view; then let me worry about decision-making tools and techniques."

Lesson 3. An Emphasis on Tools Often Distracts Us from Effective Decision Making

Tools are cool. I occasionally set aside an hour or two on weekends to visit local hardware stores to see what's happening in the world of household tools. My favorite visits are to the crammed traditional hardware stores, where every inch of shelf space and wall space is occupied with thousands of interesting doodads. These stores look like scenes out of Harry Potter movies that portray old shops filled with instruments of magic. Because tools are cool, they are seductive. When you master a set of tools, you begin to define the problems you face in terms of these tools. This is captured in the old saying, "To the four-year-old boy with a hammer, all the world is a nail," an adage that appositely describes a tendency among many decision scientists. The following dialogue reflects this tendency:

Business executive: How can we decide which new product idea we should support?

Decision scientist: No sweat. We'll run the projected cost and revenue data through a Monte Carlo simulation and see which prospect provides the best numbers.

I love Monte Carlo simulations and often run them. Sometimes I get the feeling that the Monte Carlo technique is like magic in its use of random numbers to develop solutions to problems. But I learned a long time ago that the technique's value is closely tied to the way the problem being investigated is framed. As I have emphasized in this book, proper framing of problems starts with an investigation of the problem's social space. Who are the stakeholders? What are the interests each pursues? Who are the decision-makers? What are their interests? Who are the decision-implementers? What are their interests? How qualified are they to do a job? Will they implement what the decision-makers want? What constitutes the community of affected bystanders? What are their interests? And finally, what external forces need to be accounted for?

Going through an assessment of key players operating in the social space influences the way we frame the decision problem. In the case of deciding which new product idea to support, we may determine that product D is totally repulsive to the CEO and, if selected, would get no support from the executive suite. Scratch product D, even though its pro forma financials look good. Product B would require outsourcing the production of goods to India. In view of international economic uncertainties, as well as sensitivity about exporting jobs overseas, product B should be scuttled. The analysis of product A may show that it scores highly among all key players in the social space: it will receive strong support within the organization so that it has a good chance of being produced and marketed according to plan. Although its financials as determined through Monte Carlo simulation may not rank it top among the alternatives, the fact that it will achieve strong support from stakeholders, decision-makers, and decision-implementers gives it a big boost.

Tools have an important place in decision making, but they should not be the driver of decisions. In searching for magic bullets that lead to easy decisions, decision-makers should be wary of framing their decision problems around the use of tools, no matter how cool they are.

Lesson 4. The Idea of Rational Decision Making Is Largely Chimerical When Dealing with Decisions of Consequence

In my review of the decision-making literature, I was surprised by the strong emphasis placed on the need to make rational decisions. Everyone seems to take this position. However, what constitutes rationality in decision making is a bit vague. I see two broad approaches to defining it. In one, rational decisions are those that provide correct answers to well-defined problems that actually have correct answers. These types of problems are the bread and butter of operations research, where, for example, linear programming solutions are achieved by optimizing an objective function that defines how you should allocate materials used in some kind of process in order to minimize costs. If you allocate materials that yield greater costs than projected by the objective function, you are not being rational in your allocations.

A second approach is to define rationality as making decisions that serve the best interest of the decision-maker. A nonrational decision would be one that does not work in the best interest of the decision-maker. For example, if while visiting a farmers' market you pay four dollars a pound for the same apples that are selling for three dollars a pound by a neighboring vendor, you are not deciding rationally. This perspective makes sense until you start wrestling with the matter of how to assess *best interest*. If the vendor selling the four-dollar apples is your daughter, you may be willing to pay the extra dollar in order to help her out. You've determined your best interest is to support your daughter, so your purchase is perfectly rational from your point of view. Decision scientists say you are maximizing your personal utility function, a concept that Daniel Bernoulli developed in the eighteenth century. My feeling is that while utility functions work nicely as abstract constructs, they are tough to operationalize in practice.

I believe that great concern for rationality is misplaced because when addressing decisions of consequence, we are dealing with aggregates of people who have contending interests, as suggested in lessons 1 and 2. If you consider decisions that affect only one person, assessing what constitutes rational and nonrational decisions is fairly straightforward: determine whether a given decision serves the decision-maker's interests or goes against them. Things get confused, however, when dealing with multiple players who possess contending interests, because these interests translate into contending individual utility functions, which messes up the arithmetic of determining whether a decision is rational. Optimizing the utility function of one player may lead to suboptimization of the utility functions of other players. Are we pursuing rational decision making here or not? The individual whose wants are met may view the decision as rational, but I am pretty sure that those whose utility functions were not satisfied would disagree.

The marginal relevance of rationality as a driver in decision making becomes particularly evident when dealing with highly contentious issues, such as establishing public policy on the matter of exploiting different types of fossil fuel reserves. No one disputes that the mining, refining, and shipping of fossil fuels harm the environment. What's more, the burning of these fossil fuels contributes to global warming through the greenhouse effect. However, implementing a policy that imposes major controls on the exploitation of fossil fuels will have substantial negative economic consequences, leading to loss of jobs and reduced gross domestic product. So what should public policymakers decide? Does anyone believe that the ultimate resolution of this issue will be achieved through attempts at deciding things rationally? Ultimately important policy issues like this one are resolved bit by bit over a long stretch of time. They entail political action and hard bargaining and create winners and losers. It's a messy process. In retrospect, the decision may appear imminently rational long after it is resolved. But to those who were in the decision-making trenches, the pursuit of rationality was not an action item on the decision-making agenda. And to those whose proposals were pushed aside—the losers—the final outcome was hardly rational.

Lesson 5. Take Heed of The Moral Dimension of Decision Making. Don't Be Duped by Scalawags

I touch on this lesson in the introduction to this chapter. The moral dimension of decision making is treated in detail in Chapter Five.

The gap between decision-making canon and the practical requirements of decision-making practice is greater here than anywhere else. To see this, consider the microexperiment I conducted in my home office as I prepared to write Chapter Five: I took a look at the piles of decision-making books, monographs, and articles that surrounded me and began paging through them to see what they had to say about the impact of lies, self-serving actions, corruption, illegal behavior, and other topics of this ilk on decision making. I came up empty-handed. Elsewhere in my personal library, I have plenty of books that detail the moral failings of business and government, but the lessons learned from these stories of greed, dissimulation, rapacity, and wanton illegal behavior have not made their way into the decision-making literature. This is strange, because owners of small businesses regularly factor moral failings into their decision-making processes. In the moral arena, these practical decision-makers appear to have ample lessons they can teach to adherents of decision-making canon. The assumption of this canon is that decisions are carried out in a morally neutral environment, where we don't need to concern ourselves with either Mother Teresas or Bernie Madoffs. Small business owners know this isn't so.

Two categories of moral failings warrant special attention: the problem of moral hazard and the principal-agent problem. Effective decision-makers must be alert to both. With the problem of moral hazard, we encounter people who are willing to take risks in making decisions because if the decision does not work out, they have no stake in the ensuing losses. Yet if the decision works out, they stand to accumulate substantial gains. They are, in effect, gambling with other people's money. The Nobel laureate Paul Krugman identifies moral hazard as a significant contributor to the global economic collapse of 2008–2009 (Krugman, 2009).

With the principal-agent problem, we encounter a disconnect between what the principal requires (in this case, the decision-maker) and what the agent delivers (for example, decision-implementers). The lesson here is that when making a decision, don't assume that the people charged with implementing it will do what needs to be done to realize it as planned. When making decisions, smart decision-makers figure out all the ways a decision can be misimplemented and factor this insight into the formulation of the final decision.

Lesson 6. Our Perceptions of the World Are Intermediated by the Brain. What We See, Hear, and Feel Is Not What We Get

Researching how the brain works has been a transformational experience. Two traits of the functioning of the brain have altered the way I view the decision-making endeavor.

The first is that the brain is a lazy organ. Neuroscientists make this statement, tongue in cheek. We all know that the brain is amazingly active and that its computing power puts supercomputers to shame. However, all this activity is fueled by only ten watts of power, and this power limitation requires that the brain operate with the highest degree of efficiency. One way it achieves efficiency is to work from templates in order to conserve energy. Everything you experience is matched against templates of prior experiences. If a prior experience closely matches what you are currently experiencing, the brain uses the prior experience as a template to assess your current situation.

Three consequences of this trait have decision-making implications. One is that what you experience in your day-to-day life is heavily colored by template interpretations of reality. What you see may not be what you get. A second is that the brain resists change because accommodating change requires it to consume more power. This conservative tendency that occurs at the neuronal level percolates up to the level of an individual's personality. People have an inherent adverse response to change. Assuming a fresh view of things requires special effort. Neuroscientist Gregory Berns has written a book on the conservative tendency of the brain and offers strategies for overcoming it (Berns, 2010). The third consequence is that the brain is easily fooled. While template shortcuts allow it to function with enormous efficiency, the templates that guide your actions as a decision-maker may be wildly off target. We have plenty of evidence that the brain is readily fooled: visual illusions that cause people to see things that are not there graphically demonstrate the ease with which the brain can be tricked.

The second trait is that the unconscious brain works a lot harder than the conscious brain. Studies indicate that the conscious brain processes information at 45 bits per second, roughly the processing requirement for reading a sentence in this book. In contrast, the unconscious brain processes data at 11.2 million bits per second. As Chapter Nine relates, psychologists are trying to determine whether people can tap into the processing power of the unconscious brain in order to help them make better decisions. Each of us has experienced the ability of the unconscious brain to improve our decision making when we discover that by sleeping on a problem, we sometimes make better decisions than by analyzing them carefully.

With advances in brain imaging technology, we find an increased interest among neuroscientists and psychologists to employ this advanced technology to help us determine how the brain makes decisions.

Lesson 7. We Can Learn a Lot from Honeybees: Leaderless Distributed Decision Making Is Here to Stay

Honeybees are remarkable decision-makers. In midspring, when the beehive is crowded and it is time to move half the inhabitants to new quarters, a small number of scouts are sent out to locate possible sites for the new hive. Scouts who find promising new quarters return to the swarm and carry out an energetic waggle dance that indicates their level of enthusiasm and identifies the location of the site. If other honeybees are turned on by the dance, they visit the site, then return to the swarm to offer their views using a waggle dance. Scouts who locate unattractive sites carry out tepid waggle dances and thereby attract few or no follow-up visits by other bees. Ultimately the most attractive site experiences a quorum of visitors which, when reached, affirms the site as the selected location for a new beehive. Experts say that this search strategy leads to optimal solutions. Scientists tell us that honeybees honed their group decision-making skills over a period of 30 million years. These skills have served them well: honeybees are still around.

In Chapter Seven, we encountered three books that alert us to an evolving trend in decision-making practice: James Surowiecki's *The Wisdom of Crowds* (2005), Clayton Shirky's *Here Comes Everybody* (2008), and Thomas Seeley's *Honeybee Democracy* (2010). Each offers compelling stories of how leaderless, distributed decision making can achieve remarkable results. Humans have already experienced this form of decision making, but it is so much a part of our lives that we give it little thought. I am talking here about Adam Smith's invisible hand doing its extraordinary work in the marketplace. There is no central authority that sets the price and quantity of goods bought and sold in the market. Price and quantity are established by independent buyers and sellers pursuing their selfish interests within the confines of supply and demand. Until recently, there have been few other examples of this type of distributed decision making in the human experience. But that is changing owing to the ascendance of the Internet. What the Internet does is create communities of strangers scattered all over the globe who opt to work together virtually. Open sourcing enables these strangers to work together without central direction in order to create powerful artifacts, such as Wikipedia, Linux, Moodle, Perl, Mozilla Firefox, and the Apache server. Interestingly, the Internet itself was a product of open sourcing among scientists who participated in the ARPANET initiative in the 1960s.

The successes we are encountering with leaderless, distributed decision making would have been considered implausible just twenty years ago. They arose out of the spontaneous initiatives of visionaries such as Richard Stallman and Linus Torvalds. This is an area of decision making that warrants substantial investigation by decision-making theorists and practitioners. The big question is: Can this form of decision making be employed effectively on a small scale in ordinary businesses and government agencies? If it can, then we may see a profound change in how decisions are made in organizations.

LAST WORD

In considering possible titles for this book, it never occurred to me to use something like *All You Need to Know About Decision Making*. As a decision-making practitioner and decision science professor of long standing, I am aware that what I present in this book scratches the surface of what decision-making professionals offer in books, monographs, courses, articles, and blogs on a variety of decision-making topics, using approaches that range from the heavily quantitative to the playfully anecdotal. This book is not intended as a replacement of existing canon. It is designed to supplement it. The book's subtitle captures my intent. Traditional canon tends to ignore the three components of the book's subtitle: *Decision Making That Accounts for Irrationality, People, and Constraints.* I hope that by turning their attention to irrationality, people, and constraints, decision-makers can acquire fuller insights into what effective decision making entails.

References

Allison, G. *The Essence of Decision: Explaining the Cuban Missile Crisis.* New York: Little, Brown, 1971.

Allport, G. W. *Personality: A Psychological Interpretation.* New York: Holt, 1937.

Argote, L. "A Behavioral Theory of the Firm—Forty Years and Counting: Introduction and Impact." *Organization Science,* 2007, *18,* 337–349.

Argyris, C. *Knowledge for Action: A Guide to Overcoming Barriers to Organizational Change.* San Francisco: Jossey-Bass, 1993.

Ariely, D. *Predictably Irrational.* New York: HarperCollins, 2010.

Asch, S. "Opinions and Social Behavior." *Scientific American,* 1955, *193*(5), 31–35.

Baron, J. *Thinking and Deciding.* (4th ed.) Cambridge: Cambridge University Press, 2007.

Bazerman, M. H., and Moore, D. A. *Judgment in Managerial Decision Making.* (7th ed.) Hoboken, N.J.: Wiley, 2008.

Bechara, A. "The Role of Emotion in Decision-Making: Evidence from Neurological Patients with Orbitofrontal Damage." *Brain and Cognition,* 2004, *55,* 300–340.

Bechara, A., Damasio, H., Tranel, D., and Damasio, A. R. "Deciding Advantageously Before Knowing the Advantageous Strategy." *Science,* 1997, *275,* 1293–1294.

Becker, G. "Crime and Punishment: An Economic Approach." *Journal of Political Economy,* 1968, *76,* 169–217.

Bernoulli, D. "Exposition of a New Theory on the Measurement of Risk." *Econometrica,* 1954, *22,* 23–36. (Originally published 1738.)

Berns, G. *Iconoclast: A Neuroscientist Reveals How to Think Differently.* Cambridge, Mass.: Harvard University Press, 2010.

Blake, R., and Mouton, J. *The Managerial Grid: The Key to Leadership Excellence.* Houston: Gulf Publishing, 1964.

Brooks, F. P. *The Mythical Man-Month.* (2nd ed.) Reading, Mass.: Addison-Wesley, 1995.

Burton, R. *On Being Certain: Believing You Are Right Even When You're Not.* New York: St. Martin's Press, 2008.

Changizi, M. *The Vision Revolution: How the Latest Research Overturns Everything We Thought We Knew About Vision.* Dallas: BenBella Books, 2010.

Christensen, C. M. *The Innovator's Dilemma: When New Technologies Cause Great Firms to Fail.* Boston: Harvard Business School Press, 1997.

Covey, S. R. *The Seven Habits of Highly Effective People.* New York: Free Press, 2004.

Cyert, R. M., and March, J. G. *A Behavioral Theory of the Firm.* Upper Saddle River, N.J.: Prentice Hall, 1963.

Dacey, J. "Concepts of Creativity: A History." In M. A. Runco and S. R. Pritzker (eds.), *Encyclopedia of Creativity.* Orlando, Fla.: Academic Press, 1999.

Damasio, A. *Descartes' Error: Emotion, Reason and the Human Brain.* New York: Putnam, 1994.

Damasio, H., and others. "The Return of Phineas Gage: Clues About the Brain from the Skull of a Famous Patient." *Science,* 1994, *264*(5162), 1102–1105.

Deal, T. E., and Kennedy, A. A. *Corporate Cultures: The Rites and Rituals of Corporate Life.* Reading, Mass.: Addison-Wesley, 1982.

Decision Sciences Institute, "About DSI." 2012. http://www.decisionsciences.org/about/.

DePaulo, B. M., and others. "Lying in Everyday Life." *Journal of Personality and Social Psychology,* 1996, *70*, 979–995.

Descartes, R. *Discourse on Method.* New York: Washington Square Press, 1965. (Originally published 1637.)

Dijksterhuis, A. "Think Different: The Merits of Unconscious Thought in Preference and Decision Making." *Journal of Personality and Social Psychology,* 2004, *87*, 586–598.

Dijksterhuis, A., and Nordgren, L. F. "A Theory on Unconscious Thought." *Perspectives on Psychological Science,* 2006, *1*, 96–109.

Dijksterhuis, A., Bos, M. W., Nordgren, L. F., and van Baaren, R. B. "On Making the Right Choice: The Deliberation-Without-Attention Effect." *Science,* 2006 *311*, 1005–1007.

Durkheim, E. *Suicide.* New York: Free Press, 1951. (Originally published 1897.)

Durkheim, E. *The Rules of Sociological Method.* New York: Free Press, 1982. (Originally published 1895.)

Edgington, E. S. "Statistical Significance and Non-Random Samples." *Psychological Bulletin,* 1966, *66*, 485–487.

Epictetus. *Enchiridion.* Amherst, N.Y.: Prometheus Books, 1991.

Epstein, R. "The Myth of the Teen Brain." *Scientific American Mind,* Apr.–May 2007, pp. 57–63.

Fellows, L., and Farah, M. J. "The Role of the Ventromedial Prefrontal Cortex in Decision Making: Judgment Under Uncertainty of Judgment Per Se?" *Cerebral Cortex,* 2007, *17*, 2669–2674.

Fine, C. *A Mind of Its Own: How Your Brain Distorts and Deceives*. New York: Norton, 2006.

Fine, C. *Delusions of Gender*. New York: Norton, 2011.

Frame, J. D. *Project Management Competence*. San Francisco: Jossey-Bass, 1999.

Frame, J. D. *Managing Projects in Organization*. San Francisco: Jossey-Bass, 2003.

Freedman, D. H. *Wrong: Why Experts Keep Failing Us—and How to Know When Not to Trust Them*. New York: Little, Brown, 2010.

Fukuyama, F. *The End of History and the Last Man*. New York: Free Press, 1992.

Galbraith, J. K. *The Affluent Society*. Boston: Houghton Mifflin, 1969.

Gardner, H. *The Theory of Multiple Intelligences*. (3rd ed.) New York: Basic Books, 2011.

Gladwell, M. *The Tipping Point: How Little Things Can Make a Big Difference*. Boston: Back Bay Books, 2002.

Gladwell, M. *Blink: The Power of Thinking Without Thinking*. New York: Little, Brown, 2005.

Gladwell, M. *Outliers: The Story of Success*. New York: Little, Brown, 2008.

Goleman, D. *Emotional Intelligence*. New York: Bantam Books, 2006.

Hanson, N. R. *Patterns of Discovery*. Cambridge: Cambridge University Press, 1958.

Hardman, D. *Judgment and Decision Making: Psychological Perspectives*. New York: Wiley-Blackwell, 2009.

Hastie, R., and Dawes, R. *Rational Choice in an Uncertain World: The Psychology of Judgment and Decision Making*. (2nd ed.) Thousand Oaks, Calif.: Sage, 2010.

Hawking, S. W. *A Brief History of Time: From the Big Bang to Black Holes*. New York: Bantam, 1988.

Hume, D. *An Enquiry Concerning Human Understanding*. LaSalle, Ill.: Open Court Publishing, 1988. (Originally published 1748.)

Isaacson, W. *Einstein: His Life and Universe*. New York: Simon & Schuster, 2007.

Jackson, W. D. *Glass-Steagall Act: Commercial vs. Investment Banking, Order Code 1887061*. Washington, D.C.: Congressional Research Service, June 29, 1987.

Jaques, E. *A General Theory of Bureaucracy*. London: Heinemann, 1976.

Jaques, E. *Requisite Organization*. Falls Church, Va.: Cason Hall, 1986.

Jaques, E., and Cason, K. *Human Capability: A Study of Individual Potential and Its Application*, Falls Church, Va.: Cason Hal, 1994.

Jung, C. G. *Psychological Types, Collected Work*. Princeton, N.J.: Princeton University Press, 1971.

Kahneman, D. "A Psychological Perspective on Economics." *AEA Papers and Proceedings*, 2003, *93*, 162–168.

Kahneman, D. *Thinking, Fast and Slow*. New York: Farrar, Straus and Giroux, 2011.

King, L. W. *The Code of Hammurabi*. 1915. http://www.general-intelligence.com/library/hr.pdf.

Klein, G. *Sources of Power*. Cambridge, Mass.: MIT Press, 1998.

Knight, F. H. *Risk, Uncertainty, and Profit*. Boston: Houghton Mifflin, 1921.

Krugman, P. *The Return of Depression Economics and the Crisis of 2008*. New York: Norton, 2009.

Kuhn, T. S. *The Structure of Scientific Revolutions*. Chicago: University of Chicago Press, 1996.

Lehrer, J. *How We Decide*. Boston: Houghton Mifflin Harcourt, 2009.

Lenroot, R. K., and Giedd, J. N. "Brain Development in Children and Adolescents: Insights from Anatomical Magnetic Resonance Imaging." *Neuroscience and Biobehavioral Reviews*, 2006, *30*, 718–729.

Lichtenstein, S., and Slovic, P. *The Construction of Preference*. Cambridge: Cambridge University Press, 2006.

Lowenstein, R. *When Genius Failed: The Rise and Fall of Long-Term Capital Management*. New York: Random House, 2000.

Mackay, C. *Extraordinary Popular Delusions and the Madness of Crowds*. New York: Crown, 1995. (Originally published 1852.)

MacMillan, M. *An Odd Kind of Fame: Stories of Phineas Gage*. Cambridge, Mass.: MIT Press, 2000.

MacMillan, M. "Phineas Gage: Unraveling the Myth." *Psychologist.Org*, 2008, *21*, 828–831.

Mah, L.W.Y., Arnold, M. C., and Grafman, J. "Deficits in Social Knowledge Following Damage to the Ventromedial Prefrontal Cortex." *Journal of Neuropsychiatry and Clinical Neurosciences*, 2005, *17*, 66–74.

Maia, T. V., and McClelland, J. L. "A Re-Examination of the Evidence for the Somatic Marker Hypotheses: What Participants Really Know in the Iowa Gambling Task." *Proceedings of the National Academy of Science*, 2004, *101*, 16075–16080.

Maslow, A. "A Theory of Human Motivation." *Psychological Review*, 1943, *50*, 370–396.

Maslow, A. *Motivation and Personality*. New York: HarperCollins, 1954.

McClelland, D. C. *The Achieving Society*. Princeton, N.J.: Van Nostrand, 1961.

McClelland, D. C. *Human Motivation*. Glenview, Ill.: Scott, Foresman, 1985.

Mead, M. *Coming of Age in Samoa: A Psychological Study of Primitive Youth for Western Civilisation*. New York: M. Morrow, 1928.

Miles, R. E. "The Origin and Meaning of Miles' Law." *Public Administration Review*, 1978, *38*, 399–403.

Milgram, S. "Behavioral Study of Obedience." *Journal of Abnormal and Social Psychology*, 1963, *67*, 371–378.

Mills, H. D. "Chief Programmer Teams: Techniques and Procedures (1970)." In H. D. Mills (ed.), *Software Productivity*. New York: Dorset House, 1988.

Minsky, M. L. *The Society of Mind*. New York: Simon & Schuster, 1986.

Morita, A. *Made in Japan*. New York: Dutton, 1986.

Myers, I. B. *Gifts Differing*. (2nd ed.) Palo Alto, Calif.: Consulting Psychologist Press, 1990.

Nadler, D. A., Gerstein, M. S., and Shaw, R. B. *Organizational Architecture*. San Francisco: Jossey-Bass, 1992.

Newell, B. R., Lagnado, D. A., and Shanks, D. R., *Straight Choices: The Psychology of Decision Making*. New York: Psychology Press, 2007.

Newell, B. R., and Rakow, T. "Revising Beliefs About the Merits of Unconscious Thought: Evidence in Favor of the Null Hypothesis." *Social Cognition*, 2011, *29*, 711–726.

Newell, B. R., Wong, K. Y., Cheung, J.C.H., and Rakow, T. "Think, Blink, or Sleep on It? Impact on Modes of Thought on Complex Decision-Making." *Quarterly Journal of Experimental Psychology*, 2009, *62*, 707–732.

Nicolson, A. *God's Secretaries: The Making of the King James Bible*. New York: HarperCollins, 2005.

Paulos, J. A. *Innumeracy*. New York: Hill and Wang, 2001.

Phan, K. L., Wager, T. D., Taylor, S. F., and Liberzon, I. "Functional Neuroimaging Studies of Human Emotion." *CNS Spectrums*, 2004, *9*, 258–266.

Plato. *The Republic*. Indianapolis, Ind.: Hackett, 2004.

Plous, S. *The Psychology of Judgment and Decision Making*. New York: McGraw-Hill, 1993.

Purves, D., and Lotto, R. B. *Why We See What We Do*. Sunderland, Mass.: Sinauer, 2003.

Robert, H. M., III. *Robert's Rules of Order*. (11th ed.) Cambridge, Mass.: Da Capo Press, 2011.

Sacks, O. W. *The Man Who Mistook His Wife for a Hat and Other Clinical Tales*. New York: Simon & Schuster, 1998.

Schein, E. *Organizational Culture and Leadership*. (4th ed.) San Francisco: Jossey-Bass, 2010.

Schumpeter, J. *The Theory of Economic Development*. Cambridge, Mass.: Harvard University Press, 1934.

Schumpeter, J. *Capitalism, Socialism, and Democracy*. New York: HarperCollins, 1942.

Seeley, T. D. *Honeybee Democracy*. Princeton, N.J.: Princeton University Press, 2010.

Sherif, M. "A Study of Some Social Factors in Perception." *Archives of Psychology*, 1935, *27*(187), 1–60.

Sherif, M., and others. *The Robbers Cave Experiment: Intergroup Conflict and Cooperation*. Middletown, Conn.: Wesleyan University Press, 1988.

Shirky, C. *Here Comes Everybody: The Power of Organizing Without Organization*. New York: Penguin, 2008.

Simon, H. A. "A Behavioral Model of Rational Choice." *Quarterly Journal of Economics*, 1955, *69*, 99–118.

Simon, H. A. "Rational Choice and the Structure of the Environment." *Psychological Review*, 1956, *63*, 129–138.

Simon, H. A. *Administrative Behavior*. (4th ed.) New York: Free Press, 1997.

Slovic, P., Fischhoff, B., and Lichtenstein, S. "Facts and Fears: Societal Perception of Risk." In K. Monroe (ed.), *Advances in Consumer Research*. Ann Arbor, Mich.: Association for Consumer Research, 1981.

Smith, A. *An Inquiry into the Nature and Causes of the Wealth of Nations*. (2nd ed.) Chicago: Encyclopedia Britannica, 1990.

Surowiecki, J. *The Wisdom of Crowds: Why the Many Are Smarter Than the Few and How Collective Wisdom Shapes Business, Economies, Societies and Nations*. New York: Doubleday, 2004.

Surowiecki, J. *The Wisdom of Crowds*. New York: Anchor Books, 2005.

Tversky, A., and Kahneman, D. "Judgment Under Uncertainty: Heuristics and Biases." *Science*, 1974, *185*(4157), 1124–1131.

Tversky, A., and Kahneman, D. "The Framing of Decisions and the Psychology of Choice." *Science*, 1981, *211*(4481), 453–458.

Veblen, T. *Theory of the Leisure Class*. New York: Oxford University Press, 2007. (Originally published 1912.)

von Frisch, K. *The Dance Language and Orientation of Bees*. Cambridge, Mass.: Harvard University Press, 1967.

Weber, M. *The Theory of Social and Economic Organization*. (A. M. Henderson and Talcott Parsons, trans.) London: Collier Macmillan, 1947.

Weinberg, G. *The Psychology of Computer Programming*. New York: Van Nostrand Reinhold, 1971.

Weingarten, G. "Pearls Before Breakfast." *Washington Post*, Apr. 8, 2007.

Wilson, T. D., and Schooler, J. W. "Too Much Thinking: Introspection Can Reduce the Quality of Preferences and Decisions." *Journal of Personality and Social Psychology*, 1991, *60*, 181–192.

Wilson, T. D., and others. "Introspecting About Reasons Can Reduce Post-Choice Satisfaction." *Personality and Social Psychology Bulletin*, 1993, *19*, 331–339.

Winchester, S. *The Professor and the Mad Man: A Tale of Murder, Insanity, and the Making of the Oxford English Dictionary*. New York: HarperCollins, 1998.

Yurgelun-Todd, D. "Inside the Teenage Brain." *Frontline*, Jan. 31, 2002. http://www.pbs.org/wgbh/pages/frontline/shows/teenbrain/interviews/todd.html.

Acknowledgments

In writing this book, I picked a lot of brains. Many people provided facts and insights that helped me flesh out the book's contents. My graduate students provided a great sounding board to test my ideas and to offer interesting insights. Colleagues in the management science community were generous in sharing perspectives that helped shape many of my ideas. But two people deserve special mention.

First, I thank my brother, Matthew Hugh Erdelyi, a professor of cognitive psychology at Brooklyn College specializing in recovered memory. When I needed coaching on various topics in experimental psychology as I was writing this book, he got me on the right track. I'm not sure that he agrees with some of the positions I take, but he is a good guy who tolerates different viewpoints. I appreciate his cheerful help.

I also thank my wife, Yanping Chen. She is both an M.D. and Ph.D., so I have grown accustomed to calling her Dr. Dr. Chen. Given her heavy-duty experience as a biomedical researcher, plus her expertise in science and technology policy, plus her experience as a senior manager in the education field, I couldn't resist testing my ideas on her. She was a rich resource of real-world examples that I was able to use to illustrate my points.

Thanks to the editorial and production team at Jossey-Bass who kept me on track over a period of two and a half years. I want to single out the support I received from Kathe Sweeney, Dani Scoville, and Mary Garrett. Mary shepherded the manuscript through production, and along with copyeditor Beverly Miller played a crucial role in demangling some mangled passages, gently asking from time to time, "Is this really what you intend to say?" When they raised this question, I knew I had some fixing up to do.

Finally, I thank the anonymous reviewers of the manuscript for this book. They provided valuable suggestions, and if they happen to read the published version of my book, they will see that I listened to what they said.

The Author

J. Davidson Frame is academic dean at the University of Management and Technology (UMT), where he has run the university's project management, technology management, and doctoral programs since 1998. Prior to joining the UMT faculty, he was on the faculty of George Washington University for nineteen years, where he served as chair of the Department of Management Science, director of the Program on Science, Technology and Innovation, and director of the business school's project management program.

He has written extensively on scientific productivity and the links among science, technology, and economic growth. He has also written books on project management, project competence, risk management, and contract management. His *Managing Projects in Organizations* and *The New Project Management* were business best-sellers.

Over the past thirty years, Frame has consulted with and delivered management programs to some thirty federal government agencies, including the Department of Defense, the Department of Energy, the Department of State, the Internal Revenue Service, the Social Security Administration, and the Smithsonian Institution. He has delivered management programs to major corporate clients, including AT&T, Sprint, IBM, Boeing, SITA, Fannie Mae, Freddie Mac, Morgan Stanley, Credit Suisse, and Citibank. Since 1985, he has taught extensively in the Far East, having made more than seventy trips to deliver programs in China, Australia, Taiwan, Hong Kong, Malaysia, and Singapore.

Frame served on the board of directors of the Project Management Institute for eleven years. He is a fellow of the Project Management Institute. He lives in Arlington, Virginia, just outside Georgetown, Washington, D.C. He earned his bachelor's degree at the College of Wooster and his master's degree and doctorate at the American University in Washington, D.C.

Index

Pareto optimality, 159

Participation spectrum, 141–148

Patterns of Discovery (Hanson), 48, 186

Paulos, John Allen, 229

Paulson & Co. Inc., 108, 109

Peanut-counting experiments, 168–169

People: dealing with contending interests of aggregates of, 250–252; in organizations, 71–72. *See also* Decision making by individuals; Decision-implementers; Decision-makers; Stakeholders

Perception, context as determining, 47–48, 185–186

Performance monitoring, 104–105

Perot, Ross, 75, 158

Personality: impact on decision making by individuals, 32, 118–120; Jaques's unique view of, 135–138; judgment acumen trait, 131–135; openness to change trait, 127–131; risk propensity trait, 125–127

Personality (Allport), 119

Phan, K. L., 240

Philosophy: as factor in cognitive limit, 16; perspectives on decision making, 36–38

Plato, 162, 172, 184, 213, 232

Plurality decision rule, 157–158

Politics: as component of social context, 57–58; decision-making limitations rooted in, 15; model of governmental, 54; public policy decision making and, 28–30

Predictably Irrational (Ariely), 206

Predictive coding, 207, 233

Primus inter pares, 144–145

Principal-agent dilemma, 7, 89, 107–109, 256

Problem of induction, 38

The Professor and the Mad Man (Winchester), 171

Psychological limitations, 13–14

Psychological state, 124–125

Psychology, 31–32; social, 30–31

Public goods, school of economics focusing on, 28

Public policy, 28–30, 254–255. *See also* Glass-Steagall Act

Purves, D., 184, 190

R

Rakow, T., 226, 227, 228

Rational-actor model, 52–53, 250–251

Rationality: assumed, 4, 38–42, 253–255; bounded, 5, 38–39; of criminal behavior, 46; of decisions by individuals vs. groups, 119–120; questioned in decision-making process, 5–7

Reagan, Ronald, 2

Reality, as perceived by brain, 182–186, 207–208, 233, 234, 248

The Republic (Plato), 162, 213

Requisite organization, 136

Research. *See* Empirical research

Resistance to change, 128–131, 181–182, 208–209

Ricardo, David, 213

Risk: aversion toward, with chain-of-command structure, 64; decision making with, 43–45; organizational cultures' attitude toward, 76–81; propensity toward, as personality trait, 125–127; uncertainty vs., 43

Risk, Uncertainty, and Profit (Knight), 43

Robert, H. M. III, 160

Robert's Rules of Order (Robert), 160

The Rules of Sociological Method (Durkheim), 213

S

Sacks, Oliver, 198, 234

Sampling methodologies, 206–207, 230–231

Satisficing, 5–6, 39

Scalawags, 247–248, 255–256

Schein, Edgar, 74

Schlegel, Alice, 204

Scholes, Myron, 27

Schooler, J. W., 220

Schumpeter, Joseph, 82, 120–121

Science: importance of context to theorizing in, 48, 115, 208; paradigm shift in, 3, 16–17

Scientific reasoning, 36, 37–38

Scientific revolution, 41

Scrum development technique, 69

Seeley, Thomas, 148, 258

Self-directed team structure, 65–68, 69, 70

Self-directed work units, 146–147

Setting, 30, 159–160

Shaw, R. B., 62

Shepard tabletop illusion, 195–197

Sherif, Muzafer, 30, 244

Shirky, Clay, 147, 170, 258

Simon, Herbert, 5–6, 27, 38, 42, 46, 214

Simple majority decision rule, 150, 155
Simpson, O. J., 33
Slovic, P., 231, 243
Smart mobs, 148
Smith, Adam, 4, 117, 171, 172, 213, 243–244, 258
Social context, 47–59; and Allison's perspectives on decision making, 52–54; community as component of, 50–51, 249; contending interests of aggregates of people in, 250–252; external forces as component of, 57–58, 250; implementation of decision influenced by, 56–57, 59; importance of understanding, 9–11, 48, 58; necessity of accommodating, 248–250; organizations as element of, 61, 85; sets of players in, 51, 249–250; stakeholders as component of, 49–50, 55–56, 58–59, 249; as universal element of decisions, 8, 141, 247
Social psychology, 30–31
Social space. *See* Social context
Solomonaic norm, 51–52
Spartan culture, Athenian culture vs., 74–76
Stakeholders: influence on decision implementation, 57, 250; necessity of accommodating needs of, 55–56, 58–59; represented on teams, 67; as social context component, 9–10, 49–50, 51, 249
Stalin, Joseph, 15, 142
Stallman, Richard, 147
Stein, Herb, 217–218, 219
Stigler, George, 43
Stoicism, 11
The Structure of Scientific Revolutions (Kuhn), 3, 16
Suicide (Durkheim), 213
Sullivan, Louis, 62, 105
Supermajority decision rule, 155–156
Surowiecki, James, 165–169, 170, 172, 258

T

Taylor, S. F., 240
Teams: groups vs., 148–149; self-directed, 65–68, 69, 70; virtual, 69
Techniques: as basis of decision making, 3–4, 5; caution on emphasizing, 252–253

Technologies, disruptive, 82–85
Templates: resistance to change due to, 181–182; used by brain, 180–181
Theories in use, 80
Theories of action, 80
Theory ladenness, 48, 115, 208
Thinking, Fast and Slow (Kahneman), 218
Three musketeers principle, 157
3M Corporation, 80–81
Time, limited, 14
Time span of discretion, 136–137
The Tipping Point (Gladwell), 216
Tools. *See* Techniques
Torvald, Linus, 147
Tourre, Fabrice, 108, 109
Tranel, D., 238
Truman, Harry, 143
Tversky, Amos, 5, 40–41, 230–231
Tyndale, William, 170

U

Uncertainty: decision making with, 11–12, 45–46; risk vs., 43
Unconscious decisions, 21–22
Unconscious deliberation, 214–228; blink phenomenon, 216–220, 228–229; Dijksterhuis's experiments on, 223–228, 231; examples of, 215; summary of findings on, 231–232; Wilson's experiments on, 216–220, 230–231
Unconscious thought theory (UTT), 226–228
Unknowns, 42–46; due to human behavior, 46; due to limited information, 42–43; with risk, 43–45; risk vs. uncertainty, 43; with uncertainty, 11–12, 45–46
U.S. Supreme Court, 33, 46, 112–113

V

Values: culture as composed of, 73; moral limitations rooted in, 14–15; scientific discovery influenced by, 48, 115; of time and culture, 111–113
Van Baaren, R. B., 223, 225
Veblen, Thorstein, 7
Ventromedial prefrontal cortex (VMF), 234–242; brain-scans of functioning of, 240–241; experiments on decision making and, 237–240,